GOD'S SOLUTIONS TO LIFE'S PROBLEMS

Dr. Wayne Mack
Joshua Mack

GOD'S
SOLUTIONS
TO
LIFE'S
PROBLEMS

First Timothy 5:17-18 instructs us to give the laborer his wages, specifically those who labor in the Word and doctrine. Hensley Publishing has a moral, as well as legal, responsibility to see that our authors receive fair compensation for their efforts. Many of them depend upon the income from the sale of their books as their sole livelihood. So, for that matter, do the artists, printers, and numerous other people who work to make these books available to you. Please help us by discouraging those who would copy this material in lieu of purchase.

Unless otherwise noted, all Scripture references are taken from the New American Standard Version. © The Lockman Foundation 1960, 1962, 1963, 1968, 1971, 1972, 1973, 1975, 1977. Used by permission.

HENSLEY
PUBLISHING

ISBN 1-56322-079-2

GOD'S SOLUTIONS TO LIFE'S PROBLEMS

TABLE OF CONTENTS

FOREWORD

When I heard this book was in the works, I knew it would be an extremely valuable, rich, and readable resource – and I was not disappointed. Wayne and Joshua Mack have a fervent love for the Word of God and an unshakable conviction that the only valid, trustworthy, and effective solutions to the problems of life are biblical answers. Wayne has been a skilled counselor, pastor, and teacher of biblical counseling for many years. Joshua is also a gifted pastor who shares his father's commitment to the Bible and his expertise in applying the Word of God clearly and persuasively to real life.

Wayne and Joshua themselves will tell you that what makes their counsel so effective is the inherent power of God's Word. The Bible speaks with the full weight of God's own authority. Its solutions to life's problems are perfect, sure, right, pure, clean, true, and righteous altogether (Psalm 19:7-9). No other resource addresses human problems as thoroughly and as reliably as Scripture. So when it comes to resolving personal conflicts, marital difficulties, emotional disorders, character flaws, spiritual problems, and similar issues, the Bible is the place to turn for right answers.

Unfortunately, many people today – including some who profess faith in Christ – imagine they can find more effective help elsewhere. They seek unwise, unbiblical counsel. They run after various fads in psychotherapy. They buy up whatever kinds of spiritual snake-oil or psycho-quackery are currently popular. Meanwhile, biblical counsel and biblical preaching are widely ridiculed as too simplistic, ineffectual, and old-fashioned. Even some Christians seem to lack confidence in biblical answers. I heard one influential evangelical leader offhandedly deride all biblical counseling as "nothing more than quoting Bible verses at people with serious problems."

If you have ever been tempted to give any credence to such a caricature of biblical counseling, this book will dispel the notion from your mind. Wayne and Josh Mack handle the Word of God practically and perceptively, and they show with absolute clarity how it addresses the problems of life and human behavior.

As for "people with serious problems," no problem is more serious or more desperate than the problem of sin. It is a universal problem. And despite psychologists' frantic attempts to redefine all human problems in clinical terms, the fundamental human behavioral problem is still sin. It is a moral problem, not a medical one. And the only remedy for sin is outlined in Scripture. Ultimately, then, only the biblical counselor can give people answers to life's most difficult problems.

I'm grateful for this simple, clear, and helpful guide for human problem-solving. May it provide clear answers for people who are struggling. May it increase the confidence of those who are helping people deal with their problems biblically. And may it produce a whole new generation of wise counselors who understand that God's Word is the best place to turn for solutions to the problems of life – and who know how to apply the truth of Scripture skillfully.

—Dr. John MacArthur
Pastor/teacher, Grace Community Church
President, The Master's College and Seminary
Grace To You radio program
Author

ACKNOWLEDGEMENTS

Scripture admonishes us to render to all what is due them: ...honor to whom honor is due. In keeping with that admonition, we want to recognize the help that a number of people gave us as we sought to make this book a reality.

Along the way, in my (Wayne's) Christian life and ministry, many people have encouraged me in the writing process. Numerous people have expressed appreciation for the help they have received from other books I have written, and have encouraged me to produce more written material. Some have reminded me that books can go where I can't go and can continue to minister after I am no longer around to minister. These comments have motivated me to spend more time in writing for publication.

While serving as an elder and pastor of the Joint Heirs Fellowship group at Grace Community Church in Sun Valley, California, it was my privilege to minister to a dear godly lady by the name of Melicent Hunt, "Gramma" to most of us. Gramma's love for Christ and her desire to see Him exalted was an encouragement to everyone. She was a real prayer warrior who committed herself to pray for my ministry regularly. In particular, she was so concerned that I do more writing that she instructed my wife to protect me from interruptions so that I could spend time in writing. She also promised she would pray especially for me at least two days a week – and that I had better use those days for the purpose of writing. Her commitments and admonitions were often a stimulus for me to get at the task. I knew that the next time I would see Gramma she would be quizzing me about my faithfulness in working on this project.

Dr. David Harrell, a former teaching colleague in the biblical counseling department at The Master's College and now pastor of Family Bible Church in the Nashville, Tennessee area, deserves credit for his help with the material found in chapter one.

Joshua and I would be remiss if we failed to mention a number of other people who have helped us in writing this book. First and foremost are our wives, Carol and Marda. They have supported us with their prayers and devotion and have also read the material and made valuable suggestions about its content and style. We love them dearly, and appreciate their faithfulness to Christ and us in all our endeavors. They are "suitable helpers" and models of a Proverbs 31 woman. My daughter, Beth, who is Director of the Biblical Counseling Master of Arts in Biblical Counseling modular program at The Master's College, also gave valuable assistance.

We appreciate the willingness of a number of very busy people to read the book while it was still in manuscript form and make comments about it. These people include Dr. Richard Mayhue, Executive Vice President of The Master's College and Seminary; Dr. Steve Viars, Pastor of Faith Baptist Church in Lafayette, Indiana, and President of the National Association of Nouthetic Counselors; Randy Patten, Executive Director of the National Association of Nouthetic Counselors; Jerry Marcellino, Pastor of Audubon Bible Church and President of Audubon Press and book service, Dr. Jay Adams, author, former pastor and seminary professor, president of Timeless Texts publishing company; Dr. Theodore Tripp, pastor of Grace Fellowship Church in Hazleton, Pennsylvania, author, and conference speaker; Geoffrey Thomas, pastor of Alfred Place Baptist church in Aberystwyth, Wales and frequent conference speaker in Great Britain and America; Dr. Lance Quinn, pastor of the Bible Church of Little Rock, Arkansas; Dr. Frank Catanzaro, professor of biblical counseling at Southeastern Baptist Seminary; Dr. David Powlison, editor of *The Journal of Biblical Counseling*, and biblical counseling teacher at The Westminster Theological Seminary, and Dr. John Street, chairman of the graduate and undergraduate biblical counseling department at The Master's College.

A special word of thanks goes to Dr. John MacArthur, pastor-teacher of Grace Community Church, president of The Master's College and Seminary, and Bible teacher on the *Grace to You* radio program, for writing the foreword to this book. John is one of the busiest and most productive men I know. In fact, he is so busy with such extensive responsibilities in many areas that I hesitated to ask him to write a foreword for this project. However, when asked, Dr. MacArthur responded in the way he typically responds when I ask him for help in some endeavor. He said, "I'll be glad to do it. Just send me the manuscript." Thank you, John, for being so devoted to Christ and His Word and for all the help you've been to us and countless others in our Christian lives and ministries.

We also are deeply grateful for the assistance of the people at Hensley Publishing. It has been my (Wayne) privilege to have worked with them, especially Virgil and Neal Hensley, on other projects, especially my book, *Preparing for Marriage God's Way*. I have never been associated with people in a

Christian publishing company that have been more cooperative and pleasant to work with than these people. For some time now, they have been encouraging me to do more writing. They have told me that many people who have purchased and used my book for premarital counseling have asked, "When are you going to publish more of Wayne Mack's materials?" So, they encouraged me in this project and I appreciate that encouragement. In particular, we want to express our appreciation to Terri Kalfas, who heads up the editorial aspect of their publishing. She has been a joy to work with and has done much to bring this book to fruition.

INTRODUCTION

This book, along with the others in this series, has been a long time coming. For many years I have wanted to write some books that could be used to help people deal with the inevitable problems they face as they live in this sin-cursed world. I wanted to produce some written material that could be used by individuals in their own struggles, or as counseling assignments, or in Bible study groups to help people understand and solve their problems in a biblical way.

I wanted to do this because I have discovered that many professing Christians seem to be unaware of the tremendous resources we have in the Scriptures for facing, understanding and solving life's problems. As I have presented much of this material in conferences in spoken form in various parts of the world, I have had many people tell me that they never realized how practical and helpful the Scriptures are for dealing with the nitty-gritty issues of life. Again and again, I have been asked the question, "Is this material available in any of the books you have written?" When this has occurred, I have had to say, "It's available on audio and video tapes, but to this point I haven't put it in book form." Upon hearing this, many have encouraged me to put the material in written form and make it available for Christians everywhere.

For various reasons, until now I hadn't been able to do what others encouraged me to do. This book, along with the future books in this series, is an attempt to make the requests for material in written form a reality. The title tells it all in terms of what this series of books is all about. We're going to be dealing with *God's Solutions to Life's Problems.*

To introduce the purpose and content of this and future books in this series, let's examine what the title indicates. First, it indicates that we will have problems in life. This, of course, is in keeping with the clear teaching of Scripture and is confirmed by the experience of every one of us. There is no such thing as a problem-free life. Problems are, in the words of 1 Corinthians 10:13, "common to man." In these studies, we will be discussing some of the problems that are most *"common to man."*

The title also indicates that life's problems can be solved. In other words, we don't have to go through life being overcome by the difficulties we encounter.

We can, as Romans 8:37 indicates, *"overwhelmingly conquer."* Or, in keeping with the truth declared in 1 Corinthians 10:13, the title suggests that there is a way of escape from every trial and pressure "under the sun" that we experience in our lives. We don't have to be the defeated; we can be the defeaters.

"Yes, but how can I be an overcomer?" is a question many have asked when someone makes statements like the ones in the last paragraph. The answer is found in the first two words of the title: by responding to and handling your problems "God's way." According to 1 Corinthians 10:13, *"God is faithful"* and He *"will not allow you to be tempted* (tested, pressured) *beyond what you are able, but with the temptation will provide a way of escape also, that you may be able to bear it."* Note, this text, which is part of the *"altogether true"* (Psalm 19:9) Scriptures, states definitively and conclusively that there is a way of escape. Note also that it indicates that the way of escape is provided by a faithful God, a God on Whom we can depend, a God Who is absolutely trustworthy, a God Who knows everything, a God Who is wisdom personified. Make no mistake about it. This God has provided us a way to solve our problems.

It is the purpose of this book, and all future books in this series, to explain and illustrate that way of escape. In this volume, we will be dealing with some general issues that are absolutely foundational for identifying and solving life's problems God's way. What you will find in this volume can be plugged into and used with any of life's problems. In future studies, we will explore some of the specific common problems, examining and explaining Scriptures that delineate God's way of solving them.

Our prayer is that this book and others in the series will help Christians discover afresh the sufficient and superior resources God has given us for living life "under the sun." Our prayer is that this book will help Christians live in a way that brings great glory to Him, greater joy and blessing to them, and makes them a powerful witness to a world that really doesn't have valid solutions to the problems of life.

Open pg 95
4 - Questions
Theme pg 75
Theme vs. II Tim 3:16
Prov 12:1

CHAPTER 1

The Wheat and the Tares

When the wheat sprang up and bore grain, then the tares became evident also….Allow both to grow together until the harvest; and in the time of the harvest I will say to the reapers, First gather up the tares and bind them in bundles to burn them up; but gather the wheat into my barn.
Matthew 13:26, 30

It was another typical day at my church office. I had prepared spiritually and mentally for a day of counseling – prayer, reflection and meditation on some of my favorite psalms with one of my favorite praise CD's playing in the background, and a review of the files of my counselees that I would be meeting. I thought I was ready to once again enter the dark caverns of human misery and confusion, praying that the Holy Spirit could use me to point them to the Light of the world, and allow Him to lead them to safety and a God-honoring life.

The ministry of restoring people who are caught in the web of sin – bearing their burdens and thus fulfilling the law of Christ (Galatians 6:2) – is a task which can often exhaust even the strongest of counselors. After all, *our struggle is not against flesh and blood, but against the rulers, against the powers, against the world forces of this darkness, against the spiritual forces of wickedness in the heavenly places* (Ephesians 6:12). The apostle Paul warned us *the weapons of our warfare are not of the flesh, but divinely powerful for the destruction of fortresses. We are destroying speculations* (i.e. false ideologies) *and every lofty thing raised up against the knowledge of God* (2 Corinthians 10:4-5). Certainly anyone who has even casually wrestled with their own personal life issues, much less other people's problems, will quickly concur that sin can so tenaciously grip our hearts that nothing less than the convicting hand and power of the Almighty can pry us from its grip.

But sometimes we encounter individuals who seem to be in a category all their own – a category beyond mere spiritual ignorance or even the remnants of indwelling sin patterns. People who seem to epitomize evil. Those who seem to never be able to stop the momentum of offending those they claim to love – especially God. People who never really change; who never grow into spiritual maturity. Regardless the counsel, regardless the consequence, they continue

TELL STORY OF EVANGELIST

READ
↓

OUR STRUGGLE IS NOT AGAINST FLESH AND BLOOD...THE WEAPONS OF OUR WARFARE ARE NOT OF THE FLESH.

Go to pg 22

REGARDLESS THE COUNSEL, REGARDLESS THE CONSEQUENCE, THEY CONTINUE WITH A SEEMINGLY RESOLUTE DETERMINATION TO LEAD A LIFE OF FLAGRANT DISREGARD FOR THE COMMANDMENTS OF GOD.

with a seemingly resolute determination to lead a life of flagrant disregard for the commandments of God. It's as though they enjoy their sin, and do it with impunity. What makes this even more treacherous is that more often than not, their true character is typically so well disguised with the veneer of religiosity and personal charisma that even their most intimate acquaintances have great difficulty in recognizing and confronting the insincerity and hypocrisy of who they really are.

I encountered such a person that afternoon. It was an eerie, demonic sort of experience, but one that is, tragically, becoming increasingly more common in our "everyone-who-goes-to-church-is-a-Christian" culture. The following true story illustrates the dilemma of religious externalism. This story has only been changed for confidentiality purposes without compromising the central concepts.

A GRIP AND GRIN…SHUCK AND JIVE: THE STUFF OF RELIGIOUS HYPOCRISY

As soon as I saw Tom and Lisa in the waiting room it was obvious that she was mortally wounded. I've seen that glazed over, hollow look in a person's eyes hundreds of times before. I call it the "concentration camp" look: trapped, hopeless, dying.

As I introduced myself, Tom immediately jumped to his feet, smiled gregariously, shook my hand firmly, and nervously initiated some small talk. I had to deliberately turn away from him to acknowledge Lisa, who remained seated. Had I not done so, no formal greeting or introduction would have taken place. And Lisa wouldn't have noticed it. Years of being ignored had left her numb.

Tom had a deep tan, a lot of gaudy gold jewelry, permed hair, and flashy GQ-type clothes. He had what would commonly be called the "mid-life crisis" look. It was obvious that he loved attention and got lots of it.

Lisa rose to her feet as I moved toward her. She mechanically stretched forth a trembling hand. Her handshake seemed to be an extension of her inner self – ice-cold and lifeless. Her appearance was that of one who was professionally groomed, right down to her long, painted acrylic fingernails. Though she was modestly dressed with an understated elegance, her natural beauty was

I'VE SEEN THAT GLAZED-OVER, HOLLOW LOOK IN A PERSON'S EYES HUNDREDS OF TIMES BEFORE. I CALL IT THE "CONCENTRATION CAMP" LOOK: TRAPPED, HOPELESS, DYING.

overpowered by a thick veneer of makeup, an attempt at disguising the deep wrinkles of many years of relational pain.

We entered my office and, as I expected, Tom and Lisa chose seats as far apart from one another as possible. You could have cut the tension with a knife.

Tom was a well-known evangelist and author; Lisa was the typical "ministry widow" who stayed at home to raise their three children. I soon discovered that they had been married for eighteen years. Although none of their married life had been rich and rewarding, the last eight years had been especially miserable due to Lisa's suspicions that Tom was having an affair – or affairs. She described the strange phone calls from other men and women, Tom's extensive travel without accountability, his secret collection of pornographic videos, and his repulsion when it came to anything romantic with her.

As she related her story, I was struck with the incongruency between her plastic smile and her tears. Deep lines around her mouth and eyes betrayed years of trying to project an image that everything was "fine…just fine!" when in reality, she was miserable inside.

Her tears quickly degenerated into heart-wrenching sobs as she finally told me that her worst nightmares had proven to be true. Tom had recently admitted to years of illicit relationships with women, and occasionally even with men. He had lovers scattered, literally, all over the world.

As I listened to her story, I watched Tom closely. He nodded his head in agreement with her tragic tale, but showed no emotion whatsoever. Certainly no remorse. Occasionally he would look at her, then the floor; but mostly he looked at me. It was as though he were studying my reactions to his wife's allegations. He had a disconcerting smirk on his face. A look of haughty pride. An arrogance which seemed to permeate the room like a poisonous gas. He said nothing.

I distinctly remember that old familiar feeling deep inside of me as once again I was immersed in the cesspool of human iniquity. A choking, agonizing feeling combined with an almost overwhelming urge to throw up my hands in frustration and run out of the room. But, like so many times before, the Holy Spirit constrained and comforted me as I silently cried out for strength, courage, and wisdom. I then asked them specifically about their expectations of me and of our meeting together.

Tom finally spoke for the first time. He calmly concurred that what Lisa had said was "absolutely true." His response showed no emotion, only a duplication of Lisa's plastic smile, but without the tears. He went on to say that the reason he had come to see me was to get some help for his "addictions" and, hopefully, "to rebuild" their marriage. It was apparent by the look on Lisa's face that she didn't agree, so I asked her what she hoped for.

Lisa's answer revealed both fear and guilt. She was afraid that the marriage was "dead – so dead that the corpse was rotting and burial was long overdue." Guilt, because she didn't "trust God enough to somehow miraculously heal the marriage – raise the dead, if you will." She admitted that she didn't really know why she was there, but she was quick to add her confusion over the simultaneous love and hatred she had for her husband. Her desires to "make it work" were often overshadowed by a stubborn unwillingness to even entertain the thought, especially if she had to ever "do anything sexual with him." She was not only afraid she couldn't physically respond, she was also horrified at the possibility of getting AIDS.

I then asked Tom why he wanted to rebuild the marriage now, after all these years. Before he had a chance to respond, Lisa very angrily answered for him. I suddenly saw a different side to her – a side I respected. There was at least some life left in her. "I'll tell you why he wants to rebuild the marriage," she said. "I'll tell you exactly why." She glared at her husband. "His precious bookings are beginning to suffer because word of his immorality is leaking out. No bookings, no money…and no more romantic rendezvous. And then there are the publishing contracts. Those guys are getting pretty nervous with all the rumors floating around. If the marriage falls apart, as if it hasn't already, he'll lose it all. And he's afraid I'm going to blow his cover and file for divorce. So he's here to use you just like he has me all these years."

Maintaining a condescending smile, Tom coolly replied, "Oh, don't be silly. You know as well as I do that I've had problems with my addictions for years and I've always been too busy or stubborn (said laughingly) to deal with them. I've been to several counselors over the past few years, and they agree that I take after any number of men in my family, especially dear old dad who had the same types of problems. And I've been doing a lot of reading lately." He named three or four Christian pop psychology books, then went on to say, "I can't believe how accurate they were in describing me. It's as though they've been reading my mail for years! And the good news is that I'm beginning to recover!"

He went on to say that the reason he had come to see me was to get some help for his "addictions" and, hopefully, "to rebuild" their marriage.

"He's afraid I'm going to blow his cover and file for divorce. So he's here to use you just like he has me all these years."

He then began to summarize what he had discovered through his previous counseling experiences. "Bottom line, I've been diagnosed as having a Histrionic Personality Disorder" (i.e., a secular psychological diagnosis which has as its essential feature pervasive and excessive emotionality and attention-seeking behaviors, commonly characterized by inappropriate sexually seductive or provocative behavior). Tragically, his diagnosis, indicative of all psychological diagnoses, had no authority and merely provided a sophisticated method to repackage sin. He went on to say, "I have an addictive personality. And I'm also an adult child of a family of closet alcoholics; I'm severely co-dependent, and my drug of choice is, and always has been, sex – with a little alcohol thrown in on the side. But I can't get enough sex! I'm a classic case of sexual addiction! I've discovered that virtually everything I do is a result of my shame-based, addictive personality, especially my tendencies toward bisexuality."

He then turned to Lisa, and with a sarcastic tone continued, "If Lisa would be honest with you – or maybe I should say, with herself – she would have to admit that she is also a shame-based co-dependent, highly addicted to everything but sex. Her drugs of choice are prescription drugs, fad diets, and shopping. She's also a churchaholic, addicted to women's Bible studies and seminars. And she absolutely cannot go one day without calling her mommy and daddy to bad-mouth her husband and get a little sympathy."

The veins in Tom's face and neck bulged as he continued to spew forth the venom of years of pent-up hatred toward his wife – and anything else that assaulted his conscience. Lisa just sat there. No tears. No rebuttal. No comment. She just stared out the window as if she were trying to mentally escape. It was as though she had left her body to go somewhere else and all that remained was a well-groomed corpse with a heartbeat.

THE NATURE OF TRUE SAVING FAITH... QUESTIONED

My mind was flooded with thoughts as this scenario played on. It was obvious that Tom had swallowed – hook, line, and sinker – all the clever theories which had not only provided him the necessary psycho-jargon to abdicate any personal responsibility but had also short-circuited any recognition of the heinousness of sin. He wore his labels like a badge of honor, labels which could only describe, albeit superficially, but never restore. Yet he honestly felt he was "in recovery."

TRAGICALLY, HIS DIAGNOSIS, INDICATIVE OF ALL PSYCHOLOGICAL DIAGNOSES, HAD NO AUTHORITY AND MERELY PROVIDED A SOPHISTICATED METHOD TO REPACKAGE SIN.

I COULDN'T HELP BUT NOTICE THE BLATANT ABSENCE OF ANY REFERENCE TO SPIRITUAL THINGS.

I THOUGHT ABOUT CHRIST'S PARABLE ABOUT THE WHEAT AND THE TARES, AND HOW TRUE BELIEVERS CAN BE IDENTIFIED BY THE FRUIT THEY BEAR AND THE COMMANDMENTS THEY KEEP.

HOW COULD A MAN WHO CLAIMED TO BE A NEW CREATURE IN CHRIST LIVE SUCH A CONSISTENT LIFE OF UNBROKEN AND BLATANT SINFULNESS?

I couldn't help but notice the blatant absence of any reference to spiritual things in Tom's recap of his "diagnosis." Yet there he sat: a highly visible "Christian" leader, a man who was supposedly a new creature in Christ…called according to His purpose…in the process of becoming conformed to the image of Christ…and supposedly a man who was called by God to be a minister of the gospel of Jesus Christ.

But how could this be true? My mind filled with Scripture that challenged all that this man claimed to be.

I thought about Christ's parable about the wheat and the tares, and how true believers can be identified by the fruit they bear and the commandments they keep. My thoughts especially focused upon our Lord's words in Matthew 7:22-23 where He warned:

"Many will say to Me on that day, 'Lord, Lord, did we not prophesy in Your name, and in Your name cast out demons, and in Your name perform many miracles?' And then I will declare to them, 'I never knew you; depart from Me, you who practice lawlessness.'"

Could this man sitting across from me be a man who had what James called a faith without works…a dead faith that cannot save (James 2)? Why was there no mention of sin or repentance? Why was he not even remotely sensitive to his wife's pain – not to mention God's? Why was nothing said about prayer, about the Holy Spirit and His convicting and cleansing role? Why wasn't his heart so overwhelmed with his sinfulness that he would literally cry out for forgiveness and mercy, absolutely brokenhearted over offending and mocking the One he claimed to represent?

Didn't the man have a conscience? How, in the name of heaven, could he possibly stand before an audience and extol the transforming power of Christ? How could he talk about loving a Master he so routinely disobeyed? How could a man who claimed to be a new creature in Christ live such a consistent life of unbroken and blatant sinfulness? Most Christians I know couldn't live with themselves if they had been involved in even a fraction of this man's escapades. Guilt and shame would so assault their consciences that they would eventually throw themselves at the feet of God's mercy and beg for forgiveness and cleansing. Surely this man was more than a "carnal" Christian. Far more than a "backslider." This man was seriously sinful. Something far beyond hypocrisy!

Prior to this encounter, I had wrestled with these same issues concerning others I had worked with in the past who were similar to Tom. I had to admit that people like him never really seemed to "get better." At best, they would rearrange their circumstances or substitute their symptoms with another set of equally sinful, though maybe more "acceptable," behaviors. Yet the insidious nature of their sinfulness would continue to enslave them with a treacherous bondage. Could it be that those people, and this man who sat before me, were not truly regenerate – even though they claimed to be? Was it naïve to accept their testimony as the final word on a subject of such eternal significance?

ENTERING THE RAGE

Hoping to somehow get at these issues, I calmly asked Tom to tell me about his spiritual convictions, beginning with his conversion experience. He very quickly informed me that their problems were "psychological, not spiritual," and consequently, my line of questioning was "inappropriate."

Trying to be compassionate and sensitive to his ignorance, while at the same time being forthright and decisive, I attempted to succinctly expose the false dichotomy between psychological and spiritual problems (discussed in chapter three). After I concluded my brief spiel, I proceeded with my original line of questioning.

Tom squinted his eyes, and while shaking his head he answered, "So you want me to tell you about my conversion experience? I bet you're one of those who thinks I'm not a Christian." He sneered. "Well…quite frankly, I'm highly offended! But nevertheless I'll answer your question.

"I asked Jesus into my heart when I was fifteen years old. But being saved has nothing to do with all of this. I know I'm a Christian – just a Christian with loads of baggage from a dysfunctional background! Everything from my family to the self-righteous Christian community I have had to endure all these years." He glared at Lisa. "Why don't you ask her if she's a Christian?"

Ignoring his question regarding Lisa, I decided to enter into his obvious rage by answering his original question regarding his conversion experience. So I said to him, "Tom, the reason I asked you about your conversion was because of two things. First is the noticeable absence of any spiritual remorse in your summary. I've not even heard you mention the word "sin." Second, I have a hard time

I HAD TO ADMIT THAT PEOPLE LIKE HIM NEVER REALLY SEEMED TO "GET BETTER." AT BEST, THEY WOULD REARRANGE THEIR CIRCUMSTANCES OR SUBSTITUTE THEIR SYMPTOMS WITH ANOTHER SET OF EQUALLY SINFUL, THOUGH MAYBE MORE "ACCEPTABLE," BEHAVIORS.

HE VERY QUICKLY INFORMED ME THAT THEIR PROBLEMS WERE "PSYCHOLOGICAL, NOT SPIRITUAL," AND CONSEQUENTLY, MY LINE OF QUESTIONING WAS "INAPPROPRIATE."

I HAD A HARD TIME
HARMONIZING HIS
LIFESTYLE — NOT TO
MENTION HIS PRESENT
ATTITUDE — WITH
THAT OF A NEW
CREATION IN CHRIST.

THIS MAN WAS
ATTACKING THE
TRUTH, NOT ME.

THE COUNSEL I OFFER
MUST BE GOD'S
COUNSEL, COMING
DIRECTLY FROM HIS
WORD, BECAUSE IN
AND OF MYSELF I
REALLY HAVE NOTHING
TO OFFER BUT MY
OWN PERSONAL
OPINION. AND
FRANKLY, OPINIONS
ARE LIKE NOSES —
EVERYBODY HAS ONE.

harmonizing your lifestyle – not to mention your present attitude – with that of a new creation in Christ."

His sinister smile now expanded into a silent, open-mouth laugh. As he shook his head in dismay, he reminded me of a professional basketball player arguing with the referee after he had just been called for a flagrant foul. He was utterly "dumbfounded."

He then proceeded with an epic performance worthy of an academy award: "Oh, this is just great! I come to see you to get some psychological help, and I get a sermon! I suppose you think I need to re-ask Jesus into my heart and bingo, all my problems will disappear!"

He put his head in his hands, and mumbled a string of curses too vulgar to repeat. Then he abruptly straightened up and glared at me in defiance, awaiting my response. His outright hostility triggered in me a strong, selfish desire to retreat in order to protect myself. Instead, I chose to stand my ground, knowing that my authority base was the Word of God, not mere human opinion. This man was attacking the Truth, not me.

SPEAKING THE TRUTH IN LOVE

In the power of the Spirit of God, I tried to boldly speak the truth in love: "Tom, you've come to me to seek counsel because your life, Lisa's life, and your marriage are all a colossal mess. But the counsel I offer must be God's counsel, coming directly from His Word, because in and of myself I really have nothing to offer but my own personal opinion. And frankly, opinions are like noses – everybody has one. Therefore, based upon the principles clearly set forth in the Scripture, and with a sincere desire to help restore you in the spirit of gentleness, I'm suggesting that you call sin "sin," and deal with it with all your might. I'm asking you to get serious about the wretched, vile, insidious nature of your depravity. I'm asking you to at least entertain the possibility that Satan has blinded your spiritual eyes. I'm asking you to fall on your face before a Holy God in absolute brokenness over your sin, and experience the refreshing, cleansing waters of forgiveness. The fact that you are so offended by such a request convinces me even further of the appropriateness of questioning the nature of your faith. Quite honestly, your faith is dead. Sin is your master, and you refuse to admit it!"

Tom stood up in a fury. Fearing a physical altercation, I stood as well. He then proceeded to curse me with an eruption of rage I have seldom experienced in my life. I still vividly remember the spray of his saliva on my face and the violence in his eyes. I'll never forget his concluding comment: "I've spent the last three years trying to get over my feelings of guilt. I've paid counselors thousands of dollars to help me deal with my shame. And now, thanks to you, in less than thirty minutes it's all coming back!"

With that, he stormed from my office. I followed him to the outside entrance and as he opened the door I quietly said to him, "Tom, if you ever want to deal with your life, let me know. I'll do everything I can. Meanwhile I'll be praying for you. That's a promise!" Without a word or a backward glance, he walked away.

REFLECTIONS OF SADNESS

I remember standing there at the door and watching him drive away. A deep sadness filled my heart as I reflected on what had just happened. I silently prayed that the Holy Spirit would bring great conviction to Tom's heart. My contemplation was interrupted by Lisa's broken voice behind me.

"Are you all right?" she asked.

"Yes, I'm fine. Just a little unnerved and disappointed," I replied. "How about you?"

Tears welled up in her eyes as she stared out the doorway where her husband had just departed. She softly replied, "Well, I don't know quite how to put this, but for the first time since I can't remember when, I feel there's hope. Hope for Tom, and hope for me. Not necessarily for the marriage…maybe someday, I don't know. But somehow that doesn't seem all that important right now. What's important is for Tom to give his heart to Christ. And you know, I think he knows that but is to proud to admit it."

We went back into my office where she very calmly told me about the incredibly sad and shamelessly sinful activities of her husband. The heartbreaking nature of their marriage, the hypocrisy of his "ministry," and the dreadful state of their children's lives once again exposed the grotesque consequences of sin.

"I'M ASKING YOU TO AT LEAST ENTERTAIN THE POSSIBILITY THAT SATAN HAS BLINDED YOUR SPIRITUAL EYES…. QUITE HONESTLY, YOUR FAITH IS DEAD. SIN IS YOUR MASTER, AND YOU REFUSE TO ADMIT IT!"

Tom and Lisa are now divorced. Lisa and the children are doing well. Tom has dropped out of sight, and no one really knows where he is. He surfaces only occasionally. Rumors indicate his lifestyle has remained unchanged. He has no contact whatsoever with his children. But for Lisa, "the corpse of my dead marriage has finally been buried."

A Victim of Cheap Grace Evangelism

I was intrigued with the level of defiance in the heart of a man who claimed to be called by God as an evangelist. So I asked Lisa to let me view some of Tom's evangelistic videos. Unfortunately, what I witnessed has become common fare on so-called Christian television and radio. It could best be described as a "Christian Carnival" – a religious version of professional wrestling. Tom was a performer, not a preacher, and he was obviously on stage for his own glory, not God's. His "crusade" was indicative of so many church revivals and evangelistic crusades where perspiring preachers with quivering voices and rhythmic gasps seduce naïve congregations into superficial spiritual decisions. The mesmerizing crescendo and decrescendo of spiritual clichés and choreographed gestures shame the vulnerable into all sorts of things – everything from "salvation" and rededication of their lives to foreign missionary service.

Tragically, many of these resolutions die with the emotions which bore them. But equally disastrous is the false assurance such actions perpetuate. Most have no sense of severity of guilt before God and stubbornly resist any plea to obey Christ. It's as though making Jesus Lord of their life is optional. They merely want some "fire insurance" and a supernatural resource to make them healthy, wealthy, and wise.

Tom's messages and methods were nothing more than a manifestation of his heart – a heart which had never been shattered and broken over personal sin, resulting in confession and repentance. A heart which had never experienced the transforming power of forgiveness that energizes enduring change, validated by a hunger and thirst for righteousness. Like so many people today, Tom saw Christ as his personal *blesser*, not his personal *Savior*. In his mind, Christ existed for him; he did not exist for Christ. And that is exactly the heresy he so passionately preached.

PERSPIRING PREACHERS WITH QUIVERING VOICES AND RHYTHMIC GASPS SEDUCE NAÏVE CONGREGATIONS INTO SUPERFICIAL SPIRITUAL DECISIONS.

IT'S AS THOUGH MAKING JESUS LORD OF THEIR LIFE IS OPTIONAL. THEY MERELY WANT SOME "FIRE INSURANCE" AND A SUPERNATURAL RESOURCE TO MAKE THEM HEALTHY, WEALTHY, AND WISE.

THE SUPREME IMPORTANCE OF EXAMINING OUR FAITH

How poor His story was (handwritten)

This whole scenario triggered in me a passionate desire to more fully understand the nature of true saving faith. I was becoming increasingly aware of the multitudes of people who name the name of Christ as their Lord and Savior, people who were supposedly called *"out of darkness into His marvelous light"* (1 Peter 2:9), yet who love darkness rather than light (John 3:19). People who have nothing in their lives to give evidence of such a transformation. People who are slaves to sin; whose god is their lusts. All of this directs our attention to the Holy Spirit's warning through the apostle Paul: *"Test yourselves to see if you are in the faith; examine yourselves! Or do you not recognize this about yourselves, that Jesus Christ is in you – unless indeed you fail the test?"* (2 Corinthians 13:5)

> IN HIS MIND, CHRIST EXISTED FOR HIM; HE DID NOT EXIST FOR CHRIST.

Go to work slave (handwritten)

The Scriptures are very clear as to the litmus test of true saving faith. Finish filling in the following verses:

1 John 2:3-4: *By this we know that we have come to know Him, _____ _____ . The one who says, 'I have come to know Him,_____ _____ .'*

Read (handwritten)

1 John 3:9-10: *No one who is born of God practices sin, because _____ _____. By this the children of God and the children of the devil are obvious:_____ _____.*

Read (handwritten)

1 John 5:13: *These things I have written to you who believe in the name of the Son of God, _____.*

Ephesians 5:5-6: *This you know with certainty, that _____ _____. Let no one deceive you with empty words, for_____ _____ _____ .*

Titus 1:16: *They profess to know God, but_____, being detestable and disobedient, and worthless for any good deed.*

Matthew 7:16a: *You will know them_____.*

James 2:14, 17: *What use is it, my brethren, if a man says he has faith, _____ _____ ? Can that faith save him?...Even so_____ _____.*

Romans 8:13-14: *If you are living according to the flesh,_____;* *but if by the Spirit you are putting to death the deeds of the body,_____ _____. For all who are being led by the Spirit of God,_____ _____.*

ASK
READ

WHY SOME PEOPLE NEVER CHANGE

We all know people who are just like Tom. All the godly counsel in the world will never impact their lives until Christ transforms their hearts. This is why it's a waste of time to admonish someone to become obedient to God's Word if they don't have the spiritual resources to do so. As we are informed by the Holy Spirit through the words of the apostle Paul: *A natural man does not accept the things of the Spirit of God;_____ Foolishnes _____, and he cannot understand them, because_____.* (1 Corinthians 2:14)

BASED ON THE WORD OF GOD, WHENEVER AN INDIVIDUAL IS SEEMINGLY A SLAVE TO SIN, THEIR FAITH SHOULD BE EXAMINED.

WHY is THIS

In light of this, based on the Word of God, whenever an individual is seemingly a slave to sin, their faith should be examined. This is the necessary starting point. Evangelism must always precede exhortation.

A GREAT MAN OF GOD EXPRESSES HIS FAITH

READ

There can be no better illustration to contrast the heartbreaking story of this chapter than that of the testimony of a great man of God, Charles Haddon Spurgeon. Although his words give evidence to God's transforming work of grace in his life, it was his life that validated their veracity.

In his sermon entitled "Sovereignty and Salvation," he began with a penetrating description of his salvation experience:

> Six years ago today, as near as possible at this very hour of the day, I was in the gall of bitterness and in the bonds of iniquity, but had not yet, by divine grace, been led to feel the bitterness of that bondage, and to cry out by reason of the soreness of its slavery. Seeking rest, and

finding none, I stepped within the house of God, and sat there, afraid to look upward, lest I should be utterly cut off, and lest his fierce wrath should consume me. The minister rose in his pulpit, and, as I have done this morning, read this text, "Look unto me, and be ye saved, all the ends of the earth: for I am God, and there is none else." I looked that moment: the grace of faith was vouchsafed to me in the self-same instant.[1]

Spurgeon also addressed the issue of assurance: How can we know with great certainty that we are truly in Christ? The following are excerpts regarding this crucial issue, taken from one of his sermons delivered at the Metropolitan Tabernacle in Newington, England, sometime in the late 1800's. It is titled, "The Priest Dispensed With." He wrote:

How do I know that I am a believer? Why, **by the very remarkable change** which I underwent when I believed; for when a man believes in Jesus Christ there is such a change wrought in him that he must be aware of it. As in the case of the blind man when his eyes were opened he said, One thing I know, whereas I was blind, now I see… .

Brethren, we have further evidence that we believe, for **our affections are so altered**. The believer can say that the things he once loved he now hates, and the things he hated he now loves; that which gave him pleasure now causes him pain, and things which were irksome and unpleasant have now become delightful to him. Especially is there a great change in us with respect to God. We said in our hearts, "No God." Not that we dared say, "There is no God;" but we wanted to get away from him; we would have been glad to hear that there was no God. How altered are our affections! Now our greatest joy is in God, the nearer we can approach to him the better, the very sound of his name is delicious music to us… .

We know, also, that **we believe because though very far from perfect we love holiness and strive after purity**. You that have believed in Jesus, do you not now pant after holiness? Do you not endeavor to do that which is right, and when you are conscious that you have failed does not conscience prick you? Have you not gone on your knees in bitterness of soul and said, "My God, help me and deliver me, for I delight in thy commandments; help me to keep thy statutes?" By this change of conduct we know that we have believed in Jesus Christ… .

We know that we have believed in Jesus Christ because **now we have communion with God**; we are in the habit of speaking with God in prayer, and hearing the Lord speak with us when we read his word. Some of us have spoken with our Lord Jesus so often that we have grown to be near and dear friends, and whatsoever we ask in prayer he grants us. Answered prayers are sweet testimonies to faith... .

We know that we have believed in the Lord Jesus because we have over and above all this a secret something, indescribable to others, but well-known by ourselves, which is called in Scripture **the witness of the Holy Spirit**: for it is written, "The Spirit himself also beareth witness with our spirit that we are born of God." Do you know what it means? If you do not I cannot tell you. "The secret of the Lord is with them that fear him." There comes stealing over the soul sometimes a peace, a joy, a perfect rest, a heavenly deliciousness, a supreme content, in which, though no voice is heard, yet are we conscious that there is rushing through our souls, like a strain of heaven's own music, the witness of the Spirit of God. We are sure of it, as sure as we are of our own being, and by that witness we know that we are indeed believers in the Lord Jesus Christ."[2]

THE GLORY OF GOD

Although not every denomination uses it, we would all do well to remember the foundational statement of the Westminster Catechism because it simply yet profoundly answers the crucial question, "What is the chief end of man?" – To glorify God and enjoy Him forever! This, dear friends, is the foundation of all true religion. This should be the passion of our hearts. This should rule every thought and deed of every waking moment. This must be the basis of every Christian's life.

But apart from the transformation that takes place in the human heart when we are born again, these words will be nothing more than religious platitudes. Devoid of power. Unable to save. As the Scriptures so clearly attest: *Therefore if any man is in Christ, he is a new creature; the old things passed away; behold, new things have come* (2 Corinthians 5:17).

The supernatural genius of the Gospel is its simplicity. The power to transform is in its truth. This is why the apostle Paul could so confidently extol its virtues:

READ

WHAT IS THE CHIEF END OF MAN?" — TO GLORIFY GOD AND ENJOY HIM FOREVER!

I am not ashamed of the gospel, for it is the power of God for salvation to everyone who believes (Romans 1:16).

Submitting to the gospel message gives birth to a transformation that gives us true meaning in life, and gives God the glory He deserves. Therefore, for the sake of all people everywhere who are searching for answers, the apostle Peter most effectively argues for the sufficiency of Christ and the centrality of the basics found in the Gospel.

> *Grace and peace be multiplied to you in the knowledge of God and of Jesus our Lord; seeing that His divine power has granted to us everything pertaining to life and godliness, through the true knowledge of Him who called us by His own glory and excellence.*
>
> *For by these He has granted to us His precious and magnificent promises, in order that by them you might become partakers of the divine nature, having escaped the corruption that is in the world by lust.*
>
> *Now for this very reason also, applying all diligence, in your faith supply moral excellence, and in your moral excellence, knowledge; and in your knowledge, self-control, and in your self-control, perseverance, and in your perseverance, godliness; and in your godliness, brotherly kindness, and in your brotherly kindness, love.*
>
> *For if these qualities are yours and are increasing, they render you neither useless nor unfruitful in the true knowledge of our Lord Jesus Christ. For he who lacks these qualities is blind or shortsighted, having forgotten his purification from his former sins.*
>
> *Therefore, brethren, be all the more diligent to make certain about His calling and choosing you; for as long as you practice these things, you will never stumble; for in this way the entrance into the eternal kingdom of our Lord and Savior Jesus Christ will be abundantly supplied to you.*
> *2 Peter 1:2-11*

If these words are hollow to you, maybe it's because you have never experienced the transforming power of Christ. Maybe you have never truly been born again. This is why it is so important to be able to answer the question posed in the next chapter: What is a Christian?

THE SUPERNATURAL GENIUS OF THE GOSPEL IS ITS SIMPLICITY. THE POWER TO TRANSFORM IS IN ITS TRUTH.

THE DIFFERENCE KNOWN SIN & RIGHTEOUSNESS

WE ALL WILL HAVE PROBLEMS GOD HAS SOLUTIONS LET FIND OUT WHAT

QUESTIONS FOR DISCUSSION

1. What are some of the biblical reasons emphasizing that counseling is difficult work?

_____

_____

2. What are some problems with the way that Tom responded to Lisa's accusations?

_____

_____

3. What are some of the emotions that Lisa was feeling? What was she thinking?

_____

_____

4. What did the counselor think was Tom's problem? Why?

_____

_____

5. What are some reasons people like to have unbiblical labels for their sinful behavior?

_____

_____

6. What was Tom really saying about his behavior by describing the cause in the way he did?

_____

_____

7. What is the problem with the labels Tom used for his sin?

_____

_____

8. What reasons did Tom give for rejecting the counselor's counsel?

_____

_____

9. Summarize the counselor's response to Tom's vulgarity. Do you agree with the direction the counselor took? Why or why not?

_____

_____

10. What is meant by the phrase "cheap grace?"

_____

_____

11. Why do some people never change?

_____

_____

12. Why is it a waste of time to admonish someone who is not really a Christian to become obedient to God's Word?

_____

_____

13. According to Scripture, what is the litmus test of true saving faith?

_____

_____

14. What do works have to do with salvation?

_____

_____

15. Explain why Spurgeon was convinced that he was a believer.

_____

_____

PERSONAL RESPONSE

1. Do you agree with the counselor's diagnosis of Tom's situation? Why or why not?

_____

_____

2. Why do you think Lisa felt there was hope after Tom's final outburst and exit?

_____

_____

3. How were Tom's messages and methods a manifestation of his heart?

_____

_____

4. What were some of the problems with the "gospel" that Tom preached?

_____

_____

5. Explain how Tom's view of Christ was wrong. What are some of the practical implications of such a view?

_____

_____

6. If someone were to come up to you and say, "I am a Christian because I believe in Christ. But I refuse to follow after Christ and obey Him," how would you respond?

_____

_____

7. Have you ever described the cause of your bad behavior in the way that Tom did? When and how?

_____

_____

8. Explain why evangelism must precede exhortation.

_____

_____

9. What do our affections have to do with our salvation?

_____

_____

10. Prove from Scripture that a true believer loves holiness and strives after purity.

_____

_____

11. What is the chief end of man? Explain in your own words what the Westminster Catechism's answer means.

_____

_____

12. As you reflect on the five answers Spurgeon gave to the question, "How do I know I am a believer?" can you honestly say that those five things are true in your life?

_____

_____

13. What are the most important lessons you learned from this chapter?

_____

_____

CHAPTER 2

THE FUNDAMENTAL REQUIREMENT

What is a Christian? No other question is more important, nor surrounded with as much confusion. Among the many reasons why this question is so important is the fact that you will never be able to solve your problems God's way until you have rightly understood and embraced the correct answer.

But, you wonder, how in the world does the proper answer to this question relate to solving life's problems? It's a good question. Be assured, it will be answered as you proceed through this chapter and study.

> YOU WILL NEVER BE ABLE TO SOLVE YOUR PROBLEMS GOD'S WAY UNTIL YOU HAVE RIGHTLY UNDERSTOOD AND EMBRACED THE CORRECT ANSWER.

READ

WHY

JOHN 9:31

DOES GOD NOT HEAR SINNERS AT ALL

If you ask ten people to give their perspective on what it means to be a Christian, you'll probably get five or six different answers.

Here are six of the most commonly held opinions about the essence of Christianity.

1. "Well, I certainly am a Christian; I'm doing the best I can. I try to live by the Ten Commandments, the Golden Rule, and the Sermon on the Mount."

2. "Most assuredly, I'm a Christian. If I'm not, I don't know who is. My mother and father are very religious. I even have an uncle who is a minister."

3. "Indeed I am. I have always gone to church and Sunday school. I've been baptized and confirmed. I joined the church when I was fourteen."

4. "I know I'm a Christian because when the evangelist gave the invitation I went to the front and made a decision for Christ. My counselor showed me that if I accepted Jesus as my personal Savior, I would never be lost again. I didn't want to be lost, hell is a terrible place; so I accepted Jesus, and I know now that no matter what happens, God will never reject me. I know it because I went to the altar and professed faith in Jesus Christ."

5. "I don't know if I am, and I don't see how anyone can really know for sure in this life. I guess I'll just have to wait until I die to find out."

6. "Sure, I'm a Christian. Isn't everybody? Isn't God the Father of all men? We may be going by different roads, but all of these roads lead to the same place. It doesn't really matter what you believe, just so you're sincere; everyone who is sincere in his own religion is a Christian."

These and many other answers have been given to the question, "What is a Christian?" Who is right? Can we know what it means to be a Christian, or must we be forever uncertain? If we look to human opinion we will flounder in a sea of uncertainty. But, if we look to God's Word, our confusion will be dispersed. In the Bible you'll find many statements such as these: *Thy Word is a lamp unto my feet, and a light unto my path* (Psalm 119:105). *The law of the Lord is perfect, converting the soul: the testimony of the Lord is sure, making wise the simple...the commandment of the Lord is pure, enlightening the eyes* (Psalm 19:7-8). *The Holy Scriptures, which are able to make thee wise unto salvation through faith which is in Christ Jesus. All Scripture is given by inspiration of God, and is profitable for doctrine* (to teach us what is true), *for reproof* (to make us realize what is wrong in our lives), *for correction* (to straighten out our errors), *for instruction in righteousness* (to teach us and train us in what is right) (2 Timothy 3:15-16).

These Scriptures tell us that God has given us the Bible to make us wise in spiritual matters. Therefore, it only makes sense that we should turn to the Bible to find an answer to the question "What is a Christian?" If we want to travel to a certain city we get a map. We don't turn to some person who has never been there for directions. Nor do we turn to a philosophy or science book. Instead, we turn to a map of the area where that city is located. So it is with the Bible. It was produced by the inspiration of Almighty God so that we might be made wise concerning the way of salvation.

God gave the Bible to tell us the way of salvation, so let's test the six common opinions stated previously against its standard. What does Scripture say about the six common answers given to the question, "What is a Christian?" Write out each scripture.

COMMON ANSWER NUMBER ONE:
Salvation Comes by Good Works

Ephesians 2:8-9

_____

_____

_____

From a positive point of view, these verses state that salvation is by grace. The word "grace" means unmerited favor. Positively speaking, salvation is the free gift of God. From a negative point of view, these verses teach that salvation is not of works lest any man should boast. Again, Scripture states that *not by works of righteousness which we have done, but according to his mercy he saved us, by the washing of regeneration and renewing of the Holy Ghost; Which he shed on us abundantly through Jesus Christ our Savior; That being justified by his grace, we should be made heirs according to the hope of eternal life* (Titus 3:5-6). Similarly the Bible affirms that *by the deeds of the law there shall no flesh be justified in his sight* (Romans 3:20).

THE WORD "GRACE" MEANS UNMERITED FAVOR.

COMMON ANSWER NUMBER TWO:
Salvation Comes by Heredity

John 1:12-13

_____

_____

This verse affirms that physical heritage, blood lineage, family connections, or any other such factors do not have anything to do with whether or not a person is a Christian.

COMMON ANSWER NUMBER THREE:
Salvation Comes by Religious Activity

Matthew 7:22-23

_____

_____

Other Scriptures demonstrate that a Christian is not simply a person who is active in religious matters.

Summarize each of these passages in your own words:

Mark 7:1-7

_____

_____

John 3:1-8

_____

_____

Luke 18:9-14

_____

_____

Philippians 3:6-7

_____

_____

Galatians 1:14-15

_____

_____

Psalm 51:16-17

_____

_____

COMMON ANSWER NUMBER FOUR:
Salvation Comes by Mere Mechanical Actions

John 2:23-25

_____

_____

These people made a profession of faith, but it involved mechanical actions such as walking an aisle in an evangelistic crusade or praying a certain prayer. Our Lord would not trust Himself unto them because He knew that their profession of faith was not real. Other Scripture passages teach that merely professing faith or going through certain mechanical actions does not ensure that a person is a Christian.

Summarize each of these passages in your own words:

Acts 8:12-24

_____

_____

John 3:36

_____

_____

James 2:14-26

_____

_____

2 Corinthians 5:17

_____

_____

COMMON ANSWER NUMBER FIVE:
You Just Can't Know Whether or Not You Are Saved

2 Timothy 1:12

_____

_____

1 John 5:13

_____

_____

Other scriptures teach that a person can know that he is truly a Christian.

Summarize each of these passages in your own words:

John 5:24

_____

_____

Romans 8:1

_____

_____

2 Peter 1:4-11

_____

_____

COMMON ANSWER NUMBER SIX:
Every Human Being Is a Christian and Will Most Certainly Go to Heaven

John 3:18

_____
_____

John 3:36

_____
_____

John 8:44

_____
_____

Other Scriptures teach that not everyone will go to heaven.

Summarize each of these passages in your own words:

John 8:31-44

_____
_____

Revelation 20:11-15

_____
_____

Ephesians 2:2-3

_____
_____

Colossians 3:6

_____
_____

When tested by the standard of God's Word, these six common answers to the question, "What is a Christian?" prove to be contrary to the Word of God. According to the Bible, if the basis for your hope of heaven is founded upon any one of these opinions, you're wrong. Why can we say this? Because a Christian is not simply a person who performs good works, is active in religious matters, is born of Godly parents, makes a profession of faith and is baptized, or has responded to an invitation. But if these answers are not the correct answers to the question, "What is a Christian?" how does the Bible answer this question?

RADICALLY CHANGED BY THE POWER OF GOD

The Bible declares that a Christian has been radically changed by the power of God.

Some verses assert that a Christian has been created anew in Christ Jesus:

2 Corinthians 5:17

_____

_____

Ephesians 4:24

_____

_____

Colossians 3:9-10

_____

_____

Ephesians 2:10

_____

_____

Galatians 6:15

_____

_____

Other Bible verses declare that a Christian has become a partaker of the Divine nature (2 Peter 1:2-4). This means that when people become Christians they receive a new nature from God. It is created and put within us by God (James 1:17) and is holy even as God's nature is holy (1 John 2:29, 3:7; 1 Peter 1:15-16). Still other Bible verses testify that a Christian has been begotten or born of God (James 1:18; 1 John 5:1; John 3:1-8; John 1:12-13), regenerated or made to live again (Titus 3:5), passed from death unto life and quickened from the dead (John 5:24-25; Ephesians 2:1; Colossians 2:13; Luke 15:24, 32).

These biblical phrases abundantly testify that a Christian has been radically changed by the power of God. So becoming a Christian is a supernatural operation of God upon the spirit of the person, not merely a matter of outward reformation, nor merely a turning over of a new leaf and endeavoring to live a new life, nor of education or religion. Nature might be educated to the highest standard attainable, but it cannot be developed into something of a totally different order. There is no process by which a person can be developed out of a horse, nor a beast from a bird. Likewise, there is no process by which a spiritual man can be developed out of a sinful man by education. I may gather some weeds out of a field and transplant them into my garden; I may fertilize and irrigate them, but no amount of attention will transform them into rose bushes. Education and religion cannot change man's sinful nature. They can only refine it.

Becoming a Christian is the implanting of an entirely new nature within man. It is being born again from above, being made a new creation, being remade and reoriented at the center of being. Sinclair B. Ferguson described the change that takes place when a person becomes a Christian like this:

> ... the New Testament indicates that the transforming power of regeneration is total. It meets our needs at every point. This is not to say that regeneration produces perfection. But just as total depravity means sin has influenced every area of our lives, so grace reaches into every aspect of our experience where the ravages of sin first ventured. It is through the new birth that the image of God, like an embryo in the womb, is restored. It then begins to grow to that full maturity of the later stages of Christian experience....

In regeneration the mind is illuminated. We see the kingdom of God. Is it not one of the greatest privileges of a living Christian fellowship, to witness a new Christian confessing, 'Once I was blind, but now I see'? To become a child of God by regeneration is to be given a totally new perspective on oneself and on others (how frequently young people will admit that only when they became children of God did they begin to see the needs of their parents and want to love and care for them). We see the world with new eyes: 'Something lives in every hue that Christless eyes have never seen,' we now sing!

EDUCATION AND RELIGION CANNOT CHANGE MAN'S SINFUL NATURE. THEY CAN ONLY REFINE IT.

IN REGENERATION THE MIND IS ILLUMINATED.

In regeneration the heart is purified. This is at least part of the meaning of the enigmatic words of Christ about being 'born of water' (Jn. 3:5). Many interpretations have been forwarded for this expression. Probably Jesus is referring to water as a symbol of purification. Undoubtedly that would be the major association in the mind of a Pharisee, and perhaps the recent events at Jordan would add point to his words. (Nicodemus had perhaps been to hear John the Baptist preach on the necessity of a baptism of repentance for the washing away of sins.) This, after all, was the promise God gave through Ezekiel about the New Covenant! 'I will sprinkle clean water on you, and you will be clean; I will sprinkle you from all your impurities...' (Eze. 36:25). Nicodemus, the teacher of Israel could not fail to recall the words.

IN REGENERATION THE HEART IS PURIFIED.

RBAD

But what is a purified heart? What does Paul mean when he says to the Corinthians, 'you were washed....' (I Cor. 6:11)? He means that in the work of giving us new spiritual life God creates in us new tendencies and dispositions towards right living. He puts his law in our hearts, so that the motivation to glorify and serve him in the paths of righteousness is no longer an external force, but an inward power.

In regeneration the desires are renewed. What is born of flesh is flesh, but that to which the Spirit gives birth is spirit and has the characteristics of the Spirit. This seed thought is worked out more fully by Paul in Romans 8:5-8. The mind of the flesh is hostile to God and does not submit to his Law. It cannot please God and walks on the road to death. All its desires are turned from God to self-pleasing. It has no taste for spiritual realities but turns from them and may even despise them like the Dwarfs in Lewis's Narnia. But the newly born child of God craves for pure spiritual milk so that by it he may grow. He has tasted that the Lord is Good and he wants more! (I Pet. 2:2-3). Regeneration creates new desires to worship God, know his truth, meet his people, serve his kingdom and love and honor his Son. These aspirations are not perfect. They ebb and flow. At times we lament their weakness. But however far short we confess ourselves to have fallen from what we ought to be, we are not what we once were. Our minds are now set on the things above where Christ is (Col. 3:1-2).

IN REGENERATION THE DESIRES ARE RENEWED.

In regeneration we begin to live a new life. This is a major emphasis in I John where the doctrine of regeneration is dealt with more fully. Everyone who lives righteously is born of God (I John 2:29). This righteous living expresses itself in three ways: the one who is born of God loves his fellow believers (I John 4:7), he overcomes the world (I John 5:4), and he doe not go on sinning (I John 3:9). The world around him is a chief source of temptation to sin (I John 2:15-17) but his relationship to it is radically altered. When it spreads out its enticing tentacles towards him he recognizes that his new birth has made him a new creation in which those allurements will no longer conquer him. Similarly his attitude to his fellow Christians becomes a thing of beauty – he loves them with an affection which is unparalleled. There is no more powerful testimony to the reality of a new birth than that bonding of human lives together in Christian fellowship which transcends the barriers of ordinary relationships… .

If Christ came to be our Savior; if one of the focal points of that salvation is in the deliverance of his people from the bondage of sin, then there must be some sense in which John's words can be taken at their face value. The new birth radically and totally transforms our relationship to sin. Christ Jesus makes men whole, and has begun the process of making all things new! This is what it means to be "born again" from above.[3]

The Christian, then, has been radically changed by the supernatural power of God. This wonderful work of God is usually carried on in connection with the preaching of the Bible. Write out what the following verses tell us:

1 Peter 1:23, 25

_____

_____

James 1:18

_____

_____

Romans 10:17

_____

_____

1 Corinthians 1:21

_____

_____

As the Word of God is proclaimed, the Holy Spirit wings those words like arrows into the hearts of sinners. The Word creates new life at the center of the sinner's personality. He begins to think God's thoughts after Him and to feel differently. His likes and dislikes change and his will works differently. He decides to break with sin, believe on the Lord, and follow Jesus Christ. He now begins to pattern his life according to the truth of God instead of according to his own opinions or the opinions of others. All of this is the result, not of man's own efforts, but of the supernatural power of God at work in that person's life.

AN INCREASING AWARENESS OF UNWORTHINESS
The Bible declares that a Christian is a person who has become increasingly aware of his own unworthiness.

HE NOW BEGINS TO PATTERN HIS LIFE ACCORDING TO THE TRUTH OF GOD INSTEAD OF ACCORDING TO HIS OWN OPINIONS OR THE OPINIONS OF OTHERS.

He realizes that he is a sinner by practice and has broken the laws of God and thus deserves condemnation. The Christian reads of the prodigal son who wandered away from his father and wasted his substance in riotous living and he says, "I am that prodigal son who wandered away from my heavenly Father and wasted all that God has given me in riotous living." He reads of the prodigal coming to himself and recognizing how he has grieved his father and says, "I am that prodigal who has come to the realization of how I have sinned against my heavenly Father and grieved him." He reads of the prodigal coming to the father and saying, "I have sinned against heaven and in thy sight and am no more worthy to be called thy son," and says, "I need to confess my sins to my heavenly Father." He reads the declaration of John that *"whosoever commits sin transgresses also the law, for sin is the transgression of the law"* (1 John 3:4) and he says, "I have sinned because I have transgressed the law of God. I have broken God's commandments. I am a sinner by practice."

But the Christian also realizes that he is a sinner by nature. He recognizes that the nature with which he was born is in rebellion against God. He knows Paul wrote in Romans 7:24, *"O wretched man that I am! Who shall deliver me from the body of death?"* and he in turn says, "I know what Paul is talking about, *'for when I would do good evil is present with me. I delight in the law of God after the inward man: but I see another law in my members, warring against the law of my mind'* " (Romans 7:21-23).

A Christian comes to God as David did in Psalm 51:7 and says, *"Behold, I was shaped in iniquity; and in sin did my mother conceive me. Behold, thou desirest truth*

HE IS CONCERNED NOT ONLY ABOUT SINFUL ACTIONS BUT SINFUL ATTITUDES, NOT ONLY ABOUT SINFUL DEEDS BUT SINFUL THOUGHTS.

in the inward parts; and in the hidden part thou shall make me to know wisdom. Purify me with hyssop, and I shall be clean; wash me, and I shall be whiter than show. Create in me a clean heart, O God; and renew a steadfast spirit within me." He is concerned not only about sinful actions but sinful attitudes, not only about sinful deeds but sinful thoughts. He believes that Jeremiah was describing his heart when Jeremiah said, *"The heart is deceitful above all things, and desperately wicked"* (Jeremiah 17:9). The Christian accepts God's statements about the depths, the potential, and the dessert of his sins, he believes that God would be perfectly just in condemning him to hell. Thus he comes to God not to bargain or barter but to plead as the publican in Luke 18:13, *"God be merciful to me the sinner."* The Christian is aware that his "old nature" (the nature with which he was born) is incurably wicked and capable of great wickedness. He is aware that his carnal mind was enmity against God and could not be subject to the law of God (Romans 8:7-8). He is aware of his need for a new heart, for a new nature. He is in full agreement with Jesus Christ who said, *"Ye must be born again"* (John 3:7). The Christian then is a person who recognizes that *"it is of the Lord's mercies that we are not consumed."* He rejoices that salvation is all of grace. He has no confidence in the flesh to save or to keep himself saved. He is cast completely on the Lord and upon His mercy. Scripture is replete with verses that teach that we are sinners by practice and nature.

Summarize these verses in your own words.

Romans 3:9-19

_____

_____

Romans 3:23

_____

_____

Romans 8:7-8

_____

_____

Psalm 10:4

_____

_____

Psalm 53:1-3

_____

_____

Psalm 58:3

_____

_____

Psalm 143:2

_____

_____

2 Chronicles 6:36

_____

_____

BELIEFS ABOUT JESUS CHRIST

The Christian believes that Jesus Christ is God manifest in the flesh and the only Savior and substitute for sinners.

In Matthew 21:10, when Jesus came riding into the city of Jerusalem on the day that we celebrate as Palm Sunday, the whole city was stirred and began to ask the question, "Who is this?" The Bible unmistakably tells us who Jesus Christ is.

The Bible declares the humanity of Jesus Christ. Write the following Scriptures.

Romans 5:15

_____

_____

1 Timothy 2:5

_____

_____

1 Corinthians 15:21

_____

_____

_____

go to pg 53

THE BIBLE UNMISTAKABLY TELLS US WHO JESUS CHRIST IS.

The Christian believes that Jesus Christ is truly a man – like all other men but with one glorious exception. The Bible tells us that *all have sinned and come short of the glory of God* (Romans 3:23). But Jesus Christ knew no sin. Hebrews 4:15 asserts that *he was tempted in all points like as we are, yet without sin.* In John 14:30 Jesus said, *"The prince of this world (Satan) cometh, and hath nothing in me."* In 1 Peter 2:22 we read: *Who (Jesus Christ) did no sin, neither was guile found in his mouth.* First John 3:5 asserts that *in him is no sin.* Second Corinthians 5:21 declares that *he knew no sin.* Jesus Christ perfectly, continuously, absolutely fulfilled the will of the Father. He never went to bed feeling guilty or regretting what he said, thought, or did. He lived a sinless life. In this respect he was different from all other human beings.

HE WAS GOD MANIFEST IN THE FLESH.

However, the Bible teaches that Jesus Christ was more than a perfect man, He was God manifest in the flesh – very God of very God. Not merely a great human teacher who came to show men the way, but God who came to reveal God to man. The Bible speaking of Jesus as the Word of God, the perfect revealer of the Father, says *in the beginning was the Word, and the Word was with God, and the Word was God, and the Word was made flesh and dwelt among us and we beheld his glory, the glory as of the only begotten of the Father full of grace and truth* (John 1:1, 14). It teaches that the eternal Son of God left heaven and took on human nature, being conceived of the Holy Ghost and born of the virgin Mary. Jesus Himself said, *"I and the Father are one"* (John 10:30). *"He that hath seen me hath seen the Father"* (John 14:9). Frequently in the Bible, Jesus Christ is called God. In Hebrews 1:8 God the Father speaks to Jesus Christ and says, *"Thy throne, O God, is for ever and ever."* Romans 9:5 tells us that *concerning the flesh Christ came of the fathers who is over all, God blessed for ever.* John 20:28 tells us that Thomas fell at the feet of Jesus Christ and said, *"My Lord and my God."*

FREQUENTLY IN THE BIBLE, JESUS CHRIST IS CALLED GOD.

The Bible also indicates that Jesus Christ is God by applying to Jesus Christ in the New Testament, Old Testament passages which refer to Jehovah. In Isaiah 40:3 the Bible says that *"the way of Jehovah is to be prepared."* John the Baptist quotes this verse of Scripture in the New Testament in reference to Jesus Christ. Isaiah 6:1, 4 tell us that Isaiah saw Jehovah. In John 12:41 we are told that the one that he saw was Jesus Christ. In Joel 2:32 we read that *whosoever shall call on the name of Jehovah shall be saved.* Romans 10:13 quotes this verse in reference to Jesus Christ.

These two facts, that the Bible calls Jesus Christ God and the Old Testament passages referring to God are applied to Jesus Christ in the New Testament, give abundant proof that Jesus Christ is God. Add to these facts the biblical facts that Jesus Christ possesses the attributes of God, that Jesus Christ performs the works of God, that His name is associated with God the Father in an equalitarian way, that there are biblical statements which clearly teach that He is God, that He claims to be able to do things that only God can do, and the certainty of His Godhead is irrefutably established.

Matthew 10:32, 37

_____

_____

Matthew 18:20

_____

_____

Matthew 28:19-20

_____

_____

Mark 2:5-12

_____

_____

Luke 4:16-21

_____

_____

Luke 24:27, 44

_____

_____

John 1:1, 3, 29

_____

_____

John 2:25

_____

_____

_____

John 3:13, 36

_____

_____

John 5:17, 46

_____

_____

John 6:35

_____

_____

John 8:12, 56-58

_____

_____

John 10:27-30

_____

_____

John 11:25-26

_____

_____

John 14:9-11

_____

_____

John 21:17

_____

_____

Acts 10:43

_____

_____

A Christian therefore believes that Jesus Christ is both God and man, indivisible and distinctly joined in one person, that Jesus Christ has a divine nature and human nature. Christians believe what they cannot perfectly understand. They cannot nor do they try to eradicate or erase the Biblical truth that Jesus Christ is truly God and truly man. They accept both of these facts, submitting to the clear evidence of the Word of God.

Christians believe that Jesus came to save unworthy, hell-deserving sinners. Jesus Christ explained His coming when He said, *"The son of man is come to seek and to save that which was lost"* (Luke 19:10). The angels explained his entrance into this world when they said, *"Thou shall call his name Jesus; for he shall save his people from their sins. Fear not; for, behold, I bring you good tidings of great joy which, shall be to all the people. For unto you is born this day, in the city of David, a Savior, which is Christ the Lord"* (Matthew 1:21 and Luke 2:10-11). Christians believe that Jesus Christ is the only Savior of sinners. Jesus said, *"I am the way, the truth and the life; no man cometh unto the father but by me"* (John 14:6). Christians believe that for Jesus Christ to save sinners He became their substitute, taking their place before the law of God and obeying the law they were unable to obey. In part, the atoning work of Christ consists in fulfilling the exacting requirements of God's law that Adam, and then we as his descendants, failed to obey. Jesus Christ said, *"Think not that I am come to destroy the Law, or the Prophets: I am not come to destroy, but to fulfill"* (Matthew 5:17). Romans 5:19 declares that *by the obedience of one (Jesus Christ) many shall be made righteous.* Philippians 2:8 declares that Jesus Christ became obedient unto death, even the death of the cross. The Christian then believes that Jesus Christ became man that he might perfectly keep in the stead of sinners the law of God.

CHRISTIANS BELIEVE WHAT THEY CANNOT PERFECTLY UNDERSTAND.

Christians affirm that Christ made atonement for the law that sinners had broken. The Bible asserts that Christ died for our sins according to the Scriptures; that *he was wounded for our transgressions, he was bruised for our iniquities; the chastisement of our peace was upon him; and with his stripes we are healed. All we like sheep have gone astray; we have turned every one to his own way; and the Lord hath laid on him the iniquity of us all.*

1 Corinthians 15:3

_____

_____

Isaiah 53:5-6

_____

_____

2 Corinthians 5:19, 21

_____

_____

_____

1 Peter 2:24

_____

_____

1 Peter 3:18

_____

_____

Romans 3:24-26

_____

_____

Romans 5:6-11

_____

_____

Ephesians 1:6-7

_____

_____

Galatians 3:13

_____

_____

All have sinned and come short of the glory of God; all are transgressors of God's law, and according to eternal justice all deserve to die; all deserve God's wrath and curse *for it is written, cursed is everyone that continues not in all things that are written in the law* (Galatians 3:10; Romans 3:9, 19; James 2:10). But Jesus Christ came and in the stead of His people He satisfied every charge that the law of God had against them. He paid their penalty by His death upon the cross and fully satisfied every claim that divine justice might have against His people.

In a book entitled *Right With God*, John Blanchard explained salvation this way:

> Years ago, our country had 'debtor's prisons,' to which men owing money were frequently sentenced. If the debtor could not be found, his guarantor could be jailed in his place. Now supposing I had contracted a debt, my guarantor had been imprisoned on my behalf, and later I saw him walking down the road a free man. I would now be sure that my debt must have been settled, because the man punished by

imprisonment on my behalf was free. In a much more profound way, the fact that Jesus rose from the dead is proof that God's justice was satisfied by the death of His Son on behalf of sinners. The law can no longer condemn those for whom Jesus died. Paul declares that God…"having canceled the written code, with its regulations, that was against us and that stood opposed to us; he took away, nailing it to the cross" (Colossians 2:14).

A man called Bildad once asked the most baffling of Questions, "How then can a man be righteous before God?" (Job 25:4). How can it ever be possible for man to be declared "not guilty" by God when he was born a sinner and is guilty of a life of sin? Looked at the other way, how can God punish sin and yet reverse the sentence on the sinner, declaring him to be free from His guilt? Only God could provide an answer, and He did so in the life and death of Jesus Christ acting as man's substitute. As somebody put it,

Because the sinless Savior died
My guilty soul is counted free,
For God, the Just, is satisfied
To look on Him and pardon me....

The Bible teaches that "Each of us will give an account of himself to God" (Romans 14:12). From this judgment all men will pass to one of two eternal destinies. Some will be received into the conscious presence of God. The Bible calls this "heaven." All others will be "punished with everlasting destruction and shut out …from the majesty of His power" (2 Thessalonians 1:9), and exist forever in a condition of indescribable suffering, despair and torment, which the Bible calls "hell."…

Yet in the death and resurrection of Jesus Christ, the possibility of hell and terror are removed by the gift of eternal life here and now….The man for whom Jesus Christ has fulfilled the law, and for whose sins He died on the cross, fears neither hell, judgment nor death, for Christ has given him the gift of eternal life….Physical death, although to be experienced, no longer leads to everlasting torment, but to everlasting triumph in the presence of the living God.[4]

This, every true Christian believes.

REPENTANCE AND FAITH
The Bible teaches that Christians have repented of their sins and believed on the Lord Jesus Christ.

Christians recognize that their faith and repentance do not merit them the favor of God; rather they come to God saying, "Not the labors of my hands can fulfill thy law's demands; Could my zeal no respite know, could my tears for ever flow, All for sin could not atone; Thou must save, and thou alone. Nothing in my hands I bring, simply to Thy cross I cling. Naked, come to thee for dress, helpless, look to thee for grace; Foul, I to the Fountain fly; Wash me, Savior, or I die." At the same time, they acknowledge that faith and repentance (which are gifts of God) are the means by which that salvation becomes their own personal experience and possession. Jesus Christ said, *"He that believeth on him is not condemned but he that believeth not is condemned already because he has not believed in the name of the only begotten son"* (John 3:18).

What does it mean to repent? To repent is to be sorry for sin and to hate and forsake it because it is displeasing to God. True repentance involves sorrow for sin and a hatred of sin, both internal and external sin. It is a sorrow for what we are, as well as what we do, for the corruption of our hearts as well as the perversity of our conduct, for the attitudes which prompt the actions as well as the actions themselves. Isaiah cried, *"Woe is me, for I am undone"* (Isaiah 6:5). The publican prayed, *"God be merciful to me a sinner"* (Luke 18:13). The thief on the cross said to the other thief who was mocking Jesus: *"Don't you fear God, seeing you are in the same condemnation? And we indeed are condemned justly; for we receive the due reward of our deeds: but this man hath done nothing amiss."*

Luke 23:40- 41

_____

_____

2 Corinthians 7:9-11

_____

_____

Joel 2:12; Jeremiah 31:18

_____

_____

_____

> **TO REPENT IS TO BE SORRY FOR SIN AND TO HATE AND FORSAKE IT BECAUSE IT IS DISPLEASING TO GOD.**

Psalm 119:104

_____

_____

Ezekiel 20:43

_____

_____

True repentance involves forsaking sin, not just a change of attitude toward sin, but also a change of action. The Bible tells us, *"Let the wicked forsake his way, the unrighteous man his thoughts: and let him return unto the Lord, and he will have mercy upon him: and to our God, for he will abundantly pardon"* (Isaiah 55:7). *"He that covers his sins shall not prosper: but whoso confesses and forsakes them shall have mercy"* (Proverb 28:13). Furthermore, true repentance involves sorrow for sin and a forsaking of sin because it is displeasing to God. More than anything else, the truly repentant person wants the favor of God. He hates sin and forsakes it because he knows that God hates sin.

Read the following verses and summarize each passage in your own words:

TRUE REPENTANCE INVOLVES FORSAKING SIN, NOT JUST A CHANGE OF ATTITUDE TOWARD SIN, BUT ALSO A CHANGE OF ACTION.

Ezekiel 36:25-32

_____

_____

Zechariah 12:10

_____

_____

Luke 15:18

_____

_____

Psalm 51:1-12

_____

_____

Luke 22:59-62

_____

_____

True Christians have repented of their sin. They hate their sin and they are constantly forsaking it because it is displeasing to God. Unless we have done this, we have no right to believe that we are Christians. Jesus said, *"Except ye repent; ye shall all likewise perish"* (Luke 13:3).

The Christian, however, not only turns away from sin, he also turns to Christ in faith. The Bible says, *"By grace are ye saved through faith; and that not of yourselves, it is the gift of God: Not of works, lest any man should boast"* (Ephesians 2:8-9). When people turn from something, they either do it because they have already turned to something, or because they want to turn to something. Sinners do exactly that. They turn from sin to holiness; from self to the Savior. Repentance is turning from; faith is turning to. Repentance and faith are two sides of the same coin. Repentance is the negative aspect; faith is the positive aspect. You can be sure that a person has not truly believed unless they have repented; nor have people truly repented unless they have believed on Jesus Christ.

What does it mean to believe on the Lord Jesus Christ? Well, believing on the Lord Jesus Christ means to trust in or rely upon Christ alone for salvation. The Bible declares, *"He that believeth on the Son hath everlasting life;" "He that believeth on him is not condemned"* (John 3:36; John 3:18). Notice the words "believeth on," not simply "believeth in." To believe on involves reliance upon; it involves resting your weight on Christ. It involves commitment to Jesus Christ. Commitment is the crowning element of saving faith. Commitment is simply a giving of oneself to Jesus. This is well illustrated in the physical realm when a patient actually submits to the operating surgeon by undergoing an anesthetic, thus literally putting his life into the doctor's hands. So, also, when sinners put themselves into the hands of the Great Physician, Jesus Christ, calling upon Him to heal them of the deadly disease of sin, they trust the Savior and the Savior alone for salvation. This is the exercise of saving faith, and all degrees short of this element of commitment are not saving faith. We shall not be delivered from the wrath to come by believing simply that His atonement is sufficient; but we shall be saved by making that atonement our trust, our refuge, and our all. The pith, the essence, of saving faith lies in this, a casting of ourselves on Jesus Christ. It is not the lifebuoy on board the ship that saves the person who is drowning, nor is it their belief that it is an excellent and successful invention. No! That person must have it around their body or have their hand upon it or else they will sink. So it is with saving faith. We must actually commit ourselves unto Jesus, body, soul, and spirit.

I once heard someone illustrate saving faith in this manner: Imagine that a fire breaks out in the home where a young boy is asleep on the upper floor. The boy's father and mother wake up and get all the children out, but somehow they miss little Jimmy. They don't realize that he is still in the building. Then the horrible truth dawns on them as they gather their children around and find Jimmy missing. The father tries to go back into the house to rescue his little boy, but he is blocked by a sheet of flames which he cannot get through. Meanwhile Jimmy wakes up and smells the smoke. He opens the bedroom door and is met by a wall of fire which makes it impossible for him to get downstairs. He closes the door and runs to the window. He looks down at the concrete three stories below. If he stays where he is, he will be burned to death. If he jumps, he will be dashed to pieces. It looks hopeless until his father sees him, holds out his arms, and shouts, "Jump, Jimmy, I will catch you." Jimmy knows that his father is strong enough to catch him; but does that make him safe? Jimmy knows his father loves him and is willing to catch him; but does that make him safe? Jimmy not only knows his father is willing and able to catch him but that his father is pleading with him to jump; but does that make him safe? None of these things will save him unless he trusts his father enough to jump. If Jimmy will not commit himself to his father's arms, he will perish.

Saving faith does not merely involve knowing that Jesus Christ is God manifest in the flesh Who came into the world to save sinners by perfectly keeping the law for them and by offering Himself as an all-sufficient sacrifice for sin on the cross. It does not merely involve knowing that Jesus Christ is able to save, nor that Jesus Christ is willing to save. A person may know all of this and still perish. Saving faith involves the actual casting of ourselves upon Jesus Christ and trusting Him alone for our salvation. When the Philippian jailer asked Paul, *"What must I do to be saved?"* Paul said, *"Believe on the Lord Jesus Christ and thou shalt be saved"* (Acts 16:30-31).

In another place the apostle Paul wrote: *If you shall confess with your mouth the Lord Jesus, and shall believe in your heart that God hath raised him from the dead, you shall be saved. For with the heart man believes unto righteousness; and with the mouth confession is made unto salvation....For whosoever shall call upon the name of the Lord shall be saved* (Romans 10:9-10, 13). It is not enough to believe *about* Jesus Christ. We must believe *on* and *in* the Lord Jesus Christ. We must cease from trusting in our own goodness, our own works of righteousness, our own baptism or church membership, our own keeping the law of God, and we must rest completely upon the Lord Jesus Christ Who is the all-sufficient Savior of

SAVING FAITH INVOLVES THE ACTUAL CASTING OF OURSELVES UPON JESUS CHRIST AND TRUSTING HIM ALONE FOR OUR SALVATION.

sinners. We must cease from our "do-it-yourself," "make-up-your-own-mind," "run your own life" attitudes and acknowledge Jesus Christ to be the Lord of our lives. We must commit ourselves wholly and unreservedly to Jesus Christ for time and eternity. Jesus said, *"Whosoever does not bear his cross and come after me cannot be my disciple"* (Luke 14:27). This, all true Christians have done. They have repented of their sins and believed on the Lord Jesus Christ.

At the beginning of this chapter, we stated that no question is more important than the question: What is a Christian? This is true for at least two reasons. First, it is true because a person's eternal destiny depends on a proper understanding of and right response to the true answer to this question. Second, this question is incredibly important because only Christians can solve life's problems God's way.

> IT IS NOT ENOUGH TO BELIEVE *ABOUT* JESUS CHRIST. WE MUST BELIEVE *ON* AND *IN* THE LORD JESUS CHRIST.

The Bible indicates that God has the answer to life's problems if we will understand them through a biblical grid and use His methods to handle them. The Bible indicates that it is God's will that we should be "more than conquerors," that we should be "overcomers." Write the following verses:

Romans 8:37

_____

_____

2 Corinthians 2:14

_____

_____

1 John 5:4

_____

_____

Revelation 2:7 11, 17

_____

_____

However, this "more than conqueror" experience, this "overcomer" experience, is only possible for those who are truly Christians.

What this means is that if you are going to benefit from what you learn in the rest of this study about God's solutions to life's problems, you must not only have a right answer to the question, "What is a Christian?" you must also ask and answer the question, "In light of what we have noted from Scripture about what it means to be a Christian, can I honestly say that what has been described is true of me?" Rightly answering this question is foundational for everything else that is presented in this book. It is foundational for your eternal destiny, and it is crucial for your present life in this world.

Seriously *examine yourself to see if you are in the faith* and make your *calling and election* sure (2 Corinthians 13:5; 2 Peter 1:10). Reflect on the four main factors mentioned in this chapter about what it means to be a Christian. Ask yourself the following questions: Has God impressed on me an awareness of my own unworthiness, my own sinfulness? Do I believe that Jesus Christ is Who the Bible declares Him to be and that He has done what the Bible says He has done? Have I truly repented of my sins and savingly believed on Jesus Christ in the way described in the Bible? Is there evidence in my life that I have been radically changed by the power of God?

If you can honestly answer these questions with a resounding "yes," then you are ready for the information presented in the rest of this study. You are ready to learn how to solve your problems, and help others to solve theirs, God's way.

If, however, you can't sincerely say that the description of a Christian presented in this chapter is true of you, then seriously reflect on the information presented in this chapter. Right now, call on Christ to save you, for His promise is that *whosoever shall call upon the name of the Lord, shall be saved* (Romans 10:13). Recognize and acknowledge that He is Who and what the Bible declares Him to be; ask Him to forgive your sins; thank Him for dying in the place of lost sinners; believe in your heart that God has raised Him from the dead; confess Jesus Christ before men as the Lord of your life; and dedicate yourself to continually obeying and following Him in the whole of your life. Be assured that if God has placed it in your heart to do these things, you may stand up before God and men and confess, "By the all-availing and powerful blood of Jesus Christ, and by the power of the Holy Spirit Who has now worked in my life, I am a Christian." More than that, if you are a Christian, you are ready to solve your problems God's way.

HOWEVER, THIS "MORE THAN CONQUEROR" EXPERIENCE, THIS "OVERCOMER" EXPERIENCE, IS ONLY POSSIBLE FOR THOSE WHO ARE TRULY CHRISTIANS.

QUESTIONS FOR DISCUSSION

1. What are some of the common answers that people give to the question, "What is a Christian?"

_____

_____

2. Why do you think most or all of these common answers are unbiblical answers?

_____

_____

3. What were the four main features of a correct biblical answer to the question, "What is a Christian?"

_____

_____

4. What does the phrase "a Christian is a person who has been radically changed by the power of God" mean in reference to becoming a Christian?

_____

_____

5. According to Sinclair Ferguson, what does it mean to be regenerated? What happens when a person is regenerated?

_____

_____

6. What Scripture verses support this concept of what it means to become a Christian?

_____

_____

7. When and after a person becomes a Christian how does he view himself?

_____

_____

8. When and after a person becomes a Christian what are his beliefs about Jesus Christ?

_____

_____

9. What illustration does John Blanchard use to describe what it means to be saved by Jesus Christ?

_____

_____

10. What Scripture verses support this concept of what it means to become a Christian?

_____

_____

11. What roles do repentance and faith play in becoming a Christian?

_____

_____

12. What does it mean to repent?

_____

_____

13. What does it mean to believe?

_____

_____

14. How does this story illustrate saving faith to you?

_____

_____

15. What Scripture verses support the concept (repent and believe) of what it means to become a Christian?

_____

_____

16. What relevance does becoming a real Christian have to do with solving life's problems God's way?

_____

_____

_____

PERSONAL RESPONSE

1. If being a Christian involves the four things described in this chapter, can you honestly say you are a Christian?

_____

_____

2. If you can't, will you now embrace these truths, repent of your sins, and believe on the Lord Jesus Christ in the way described in this chapter?

_____

_____

3. What other answers have you heard (or at least know of) that people give to the question, "What is a Christian?"

_____

_____

4. Are there any other important facts about what it means to become a Christian that you would like to add?

_____

_____

5. If you do believe you are a Christian, what radical changes have taken place in your life since you became a Christian?

_____

_____

6. How has the Bible's teaching about your unworthiness before God affected you? What real difference has this made in your everyday life?

_____

_____

7. How does this teaching about our unworthiness relate to the modern concept of self-esteem?

_____

_____

8. Why doesn't this teaching, when rightly understood, promote a depressed, morose, melancholic, groveling, miserable person?

_____

_____

9. What relevance does the fact that Jesus Christ was both perfect God and perfect man have to you in your everyday life? What difference do these facts make in your life on a daily basis?

_____

_____

10. What reasons do you have for believing that you have really repented of your sin and believed on the Lord Jesus Christ?

_____

_____

11. For you personally, in your daily life what does it mean to confess Jesus Christ as Lord?

_____

_____

12. In what ways has the fact that you claim to be a Christian helped you to solve your daily problems God's way? What relevance does all this have to do with you as you face the inevitable problems of life in this world?

_____

_____

CHAPTER 3

WHERE TO FIND GOD'S SOLUTIONS

Some time ago I heard a story about a man carrying a brown paper bag who visited a theatrical agent. He walked into the agent's office and began to demonstrate the act that he had developed. He opened his brown paper bag and pulled out a miniature piano and a piano stool. He then placed the objects on the agent's desk. Next he reached back into his brown paper bag and pulled out a little frog. He sat the frog down on the piano stool and said to the little frog, "Okay Frankie, now play."

Obediently, Frankie flapped his flappers and out of that little piano came beautiful music. As you can imagine, the agent had never seen anything like this before. A frog playing a piano? This was fantastic! Enthusiastically, he said, "You've come because you want me to become your agent. Well, I'll be glad become your agent. This is tremendous." At that point, the frog's owner said, "Just wait a minute, you haven't seen anything yet. Let me show you the next part of my act." Reaching back into his brown bag he pulled out a female mouse and sat that little mouse down on top of the piano. She dangled her legs over the side of the piano. Then the man said, "Okay, Frankie, now play. Okay, Minnie, now sing." Frankie flapped his flappers and played the piano. And Minnie reared back and sang. Together, the two little animal musicians made beautiful music.

Well, if the agent was excited previously, now he was ecstatic. A frog playing a piano and a mouse singing. What an act! What a duet! "This is fantastic," he said. "This is one of the most sensational acts I've ever seen. With an act like this, I'm sure I can book you on the Oprah show, the Rosie show, the Regis show, the Letterman show, the Good Morning America show, the Today show, any of those kind of television shows. I can get you appearances in the best nightclubs. This is great! When do you want to start?"

At this point, the man hung his head and began to put Frankie, Minnie, and the piano back into the brown paper bag. The perplexed agent asked, "What are

YOU HAVEN'T SEEN ANYTHING YET.

you doing?" "I'm sorry, but I've changed my mind," the man with the frog and mouse said. "I can't let you become my agent. It wouldn't be right for me to have you do that." Quickly, the agent responded. "What's the matter with you? Why wouldn't it be right? You at least owe me the courtesy of telling me why it wouldn't be right." Finally, after much cajoling the man said, "It wouldn't be right because I lied to you about my act. It's not what you think it is. I deceived you." "What do you mean you lied to me?" the agent asked. "I heard music coming out of that piano. I heard that mouse sing. If you lied to me, at least tell me how you lied." "You're right, I should tell you the truth about how I lied," the man said. "I owe you that much. I'm sorry I lied to you about what Minnie and Frankie were doing. Minnie really wasn't singing at all. In fact, she can't sing a note. Frankie was actually doing the playing and singing. You see, Frankie's a ventriloquist. He was doing it all!"[5]

MANY CHRISTIANS ARE UNAWARE OF THE TREMENDOUS RESOURCES IN GOD'S WORD.

PROFICIENT

THEY'RE CONSTANTLY RUNNING TO THE WORLD'S TABLE TRYING TO PICK UP CRUMBS THAT DROP TO THE FLOOR, HOPING TO FIND HELP FROM THE WORLD'S IDEAS, THEORIES, AND SUPPOSED SOLUTIONS TO PROBLEMS.

The attitude of many professing Christians toward the Bible is like the attitude of the man in this story toward his frog. He failed to realize the tremendous resources he had in that little frog. And, like that man, many professing Christians are unaware of the tremendous resources for solving life's problems God's way that He has given us in His Word.

Many professing Christians don't understand how greatly God has blessed us. They don't understand the fantastic wealth we have in the Scriptures. They don't realize that in the Scriptures we have resources nobody else has. They go limping around with an inferiority complex about their Christianity. They're constantly running to the table of the world trying to pick up a couple of crumbs that drop to the floor, hoping to find help from the world's ideas, theories, and supposed solutions to problems. They either forget or ignore the fact that God has given us resources that are sufficient and superior.

We could spend a lot of time describing the variety of sufficient and superior resources we have as Christians, because they are many. In this chapter, however, we will to limit our focus to just one aspect of all of the resources we have as Christians. We will focus on the magnificent, powerful resource described for us in 2 Timothy 3:14-17.

Many professing believers think they are doomed to a life of failure. They live defeated lives because they do not realize that God has given them the resources to be victorious in their fight against sin. How sad to be constantly defeated and overwhelmed by problems instead of finding and utilizing God's resources in His Word for solving them!

If anyone in Scripture might have been tempted to feel overwhelmed by problems, it would have been Timothy. He was a timid young pastor with tremendous responsibilities in a very challenging situation. In 2 Timothy 3:1, Paul himself wrote, *"Realize this, that in the last days difficult times will come."* He was not only looking to the future, he was also speaking about Timothy's present situation.

"Timothy," he was saying, "you're in a difficult spot. Times are tough. You're part of a great battle. Look around you. Men are lovers of themselves, lovers of money, boastful, arrogant, revilers, disobedient to parents, unholy, ungrateful, unloving, irreconcilable, brutal, haters of good, treacherous, reckless, lovers of pleasure rather than lovers of God. They put on the mask of godliness but underneath they are corrupt and have denied its power. They may profess to know God, but they don't. They go around opposing the truth and bringing weak people down. But Timothy, you are different. You are not just going with the flow. You followed me and you obeyed the gospel message. You know that's not easy. Remember how I was persecuted. Think about all the terrible persecutions I had to endure in order to proclaim the Gospel. And the truth of the matter is, if you are going to follow after Christ and be godly, you will be persecuted. You need to know that. It's actually going to become even more difficult, because men aren't getting better, they are getting worse. Timothy, make no mistake about it: True Christianity is a fight!"

> HOW SAD TO BE CONSTANTLY DEFEATED AND OVERWHELMED BY PROBLEMS.

How would you like to receive those encouraging words from your mentor? Imagine Timothy's reaction! "How can I possibly overcome all these obstacles? Paul, I don't have the resources to be victorious in this battle." If Paul had stopped with verse 13, Timothy might have been tempted to give up. But fortunately, he didn't. Paul didn't merely acknowledge that Timothy's situation was difficult; instead, Paul reminded Timothy, in verses 14-17, of the resources God had provided so that he could be victorious in his battles.

> MAKE NO MISTAKE ABOUT IT: TRUE CHRISTIANITY IS A FIGHT!

Paul wrote,

> *You however continue in the things you have learned and become convinced of, knowing from whom you have learned them; and that from childhood you have known the sacred writings which are able to give you the wisdom that leads to salvation through faith which is in Christ Jesus. All Scripture is inspired by God and profitable for teaching, for reproof, for correction, for training in righteousness; that the man of God may be adequate, equipped for every good work.* (2 Timothy 3:14-17)

PROFICIENT

Paul was saying, "I know that the world in which you minister is difficult; the problems of people are great; there are going to be problems from without and from within. I know all of that. But Timothy, God has given you the resources you need to minister in a world like that. And those resources are found in the Word of God! Don't forget to use your weapon!"

Christian, you should take heart! These verses weren't written only for Timothy. They are for you! Yes, your problems are difficult. Yes, you have struggles with your lusts, with the world and even with the devil. Yes, there are times when you feel like giving up because you just don't think you have what it takes to overcome. Don't become hopeless! God has provided everything you need in order to achieve victory over temptation and live a godly life in an ungodly world! God never promises the battle will be easy, but He does promise that He has provided everything you need to overcome!

GOD'S MESSAGE TO YOU

Imagine going to your mailbox, and finding inside a letter written to you by the President of the United States. How would you react? You would probably take it out of its envelope very carefully, read it very slowly, and then go and call all your friends to come over and see what the President wrote you. That letter would be a prized possession!

The importance of a president can't even compare to the importance of God; thus, the value of a letter written by a human president can't even compare to the value of a book written by God. The worth of the Scripture is far greater than that of any letter from an earthly ruler, because in the Bible we have a message from the Ruler of the entire Universe.

That's exactly what Paul was reminding Timothy. He wrote, *"All Scripture is inspired by God…"* (2 Timothy 3:16). Or, to put it another way: God wrote a book for you!

The word "inspire" is used in many different ways. We sometimes use the word to describe something that exhilarates or enthuses us. Maybe you've gone to a concert or a play and left saying, "Wasn't that inspiring?" Or perhaps you've read a powerful piece of fiction and said, "That inspired me." But that's not what Paul meant when he wrote: *"All Scripture is inspired by God."* He wasn't simply saying that the Bible is a very inspiring book, or that if you read the Bible you are sure to go away enthused and encouraged. That may be true, but that wasn't Paul's point.

Most of the time we use the word "inspire" to describe someone who has done something extremely original or creative. We say things like, "That person must have been inspired." Or when we do something creative, we might say, "I just felt inspired." What we mean is that we were able to do something out of the ordinary, better than what we usually would have done.

But when the Bible refers to inspiration, it isn't referring to the writers, it's referring to the writings. So Paul didn't mean that these men were lifted up and enabled to do something better than they normally would have done. No, notice that he wrote, "All *Scripture* is inspired…".

The Greek word for "inspired" is actually a combination of two Greek words, one that means "God" and another that means "breath." So literally translated, 2 Timothy 3:16 is saying, "All Scripture is God-breathed." B.B. Warfield explains that the Greek term for inspiration says of Scripture…not that it is "breathed into by God," or is the product of the Divine "inbreathing" into its human authors, but that it is breathed out by God. "God-breathed" is the product of the creative breath of God. In a word, what is declared by this fundamental passage is simply that the Scriptures are a Divine product…No term could have been chosen…which would have more emphatically asserted the Divine production of Scripture than that which is here employed.

ALL SCRIPTURE IS GOD-BREATHED.

Paul is saying that God is the author of Scripture. Yes, God did use men to write the Bible. No, He did not obliterate their personalities in doing so. When you read Paul's writings, the personality of Paul comes through. When you read Peter's writings, the personality of Peter comes through. The writers of Scriptures were not typewriters, where God pressed the keys and the Bible came out in a very mechanical fashion. Instead, God in His wonderful and sovereign way so superintended the lives of these people that He used their personalities and their various writing styles *to say exactly what He wanted to say*, so that what we have in this Book comes from God Himself.

WHAT WE HAVE IN THIS BOOK COMES FROM GOD HIMSELF.

Dr. Martin Lloyd Jones once told a story about a man who went into an antique shop and saw a painting on the wall. The painting was dingy and dirty, but there was something about it that he really liked. So he decided to buy it. He paid a few dollars for it, took it home, cleaned it up, and put a new frame on it. He hung it up on the wall in his living room. Some time after that a friend who was a connoisseur of art came to visit him, walked into his living room, and looked at the painting on the wall. He was stunned. "Do you know what you have there? That's a painting by the famous Spanish painter El Greco." They ended up taking the painting to an art expert who confirmed that it was an original El Greco painting. The man had bought the painting for a few dollars. Two weeks later he sold it for over thirty five thousand dollars. What changed the worth of the painting? The knowledge that El Greco had painted it.

Some people don't have much of an appreciation for the Bible. For them it is just a dry, old, boring, dead book written by people who lived long ago. One of the reasons they don't appreciate the Scriptures is because they don't understand Who the author is. Sometimes, even believers call the Bible "God's Word" but fail to stop and grasp just how significant that statement really is. God, Who created the entire universe, Who is so immense that He can hold all the oceans of the world in the palm of His hand, Who knows all things, Who never has had to learn anything, Who never needed any advice, before Whom all the nations of the world are like a small drop in a bucket, Who is absolutely incomparable, Who sits above the earth, Who controls all of creation, Who designed the stars and keeps them in their place, He has spoken, and we can discover what He has to say in the Scriptures!

Satan's been attacking God's Word since the Garden of Eden. Go all the way back to the very first temptation, and you'll see that he began by casting doubt on God's Word, and then offering ungodly counsel in its place. He tempted Eve by saying, *"Indeed, has God said...You surely shall not die?..."* (Genesis 3:1, 4). "You know better than God what is good for your life! God made it absolutely clear that eating of the fruit would bring death and judgment, but He doesn't know what is best for you. Don't trust His Word!"

ONE OF THE WAYS THAT SATAN ATTACKS GOD'S WORD IS BY ATTACKING ITS INSPIRATION.

One of the ways that Satan attacks God's Word is by attacking its inspiration. Sometimes he spreads his lies through the "wise men of the world," who call the message of God foolishness, saying things like, "The Word of God? I don't think so! That's just a useless old book!" They attack the inerrancy, infallibility, and authority of Scripture with all sorts of "clever" and "sophisticated" arguments. Christians should not be intimidated by the world's attacks on Scripture. Paul wrote, *"Let no man deceive you. If any man among you thinks that he is wise in this age, let him become foolish that he may become wise. For the wisdom of this world is foolishness before God"* (1 Corinthians 3:18-19). The wisdom of the world is foolishness to God and the wisdom of God is foolishness to the world. Take your pick!

Many times Satan uses a somewhat more subtle strategy. He doesn't deny the inspiration of Scripture; instead he denies its usefulness. Paul tells us that God gave us this message (the Bible) for a reason. He writes, *"All Scripture is inspired by God and is profitable…"* (2 Timothy 3:16). God did not give you the Bible just so you could load your mind with all sorts of useless facts. He gave you the Bible so that it would be of practical benefit for you. Satan mounts all sorts of different attacks on the profitability of Scripture.

THE GREAT DECEPTION

Many years ago I enrolled in a graduate program in psychology at a secular university. In one of the courses I took, the professor announced at the beginning of the course that one of her intentions was to systematically desensitize us to any traditional values. In other words, she wanted to pull us away from believing anything the Bible said. And that's exactly what she attempted to do. Time and time again throughout the course, she sought to undermine the authority and value of Scripture. Why? She didn't think the Bible was profitable. According to her, if you really wanted to help people, you had to forget everything you ever learned from the Word of God.

When you get right down to it, that's what most of the world thinks about Scripture. "The Bible? That's just an outdated book written by a bunch of men a long time ago. It has caused lots of problems, contains lots of funny ideas, and may look nice on your shelf, but it's useless to read. Get with the times!"

But others won't go that far. They won't say that the Bible is altogether useless. In fact, they even think the Scriptures are rather interesting. Take a look throughout history and you'll find that many leaders of the past professed a high regard for Scripture. For example, Benjamin Franklin loved to go hear George Whitefield preach the Word of God, and Thomas Jefferson actually created his own version of the Bible; but neither man was a Christian.

Instead of completely rejecting the Bible, these people cheapen it. "The Bible is an incredible piece of literature. Everyone should read it. Just don't get too excited about it. Keep it in its place. Learn from it what you can and then place

OTHER TIMES HE DOESN'T DENY THE INSPIRATION OF SCRIPTURE; INSTEAD HE DENIES ITS USEFULNESS.

GOD DID NOT GIVE YOU THE BIBLE JUST SO YOU COULD LOAD YOUR MIND WITH ALL SORTS OF USELESS FACTS.

MOST OF THE WORLD THINKS OF THE BIBLE AS JUST LITERATURE.

it on your bookshelf alongside other great works of the past like Plato and Aristotle. Remember, it's just another book!"

Still others say the Bible is profitable, but live like it isn't. It's easy to shake our heads and point our fingers at the world for rejecting the Bible, yet in reality we do exactly the same thing. If you've been a believer for any length of time you know that you can't even begin to compare the value of the Bible with the works of men. You realize that you can't treat the Bible as though it is just another book from ancient times. You understand that Scripture is not just another idea coming from the mind of man; it's absolute truth coming straight from the mouth of God! You may even be able to quote a great definition of inspiration, and be willing to defend the inerrancy and infallibility of Scripture to your final breath. But when the rubber meets the road, does your profession really make any difference in your life?

When it comes to the matter of rearing children, do you run to the bookstore to find out what the latest child-rearing guru has to say, or turn to popular magazines to get the latest advice from a non-Christian psychotherapist, but fail to turn to the Word of God? When you have a problem with depression or anger, do you turn to the world for answers and neglect God's Book? When you are struggling to make an important life decision, do you even consider looking to the Bible for help?

Many believers have never been taught the Bible's real value. They go to churches that profess to believe the Bible is the Word of God, but whose pastors are proclaiming the opinions of man. Oh, they may be very good at using religious language and quoting Scripture verses, but when their messages are closely examined, they are nothing more than the world's philosophies dressed up in Sunday suits. The results are tragic: The pastor doesn't preach the Word of God, so the people don't look to the Word of God for answers to life's problems.

Still others go to churches where the pastor teaches the Word of God, but fails to show the congregation how the Bible relates to the everyday issues of life. The pastor teaches in such fuzzy generalities that the people have no idea that God's Word has anything at all to say about the way they ought to live their lives. The Bible is good for Sunday, but that's where it stays. As a result, these Christians begin to think that the Bible can tell us how to pray and how to get saved, but when it comes to dealing with the really nitty-gritty practical issues of life,

SCRIPTURE IS NOT JUST ANOTHER IDEA COMING FROM THE MIND OF MAN; IT'S ABSOLUTE TRUTH COMING STRAIGHT FROM THE MOUTH OF GOD!

DOES YOUR PROFESSION OF FAITH REALLY MAKE ANY DIFFERENCE IN YOUR LIFE?

WHEN YOU ARE STRUGGLING TO MAKE AN IMPORTANT LIFE DECISION, DO YOU EVEN CONSIDER LOOKING TO THE BIBLE FOR HELP?

Scripture doesn't have much to say, and if it does say something, it sure doesn't say enough.

Sadly, the attitude of a Christian woman who once came to interview me about biblical counseling represents that of many Christians. She asked me about the basis for my counseling, and I explained what the Bible says about its sufficiency for dealing with the issues of life. She looked at me rather quizzically and said, "That's fine for the small problems. But what do you do when someone has a really big problem?" In other words, sure, sure, the Bible is profitable for the surface problems, but what do you do when someone is struggling with the hard problems? That dear lady had an inadequate view of the adequacy of Scripture!

Satan doesn't always spread his lies through worldly intellectuals. Sometimes he uses false teachers in the church. We see this so often throughout the New Testament. Paul left Timothy in Ephesus for a very specific reason: To stop certain men who were distracting believers from a profitable study of the Word of God by focusing on fruitless "not-in-Scripture" discussions. Do you see a recurring theme? Whether the lie is coming from a university professor or a false teacher, whether the lie is attacking the authority of Scripture or its sufficiency, Satan's goal is the same: Get people to reject the Word of God.

> SATAN'S GOAL IS TO GET PEOPLE TO REJECT THE WORD OF GOD.

THEME

In 2 Timothy 3:15-17, Paul describes at least five ways in which the Scriptures are profitable. Knowing these five ways is important if you are going to profit in a maximum way from hearing and reading the Bible. Every time you hear the Word of God, every time you read the Word of God, you should be expecting to be challenged and helped in at least these five ways.

God never gave you the Bible to merely fill your mind with facts. God never gave you the Bible to merely satisfy your intellectual curiosity. God gave you the Word of God for very practical reasons. If you come to the Bible merely to learn abstract doctrine, facts, or stuff your mind with information, you will be using the Bible in a way that God never intended you to use it, and you will not receive the maximum benefit from your study. Remember, God intended you to use the Bible so that it would be profitable for you.

> GOD NEVER GAVE YOU THE BIBLE TO MERELY FILL YOUR MIND WITH FACTS. GOD INTENDED YOU TO USE THE BIBLE SO THAT IT WOULD BE PROFITABLE FOR YOU.

QUESTIONS FOR DISCUSSION

1. How did Paul describe the kind of world in which and the kind of people to whom Timothy was ministering? Give some details about the problems of the people to whom Timothy would be ministering.

_____

_____

2. How might this reminder have affected Timothy?

_____

_____

3. What did Paul do to encourage Timothy in his difficult ministry?

_____

_____

4. What are some of the ways the word "inspired" is used in our day?

_____

_____

5. What does the word mean as it used in 2 Timothy 3:16?

_____

_____

6. What doesn't the biblical concept of inspiration mean?

_____

_____

7. What point was the illustration about a painting of El Greco making?

_____

_____

8. What are some of the wrong attitudes that people have toward the Bible?

_____

_____

9. What are some of the ways that Satan uses to attack the Bible?

_____

_____

10. How do some Christians manifest their lack of respect for and confidence in Scripture?

_____

_____

11. What is meant by the "authority" of Scripture?

_____

_____

12. What is meant by the "sufficiency" of Scripture?

_____

_____

13. What view of the Bible held by some does the word "profitable" contradict?

_____

_____

PERSONAL RESPONSE

1. What kind of world do we live in, and what kind of people do you see all around you in this world? Which of the words used by Paul to describe the problems people have are true of people today?

_____

_____

2. Which of these sin-related problems do you personally struggle with the most?

_____

_____

3. How are your emotions, attitude and behavior personally affected by what you see in the lives of people, even in the lives of professing Christians and in your own life?

_____

_____

4. How does the truth about the Bible being inspired by God really affect you in a very practical way? What evidences are there in your life that prove you value the Bible above all other sources of information?

_____

_____

5. Have you ever been affected or influenced by any of Satan's attacks on the Bible? If so, how and when?

_____

_____

6. How does your life demonstrate that you believe the Bible is authoritative? If the Bible is authoritative, what difference will this make in your life?

_____

_____

7. What is your personal view of the sufficiency of Scripture? How does your life demonstrate that you believe the Bible is sufficient or insufficient? If the Bible really is sufficient, what difference will this make in your life?

_____

_____

CHAPTER 4

SALVATION IN ITS FULLEST SENSE

In his book, *Our Sufficiency in Christ*, John MacArthur tells the true story of Homer and Langley Collyer who inherited an incredible amount of wealth from their father and yet lived their entire lives and died as though they had no resources at all. Concerning this sad and unnecessary situation, John MacArthur writes:

> Homer and Langley Collyer make a sad but fitting parable of the way many people in the church live. Although the Collyer's inheritance was sufficient for all their needs, they lived their lives in unnecessary, self-imposed deprivation. Neglecting abundant resources, Homer and Langley instead turned their home into a dump. Spurning their father's legacy, they binged instead on the scraps of the world. Too many Christians live their spiritual lives that way.[6]

This statement by John MacArthur accurately describes the way many Christians live. I've met many of them in the church, in the classroom, and in my counseling office – professing believers who thought that they were doomed to lives of failure. They live defeated lives: they are anxious, angry, discouraged, depressed, bitter, resentful, inconsistent, unstable, and accomplishing very little for the Lord. Like Homer and Langley, they either are unaware of or don't know how to access the great resources God has made available in His Word for solving their problems His way.

As we began to study and apply 2 Timothy 3:14-17, you learned that this text establishes the fact that God gave us His Word to be useful or profitable. Then you learned that this text mentions at least five ways in which the Scriptures are useful to us. In this and the next two chapters you'll discover the five ways these verses say the Bible is profitable for us.

MANY PROFESSING BELIEVERS THINK THEY'RE DOOMED TO A LIFE OF FAILURE.

IT IS PROFITABLE FOR GIVING US WISDOM

In verse 15, Paul wrote that the Scriptures are profitable in that they are able to *"give you … wisdom."* In another place, Paul wrote of this wisdom that it is:

...a wisdom not of this age, nor of the rulers of this age, who are passing away; but we speak God's wisdom in a mystery, the hidden wisdom, which God predestined before the ages to our glory....we also speak, not in words taught by human wisdom, but in those taught by the Spirit....But just as it is written, Things which eye has not seen and ear has not heard, and which has not entered into the heart of man, all that God has prepared for those who love Him." (1 Corinthians 2:6-9, 13)

Through the Scriptures God has given us a wisdom that no one, not even the most intelligent and learned men throughout all of history have ever discovered. It is a wisdom that has been hidden and kept secret from men apart from divine revelation.

IT IS A WISDOM THAT HAS BEEN HIDDEN AND KEPT SECRET FROM MEN APART FROM DIVINE REVELATION.

John MacArthur says that this wisdom given to us in Scripture is a wisdom that can't be found either externally or internally, objectively or subjectively through empirical or experimental research. "God's truth is not observable by the eye or ear, no matter how many sophisticated instruments we may use....Rationalism cannot reason out God's truth. Man's two greatest human resources, his observation and his reason, are equally useless in discovering divine truth."[7]

Throughout history, men have earnestly sought many things. Some have valued material things highly and made accumulating possessions their life's quest. Other have sought power and control as the ultimate goal in life. Still others have valued the acquisition of what they considered to be wisdom as the highest and noblest good. Unfortunately, as Paul mentions in 2 Timothy, many of these people are always *"learning and never able to come to the knowledge of the truth"* (3:7). These people, according to Paul, profess to be wise. In reality, however, they are fools because they reject or ignore God Who is the only source of the highest kind of wisdom. Still more, they are fools because they reject or ignore the Bible, which is the place where the all-wise God has chosen to reveal His wisdom. Amazingly, instead of humbly believing and receiving the truth, they suppress it, devalue it, distort it, deny it, and exchange it for a lie (Romans 1:18, 22-25).

According to the Bible, many of the people whom the world would consider to be the wisest are, from God's perspective, the biggest fools. They are fools for all of the reasons we've already mentioned, but they are also fools in that in neglecting the Bible they are robbing themselves of all the benefits that true wisdom brings. True wisdom brings life to the soul; it provides you with security and stability; it keeps you from stumbling; it frees you from fear and makes you a confident person; it guards and protects you; it exalts and honors you; it makes you a blessed person who experiences the favor of the Lord.

Write the following verses:

Proverbs 3:22-26

_____

_____

Proverbs 4:59

_____

_____

Proverbs 8:18-36

_____

_____

TRUE WISDOM BRINGS LIFE TO THE SOUL.

No wonder the writer of the book of Proverbs frequently exhorts us to receive, seek, acquire, keep and love it (Proverbs 1:3; 2:2; 3:13, 21; 4:5; 8:5; 29:3). And, since the Scriptures are the repository in which true wisdom is found, it's no wonder that Paul extolls the value of Scripture in this passage.

IT IS PROFITABLE FOR SALVATION

In particular, Paul wants us to know that the Scriptures are profitable because the wisdom they give is a *"wisdom that leads to salvation through faith which is in Christ Jesus."* The word "salvation" is used a couple of ways in the Bible. Sometimes it is used as a synonym for justification, i.e., how sinful men become right with God or come into a right relationship with Him. Sometimes you hear people say, "Look within yourself; you'll find the answers to your questions there." The Bible makes it clear, however, that if you're looking within yourself for answers, you may get answers, but they are all going to be wrong!

IF YOU'RE LOOKING WITHIN YOURSELF FOR ANSWERS, YOU MAY GET ANSWERS, BUT THEY ARE ALL GOING TO BE WRONG!

Every single idea that man comes up with about God, apart from God, is worthless. That's because before God saved us we were foolish, disobedient, deceived, enslaved to various lusts and pleasures, living in malice and envy, and full of hate toward one another (Titus 3:3). There was no spark of inner wisdom or truth in the deep recesses of our souls. An unbeliever can have a Ph.D. in rocket science but when it comes to the things of God, he is completely bereft of understanding. Unsaved people are out of touch with reality. They hate God, love sin, enjoy lies, and are in bondage to their own sinful desires. There is no way they can discover God in and of themselves.

But from before the beginning of time God made a plan to save mankind and give believers eternal life. Since we can't discover that plan by ourselves, God graciously stooped down to reveal it to us in the Scriptures. Paul explained in Titus 1:2-3 that *the hope of eternal life, which God, who cannot lie, promised long ages ago, but at the proper time revealed His Word....* In other words, God promised eternal life ages ago. He made a covenant with God the Son to redeem the elect and give them to Him as His special possession. This plan was hidden in the eternal counsels of God. But throughout the Old Testament, He slowly revealed glimpses of this great plan and now at just the right time – or in His own time – He has made that eternal life clear.

How did God reveal this promise of eternal life? Paul explained it this way: *"He manifested His word in the proclamation with which I was entrusted..."* Paul was saying that God promised eternal life, but He revealed His Word. What does that tell us? The Word and eternal life are so intimately connected that Paul can use the two terms interchangeably! God revealed the truths about eternal life through His Word. The promise of eternal life can't be separated from His Word. If you want to have eternal life in heaven with God, there is only one way to come to that – and that is through His Word. The Word provides the wisdom that leads to salvation.

If someone wrote a book explaining how to escape poverty and find financial bliss, you can be sure that even if it didn't work for anyone else, the author, at least, would become a rich man. If someone wrote a book that provided a miraculous cure for blindness, bookstores wouldn't be able to keep it on their shelves! If someone wrote a book explaining how to successfully defeat physical death, it would be a bestseller! People would wear the pages thin trying to understand its contents.

God has written about something, much more important than any of those subjects. In the Bible, He gives the wisdom that leads to salvation. And the salvation the Bible reveals is absolutely marvelous. We discover in Scripture the way to be *saved from spiritual poverty:* We were slaves to sin whose wages is death, and the Bible tells us how to become children of God who possess every

UNSAVED PEOPLE ARE OUT OF TOUCH WITH REALITY.

spiritual blessing in the heavenly places. God's Word explains how to be *delivered from spiritual blindness:* We were spiritually blind, utterly incapable of seeing the light; God uses the Bible to open our eyes and provide the light for our path. The Scriptures explain the only way to be *saved from spiritual death:* We were dead in our sins with no spiritual pulse; in the Scriptures God shows us the way that we can be quickened, raised from the dead!

The Bible is the way that you find out how to be saved, how to get right with God. That's the biggest question that anybody will ever face in life: How can I get right with God? One day, I'm going to stand before my Creator. One day, I'm going to give an account of myself. One day, I'm going to stand before God in judgment. Since that's true, "How can I get right with God?" is a question every human being ought to be asking.

How can you be sure that when you stand before God, God will accept you? How can you be saved? How can you be delivered? How can you know for sure that you're going to heaven?

There's only one way to know for sure, and that's by turning to the Scripture. It can make you wise unto salvation. This Book's author is God. And this Book tells you how to be saved. God tells you in this Book that you are a sinner: *"All have sinned and have come short of the glory of God."* There's not a person on the earth who does good. "No, not one" is the message of Romans 3:10-18. The Bible says *there is none righteous; not even one.* So here we are as sinners, unrighteous people trying to come into the presence of a holy God. God hates sin. His eyes are so pure that He cannot look upon sin. How then can we as sinners come into the presence of God and be accepted by One who is so holy and so pure?

The Bible tells us there's only one way. Only one way! Write what John 14:6 tells us:

_____

_____

There is no name under heaven by which we can be saved except the name of Jesus (Acts 4:13). The Word of God says we are declared righteous the redemption that is in Christ Jesus (Romans 3:24-25).

GOD USES THE BIBLE TO OPEN OUR EYES AND PROVIDE THE LIGHT FOR OUR PATH.

HOW CAN YOU KNOW FOR SURE THAT YOU'RE GOING TO HEAVEN? THERE'S ONLY ONE WAY TO KNOW FOR SURE, AND THAT'S BY TURNING TO THE SCRIPTURE.

How do we become right with God? Through Jesus Christ Who loved sinners and died as their substitute on the cross. Jesus Christ became the sacrifice. He took the punishment that we deserve. God, Whose very nature is holy, righteous and just, Whose very nature makes it impossible for Him to overlook sin, poured out His wrath against our sins on Jesus. We had seriously and continuously broken God's law. We were sinners by practice and by nature. God's very nature cried out for justice.

Understand this: For God to overlook our sin, He would have had to deny His very nature; He would have had to cease being God.

Read and write the following verses:

Romans 8:32

_____

_____

2 Corinthians 5:21

_____

_____

Romans 3:25-26

_____

_____

In order for God to remain true to His nature, the penalty for sin had to be paid. We had broken God's law externally (through our behavior) and internally (in our hearts, thoughts, affections, and desires). God, being Who He is, could not simply look the other way. So He sent His Son, Who became flesh and dwelt among us as man (a sinless man, to be sure), to be our righteous substitute through His life and death. Then, after Jesus died to pay the penalty for the laws we had broken, God raised Him from the dead to indicate that the sacrifice and the payment had been accepted. Consequently, the Bible says, when a person repents of his sins and believes on the Lord Jesus Christ, God puts the righteousness of Jesus to their account. God then sees the sinner in the righteousness of Christ. God accepts the sinner because of Jesus. My friend, according to the Word of God, that's the only way that God will ever accept you.

When you die and stand in the presence of God on judgment day, and God asks you, "What right do you have to enter into My heaven?" what would you say? Make no mistake about it, you will stand before God on judgment day and you need to know what your answer would be.

I've asked a lot of people that question, and I've heard a lot of different answers…many times answers that were not based on the Bible. According to the Scripture, the only satisfactory answer to that question is, "My hope is built on nothing less than Jesus' blood and righteousness. I dare not trust the sweetest frame (i.e., my best and most enjoyable feeling or my best efforts, my own best works), but wholly lean on Jesus' name."

According to the Bible, unless your answer to that question is, "I'm relying on and trusting entirely in Jesus Christ and the work He did for me – in His life, His death, and His resurrection," you'll never get to heaven.

Your only hope of heaven is to fall on your face as a guilty sinner and plead the mercy of God which has been extended through Jesus Christ and to submit to Him as your Lord and Savior. That's what this Book, the Bible, that was inspired by God, declares. This Book is profitable to bring us to salvation in the sense that it tells us how to come into a right, justified relationship with God.

Read the following verses and write them down.

Hebrews 9:27

_____

_____

Romans 14:10, 12

_____

_____

2 Corinthians 5:10

_____

_____

Now read and write down the following verses.

> ACCORDING TO THE WORD OF GOD, THAT'S THE ONLY WAY THAT GOD WILL EVER ACCEPT YOU.

Acts 4:13

_____

_____

Romans 10:9-10

_____

_____

Romans 3:24-25

_____

_____

BUT WHAT DOES BEING SAVED HAVE TO DO WITH SOLVING LIFE'S PROBLEMS?

As you've been reading, you may have thought, "That's all very well and good, but what does being saved have to do with solving life's problems? So far this seems like just a lot of religious mumbo-jumbo with little or no practical implication for living life in the present." Good observation! In reality, many people are having serious, here-and-now problems as well as there-and-then unresolved problems, **because they lack salvation**.

WHEN YOU ARE MADE WISE UNTO SALVATION, YOU ARE GIVEN NEW RESOURCES FOR SOLVING LIFE'S PROBLEMS.

What you've learned thus far has everything to do with solving life's here-and-now problems because when you are made wise unto salvation, an innumerable amount of privileges are opened to you – privileges that are of value to you now and forever. When you are made wise unto salvation, you are given new resources for solving life's problems; resources that, according to the Bible, no one else has. For example, when you are made wise unto salvation, you become a new creature with new potential and power in Christ Jesus; you receive the indwelling presence of the Holy Spirit Who is able to strengthen, sustain, renew, and change you; you receive, through the Word and by His Spirit, new insights and wisdom about life in the present as well as in the future; you have guaranteed access to God through prayer; you cease from being an enemy of God and become a son with all the privileges thereof; and you become part of the church of Christ with access to all of the gifts and abilities of other believers who can assist you in the struggles you face in life.

Read and note what the following verses tell you:

2 Corinthians 5:17

_____

_____

Ephesians 3:16-17

_____

_____

Galatians 5:22-23

_____

_____

Ephesians 1:9-11

_____

_____

Ephesians 2:13-18

_____

_____

1 Peter 3:12

_____

_____

Psalm 50:15

_____

_____

Psalm 55:22

_____

_____

John 1:12

_____

_____

Romans 8:15

_____

_____

Galatians 4:6

_____

_____

Ephesians 2:19

_____

_____

Colossians 1:14

_____

_____

1 Corinthians 12:13-26

_____

_____

Romans 12:4-8

_____

_____

1 Peter 4:10-11

_____

_____

Galatians 5:13

_____

_____

Earlier in this chapter you read that the word "salvation" is used in a couple of senses in the Bible. It's often used in a narrow sense, referring to being saved from the penalty of our sin and our alienation from God (Colossians 1:21-23). There is, however, a broader, more comprehensive way in which the Bible uses this word. The word "salvation," originating from the Greek word *soteria*, includes the idea of being made whole, complete, or sound. In salvation, God not only saves us from the penalty of our sin – estrangement from Him, hell. He also wants to save us from the corruption of our sin. He wants to transform and change us on the inside as well as the outside. He wants to change our internal condition as well as our legal position before Him, our condition as well as our position, our state as well as our standing.

According to the words of Paul found in Romans 8:29 and 2 Corinthians 3:18, in salvation God wants to conform us into the image of Christ. In salvation, His purpose is to make us complete in Christ (Colossians 1:28). He intends to so

THE WORD "SALVATION," ORIGINATING FROM THE GREEK WORD *SOTERIA*, INCLUDES THE IDEA OF BEING MADE WHOLE, COMPLETE, OR SOUND.

work in us that we will *grow up in all aspects into Him ... even Christ* (Ephesians 4:15). Used in this way, God's so great salvation (Hebrews 2:3) includes sanctification (being made actually holy in our hearts and conduct) as well as justification (being declared righteous in our standing before a Holy God through the righteousness of Christ). From God's perspective, salvation includes being made like Christ as well as being declared legally righteous in Christ.

This is the way the word "salvation" is used in 1 Timothy 4:16 when Paul wrote about ensuring the "salvation" of Timothy and the members of the Ephesian church. Certainly, in this text Paul is not questioning whether Timothy or others are in a right relationship with God – that they have been justified, that their sins have been forgiven. He is talking about "salvation" in the sense of growing more and more into the likeness of Christ, which is the end that God has in mind when He justifies us.

In salvation, God is not interested only in saving us from the punishment of hell. Neither is He interested only in getting us to heaven. It goes beyond that. He wants to change us from the inside out so that our thoughts, affections, desires, feelings, attitudes, and aspirations – everything about us – becomes Christlike. He intends that our life, like that of our Lord Jesus Christ, should be filled with the fruit of the Spirit – love, joy, peace, patience, kindness, goodness, faithfulness, gentleness, and self control (Galatians 5:22-23). This is "salvation" in its fullest sense. And this is why being made wise unto salvation is such an important, useful, and critical aspect of solving life's present as well as eternal problems.

What instrument does God use in this internal transformation process, in this broader sense of salvation? The same one He used to make us wise unto salvation in terms of changing our relationship with Him. He uses the Word of God to change us on the inside, to tranform us into the image of Christ. *We all...beholding as in a mirror the glory of the Lord, are being transformed into the same image from glory to glory...* (2 Corinthians 3:18). *Sanctify them* (make them holy and righteous in their hearts and conduct) *by Thy truth; Thy Word is truth* (John 17:17). *Christ also loved the church and gave Himself up for her; that He might sanctify her, having cleansed her by the washing of the water of the Word* (Ephesians 5:25-26).

Many years ago, Thomas Chisholm expressed what should be the heart cry of every believer in this way:

IN SALVATION, GOD IS NOT INTERESTED ONLY IN SAVING US FROM THE PUNISHMENT OF HELL.... HE WANTS TO CHANGE US FROM THE INSIDE OUT.

O to be like Thee! Blessed Redeemer, This is my constant longing and prayer. Gladly I'll forfeit all of life's treasures, Jesus, Thy perfect likeness to wear. O to be like Thee! Full of compassion, loving, forgiving, tender and kind; helping the helpless, cheering the fainting, seeking the wandering sinner to find. O to be like Thee! While I am pleading, pour out Thy Spirit; fill with Thy love, Make me a temple, meet for Thy dwelling; Fit me for life and heaven above. O to be like Thee, Blessed Redeemer, pure as Thou art! Come in Thy sweetness, come in Thy fullness; Stamp Thine own image deep on my heart.

The constant heart cry of every believer should be, "Lord Jesus, I want to be like You. Please work in me, transform me, change me, and make me like You." That should be our constant longing and prayer. The good news is that as we become more like Jesus, as that becomes more of a reality in our lives, we will be experiencing the greatest good that any person could ever experience. The most beneficial, profitable thing that could ever happen to anyone is to increasingly become like Jesus Christ in the way the Bible and this poem describe it. Imagine what our lives would look like, what would happen in our relationships with people, what would happen in our families, what our churches would be like, what our impact on the world would be like...if we were more like Jesus.

THE GOOD NEWS IS THAT BECOMING MORE LIKE CHRIST IS NOT A PIPE DREAM.

Think of the impact believers would have for Christ if we, like Him, were full of compassion, loving, tender, and kind; if we, like Him, were as dedicated to helping the helpless, cheering the fainting, and seeking the wanderer as He was. That's something to get excited about and long for! The good news is that becoming more like Christ is not a pipe dream. For all of us who have experienced salvation in the justification sense, experiencing salvation in terms of growing more and more into His likeness is something that can be our continuing experience right here and now. We can change! We can be different! We can solve our sin-related problems! We can become more like Jesus! How? Through the regular, diligent, faithful, earnest, fervent study of God's Word. It's the only way it will happen; but it can happen because the God-inspired Scriptures are useful to make us wise unto salvation in both of the senses discussed in this chapter.

QUESTIONS FOR DISCUSSION

1. What was the point of the Homer and Langley Collyer illustration?

_____

_____

2. How does the wisdom found in the Bible differ from the so-called "wisdom of the world?"

_____

_____

3. Why is the person who rejects or ignores the wisdom found in Scripture a fool?

_____

_____

4. In what two ways is the word "salvation" used in Scripture?

_____

_____

5. What are the implications of the fact that the Scriptures are able to make us wise unto salvation?

_____

_____

6. From what does God save us?

_____

_____

7. How is a lack of salvation related to many of the problems people have? What do people who are not wise unto salvation lack that Christians have?

_____

_____

8. What is God's ultimate purpose for us personally in salvation?

_____

_____

9. Why is being saved in the justification sense of the word such a beneficial thing?

_____

_____

10. Why is being saved in the sanctification sense such a wonderful thing?

_____

_____

PERSONAL RESPONSE

1. What impact does the fact that God gives us true wisdom in the Scriptures have on you? What is your response to this fact?

_____

_____

2. Why should you want to know more of God's wisdom given through the Word?

_____

_____

3. What role did the Bible play in your salvation in the justification sense?

_____

_____

4. Were there any special verses that God used to bring you into a relationship with Himself?

_____

_____

5. What role does the Bible play in your salvation in the "becoming like Jesus" sense?

_____

_____

6. What passages of Scripture have been and are most meaningful to you in the process of becoming like Jesus?

_____

_____

7. In practical, specific terms, what would it mean, what would it look like for you to be like Jesus in your thought life, in your desires, in your family relationships, in your church relationships, in your work or school relationships, in the use of your time and money, in your attitudes, in your speech, etc.?

_____

_____

8. What are the main lessons you learned or challenges you received from this chapter?

_____

_____

CHAPTER 5

JUST WHAT YOU NEED

In this book we're learning about solving life's problems God's way. That title indicates several things: it indicates that (1) as we go through life we will face problems; (2) the problems we face can be solved; (3) we should want to solve our problems God's way; (4) we can learn God's way to solve our problems.

But, someone might ask, what does it mean to solve life's problems God's way? How can we know what God's way of solving problems is? How do we find God's solutions to life's problems? The answer: We can know what God's way of solving problems is by turning to the only Book that has been inspired by God, the Bible. *All Scripture (and only the Scripture) is inspired by God and is profitable* for helping us to understand what our problems are and to provide the solutions to them. Only the Scriptures can make us *adequate, and thoroughly equip us for every good work* (2 Timothy 3:16-17).

In commenting on the meaning of several words in this passage, counselor Jay Adams has written: "What does the word 'adequate' mean? The term is *artios* meaning 'capable, fitted, complete, proficient;' or as Arndt and Gingrich sums it up, 'able to meet all demands.'[8]

"Even more extensive is the second term, *exartizo*. This powerful and expressive word means to 'thoroughly equip' for a task. In the papyri it is used of an oil press completely furnished. Also, before a ship was to sail, all contingencies on the journey would be considered, and supplies to meet each would be stowed on board (e.g., extra canvas from which to make new sails should the original sails be damaged); the ship would be thoroughly 'rigged out'. ... In the pages of Scripture are stowed every principle (men) might ever need to perform their tasks."[9]

In other words, Paul was saying that the Scriptures are profitable in equipping us to handle any problem, any challenge that comes to us in life. In chapter three we learned that God gave us His Word to be useful or profitable; and in chapter four we began to study specific ways in which God intends His Word to be useful to and profitable for us. Chapter four explained and applied the first of those ways. There we learned that the Scriptures are useful in making us wise unto salvation and why that is so beneficial for us in the here and now. In this chapter, we will focus on two other ways in which Paul indicates the Scriptures are profitable for us as believers.

It Is Profitable for Teaching

As Paul continues to expound on the usefulness of Scripture, he tells us in verse sixteen that in addition to being profitable to make us wise unto salvation, the Scriptures are also profitable for "teaching." When God saves us, He doesn't magically infuse all sorts of knowledge and information into our minds. We must learn, and what we must learn are the truths of God's Word, the whole counsel of God (Acts 20:27).

What does the Bible teach us? It teaches us about life. It teaches us truth (John 17:17). The Bible teaches us the truth we need to know in order to begin living a life that honors and glorifies Him. It teaches us what is right and what is wrong, what is valuable, what is wise and what is unwise. It teaches us how to escape the corruption that is in the world and in our own hearts. It teaches us how to be effective in Christian ministry; how to be good husbands and wives, parents and children; how to be good citizens; how to love God and love our neighbors (2 Peter 1:3-4). It teaches us how to solve our problems God's way (1 Corinthians 10:13; Romans 8:32-39). It teaches us how to have joy, peace, patience, gentleness, goodness, kindness, self-control, and trustworthiness (2 Peter 1:5-7; Galatians 5:22-23). It teaches us about God, heaven, hell, the present life, and the life to come. In fact, there is nothing that we need to know in order to live effectively and successfully, as God defines success, that is not taught (at least in principle form) in God's Word (2 Peter 1:8-9; 1 Timothy 4:7; John 10:10).

The Bible is our infallible, inerrant standard in matters of faith and practice. God's Word is *perfect, restoring the soul, sure, making wise the simple, right, rejoicing the heart, pure, enlightening the eyes. Its teachings are more to be desired than gold, yes, than much fine gold.* By them God's people are warned and protected from error and harm and *in keeping them there is great reward* (Psalm 19:7-11).

Psalm 119, the longest chapter in the Bible, is all about the Word of God. In almost every one of the one hundred seventy-six verses of this psalm, the writer extols the profitableness of the teachings found in God's Word. Knowing and

WHAT DOES THE BIBLE TEACH US?

IT TEACHES US HOW TO SOLVE OUR PROBLEMS GOD'S WAY.

obeying the teachings of God's Word produces a blessed life, a grateful heart, freedom from shame, purity of heart, deliverance from sin, incomparable joy and delight, deliverance from reproach and contempt, inner strength and fortitude, boldness and courage, comfort and refreshment, freedom and security, and a host of other beneficial things. No wonder the Psalmist wrote, *"I shall delight in Thy commandment, which I love"* (Psalm 119:47). *"I shall delight in Thy statutes; I shall not forget Thy Word"* (Psalm 119:16). *"Thy testimonies are also my delight; they are my counselors"* (Psalm 119:24). *"Thy Word is a lamp to my feet, and a light to my path"* (Psalm 119:105). *"My soul keeps Thy testimonies, and I love them exceedingly"* (Psalm 119:167). *"I esteem right all Thy precepts concerning everything"* (Psalm 119:128).

What a blessing to have the inerrant teaching of the inerrant, infinite God as a guide for life and as a help for understanding our problems and the solution to them!

This blessing was made especially real to me some time ago when, as mentioned previously, I was involved in a psychology graduate studies program at a secular university. While in that program, I heard a lot about the theories and opinions of many supposedly learned people, regarding people and their problems. After presenting the various and often conflicting views that respected leaders in the field of psychology taught about people and their problems, one professor said, "We can't know for sure which one of these theories is altogether true, but if you're going to counsel people you need to study these theories and then decide which one makes the most sense to you. You need to do this because when people come to you for counseling, they will want some explanation of why they are having the problems they're having."

I appreciated this professor's honesty, but I grieved over the fact that counselors were going to be trying to help people understand their problems and find the solution to them without any solid reason to believe that what they believed had any real validity. At the same time, I rejoiced to know that God's Word was profitable to infallibly teach us *everything we need for life and godliness* (2 Peter 1:3-4).

In another psychology course the subject of values was discussed. We were told that the only legitimate way to determine what was right and what was wrong was to operate by the maxim, "Right is whatever is meaningful and fulfilling to you and doesn't hurt anyone else." This leaves us in a terrible, relativistic, uncertain quandary about determining right and wrong. In my response paper to this class, I wrote in as kind and as respectful a way as I knew how:

> This way of determining right and wrong is very relativistic and subjective in that what I think is meaningful and fulfilling may be quite different from what somebody else thinks is meaningful or fulfilling. And besides, how do I know that something is really meaningful and fulfilling? After all, I may be wrong about what is meaningful and fulfilling. Because I am a finite human being, what I think is meaningful and fulfilling may not be an accurate evaluation at all.

In the same paper, I asked, "What standard do I use to determine whether something will truly not hurt someone else? How do I know for sure that someone else won't be hurt by what I do or don't do? I am finite and fallible, and my understanding of what is hurtful may be totally or at least partially errant."

WE CAN SAY, NOT PROUDLY, BUT BOLDLY, THAT WE DO HAVE ANSWERS!

In response to my paper, the professor wrote, "You have raised some serious and interesting issues to which we don't have the answer, but we must continue to wrestle with them."

In other words, if we scrap this standard of right and wrong, we have no standard at all.

IF ALMIGHTY, ALL-WISE, ALL-KNOWING, INFALLIBLE GOD TEACHES SOMETHING, WHAT DOES IT MATTER WHAT THE REST OF THE WORLD SAYS?

Again, how sad that people who are in the people-helping field are so lacking in anything that is solid when it comes to understanding people and their problems and providing the solutions to them. How grateful and how humbled we should be by the fact that we have God's Word which is profitable for teaching. Friends, we can say, not proudly, but boldly, that we do have answers! We do have truth in God's Word.

In His book, the Bible, Almighty God tells us what is right and what is wrong. When we base our understanding on this Book we don't have to wonder, "Is what I am doing right or is it wrong?" If the teachings of this Book are inspired by God, we can have peace, confidence, and security if what we believe, what we say, and what we do is in accordance with what it says. If almighty, all-wise, all-knowing, infallible God teaches something, what does it matter what the rest of the world says? It's to the law and the testimony of God's Word that we go for truth, and anything that contradicts God's Word is patently false (Isaiah 8:9-10).

Without the certitude that comes from knowing that what you believe is the teaching of God, you go through life like a ship without an anchor. You are constantly being tossed to and fro with no real grounds for certainty about anything. The result when you think realistically about your situation: uncertainty, fear, anxiety, depression, confusion, perplexity, and many other unpleasant experiences. On the contrary, when you know that the teachings of the Bible have been inspired by God, and you understand, believe, and apply those teachings to your life, you have the basis for peace, confidence, certainty, contentment, boldness, courage, joy, gentleness, goodness, kindness, self-control and trustworthiness.

In reality, if you don't know for sure what's true, you should be anxious; you should be fearful; you should be insecure, because you're building your life on shifting sand. But when you are lining your life up with the Word of God – living according to the standards of God's Word; operating your family according to God's Word; conducting your business according to God's Word; relating to other people according to God's Word – you can have security because you know what God has said is the truth. Ah yes, this Book inspired by God is profitable for teaching.

IT IS PROFITABLE FOR REPROOF

Paul continues, *"All Scripture is inspired of God and is profitable … for reproof."* Reproof is profitable? We don't like to be reproved. But the Bible is profitable for reproof. And really, nothing is more beneficial than the right kind of reproof. There are people, for example, who live all of their lives thinking the wrong things, believing the wrong things, living the wrong way, only to discover too late that they were wrong.

The man described in Luke 16 is probably an example of such a person. This man was rich; he lived all of his life in an extravagant manner, focusing only on the pleasures and satisfactions that come from this world, giving little if any thought to God or the things of eternity. His money gave him material and social privileges in this world that poorer men never have. He had power, control, worldly success, and respect from people. He could do almost anything he wanted to do, and apparently he did. That's how he lived. In the words of Psalm 17:14, he was a man of this world; his portion was in this life; he satisfied his appetites with God's good things, but never acknowledged that it was God who gave him the power to get these things. He never stopped to think seriously

WITHOUT THE CERTITUDE THAT COMES FROM KNOWING THAT WHAT YOU BELIEVE IS THE TEACHING OF GOD, YOU GO THROUGH LIFE LIKE A SHIP WITHOUT AN ANCHOR.

about the fact that the food he ate, the water he drank, the air he breathed, the health he had, and the land he farmed were given to him by God. He had no relationship with God, and he didn't seem to care. Then, the Bible says, he died and went to hell.

The words of Luke 16:31 seem to indicate that this man had been reproved. He had been warned, but he hadn't listened. Prior to his death and entrance into hell, he had not seen the value of reproof. He avoided it, ignored it, refused it, and rejected it as much as possible. But in hell, he saw the value of reproof, and he begged to have someone go and reprove his brothers. At that point, it was too late for him to benefit from reproof.

All of his life he had been wrong. Previously, according to Jesus, he had had the Scriptures to reprove him, but he had not listened. He just had not paid any attention. He had shut his ears to the truth. Then he died and went to hell. And then it was too late! The right kind of reproof is profitable when heeded, but it is only of value this side of the grave.

Numerous Bible verses extol the value of reproof. Proverbs 10:17 says, *"He is on the path of life who listens to instruction, but he who forsakes reproof goes astray."* There is value in the right kind of reproof, because it keeps you from going astray. It keeps you away from the path of ruin and death – physical death, spiritual death, ministerial death, emotional death, marital death, familial death. It puts you on the path of real life – abundant life, eternal life, the blessed life. No reproof, no improvement, protection, correction, improvement, no real life. That's the teaching of Proverbs 10:17. It's no surprise then that 2 Timothy 3:16 would mention reproof as one of the profitable things the Scriptures are able to do for us.

Proverbs 12:1 reminds us that *he who loves discipline loves knowledge, but he who hates reproof is stupid.* The person who hates reproof is stupid (ignorant) and will remain so. Acquiring knowledge requires being reproved. No reproof, no real knowledge is the teaching of this verse. Through reproof we gain a knowledge of how we're thinking wrongly, acting wrongly, reacting wrongly, and relating wrongly. Through reproof we gain a knowledge of our wrong motives, and our wrong ways of thinking about God, ourselves, the world, our values, anything we're wrong about. Through reproof we find out how we need to change. We learn things that are hindering us in our relationships with God, with people, and with ourselves. According to Proverb 12:1, no reproof equals no real

THERE ARE PEOPLE, FOR EXAMPLE, WHO LIVE ALL OF THEIR LIVES THINKING THE WRONG THINGS, BELIEVING THE WRONG THINGS, LIVING IN THE WRONG WAY, ONLY TO DISCOVER TOO LATE THAT THEY WERE WRONG.

THE PERSON WHO HATES REPROOF IS STUPID (IGNORANT) AND WILL REMAIN SO.

knowledge, no real change, no improvement, little or no usefulness. It's no surprise then that 2 Timothy 3:16 would mention reproof as one of the profitable things the Scriptures are able to do for us.

Proverb 12:15 instructs us that *the way of a fool is right in his own eyes. But a wise man is he who listens to counsel.* The person who thinks his understanding and opinion is always right and that he always does everything right is a fool.

He's a fool because God, Who knows everything as it really is, says he's not always right. It is an extremely foolish thing to argue with an all wise, all knowing God Who always is right.

He's a fool because his own experience, if he's lived any period of time at all, would tell him it is otherwise. He knows he's made mistakes in judgment and in living.

He's a fool because he is finite and very limited in terms of what he does know about all there is to know.

THE PERSON WHO THINKS HIS UNDERSTANDING AND OPINION IS ALWAYS RIGHT AND THAT HE ALWAYS DOES EVERYTHING RIGHT IS A FOOL.

He's a fool because he never will change for the better; he never will improve; as long as he thinks the way he does, he never will benefit from the insights of others who know more about many things.

This kind of person is a fool because he is *quarrelling against all sound wisdom* (Proverb 18:1).

He's a fool because he's inviting destruction – eternal, temporal, relational (Proverb 14:12).

He's a fool because *pride goes before destruction, and a haughty spirit before stumbling* (Proverbs 16:18).

He's a fool because he will not *listen to counsel,* and *without counsel, plans are frustrated, but with many counselors they succeed* (Proverbs 15:22).

He's a fool because *he who listens to reproof acquires understanding whereas he who neglects discipline* (reproof) *despises* (is hurting, demeaning, restricting, harming) *himself* (Proverb 15:32).

He's a fool because he is excluding himself from the fellowship of the wise (Proverb 15:31). Without reproof, there is no wisdom, no improvement, no growth, no true success.

Again, it's no surprise then that 2 Timothy 3:16 would mention reproof as one of the profitable things the Scriptures are able to do for us.

Proverb 13:18 tells us that *poverty and shame will come to him who neglects discipline. But he who regards reproof will be honored.* Rejecting or ignoring reproof brings poverty. Sometimes it brings financial poverty, sometimes then it brings other kinds of poverty such as marital, familial, emotional, relational, ministerial, spiritual poverty. On the other hand, paying attention to reproof is an honorable thing and leads to being honored by usefulness in the kingdom, personal growth, marital, relational, familial, and emotional success. According to the Bible, achieving true success as God would define it necessitates being reproved. As far as God is concerned, without reproof, there is no honor. Being properly reproved is one of the most necessary and beneficial things in terms of making spiritual progress.

Once again, it's no surprise that 2 Timothy 3:16 would mention reproof as one of the profitable things the Scriptures are able to do for us.

ACHIEVING TRUE SUCCESS AS GOD WOULD DEFINE IT NECESSITATES BEING REPROVED.

That the psalmist recognized the value of reproof is indicated by his statement in Psalm 141:5: *Let the righteous smite me in kindness and reprove me; it is oil upon my head; do not let my head refuse it....* Much can be learned from this verse about the way we should seek, give, and regard reproof.

In this verse David did several exemplary things:

1. He saw the importance of being reproved, and he invited the righteous to reprove him. He had previously been the beneficiary of reproof from the prophet Nathan (2 Samuel 12:1-15) and even from a woman by the name of Abigail (1 Samuel 25:14-33).

2. He recognized that the most valuable kind of reproof comes from righteous people – people who are right with God, people who will use God's standards (not the world's standards, or even their own opinions) as their standard of right and wrong.

3. He indicated that the best kind of reproof is motivated by kindness (genuine concern) and presented in a kind and humble way. Long before Paul ever wrote the words of Galatians 6:1 about seeking to help erring people in a spirit of gentleness, David already understood the importance of giving reproof out of kindness and in a kind manner.

4. He realized that sometimes even the right kind of reproof will hurt – sometimes it will smite. Sometimes, even if you use a soft tongue, bones get broken, as Proverb 25:15 indicates should be the case: *A soft tongue breaks the bone.* Sometimes, in a figurative sense, bones need to be broken for good to be achieved. And, even if you use a soft, gentle tongue, it hurts when bones break. David knew that, but he realized that although reproof may hurt, it is a helpful and beneficial pain; it is something that is needed, that is for the good of the person being reproved.

5. He understood the incredible value of the right kind of reproof. *It is oil upon my head.* These words may be understood in two ways. First, they may be referring to the Old Testament practice of anointing with oil the head of a person, or even objects that were set apart for special service. Exodus 29:7 speaks of "anointing oil," oil used to anoint or set apart a person or object for special ministry. Psalm 133:2, for example, indicates that when Aaron became the high priest his head was profusely anointed with oil. To be set apart for special service by having your head anointed with oil was a tremendous privilege. If this is what David was referring to, he was saying that reproof is a way of preparing you, equipping you, and setting you apart for special use in the service of God. In other words, he is indicating that when you are appropriately reproved, you are being prepared for unique ministry in the Kingdom of God.

> REPROOF IS A WAY OF PREPARING YOU, EQUIPPING YOU, AND SETTING YOU APART FOR SPECIAL USE IN THE SERVICE OF GOD.

Second, the words "oil upon my head" may call our attention to Psalm 23:5 where the psalmist said that God had anointed his head with oil. In this instance, the psalmist, who has pictured His Lord as his Shepherd and himself as a sheep, was referring to the medicinal, healing, soothing function of oil. As sheep traveled through rough terrain where there were rocks with jagged edges or bushes with sharp thorns on them, they would often get cuts on their heads. The rest of their bodies, protected by wool, seldom got scratched, but their heads often did. So, in the evening when they bedded down for the night, the shepherd would walk among his sheep to examine them for cuts that might become infected and cause them to get sick or even die. Pouring oil upon their wounds had a medicinal, healing, protective, and restoring function, which enabled them to get better, travel with the flock, and produce an abundance of wool and mutton. As a protection against further damage, the sheep were examined for blemishes and oil was applied to them. In Psalm 141:5 David might have been saying that being appropriately examined and reproved was a necessary activity in order for him to deal with his defects, to be restored to good spiritual health, and to be productive in God's service. In reality, whether you understand what David is saying in the first or second way doesn't make much difference in terms of the main point he is emphasizing. In either case, the oil representing reproof is being portrayed as a beneficial thing – something to be desired, something that prepares, equips, and enables us for productive service for Christ.

We won't naturally welcome or seek reproof — and that is to our detriment.

6. Notice from this text one more thing that David knew about reproof. He knew his instinctive propensity to not want to be reproved. He was aware of his tendency to negate the value of reproof, to avoid it if possible, to refuse and reject it. So in effect, he stepped outside himself, sat himself down in the chair of a counselee, and began to give himself good counsel. "Do not let my head refuse it" were words he spoke to himself. In other words, he decided he was not going to allow his feelings to control him or dictate how he would think of or respond to reproof. He decided that he would take control of his feelings and thoughts and make himself think scripturally about the benefits of reproof. So it must be with us; we won't naturally welcome or seek reproof – and that is to our detriment. We must choose to view it from the perspective of the God Who knows things as they really are. He says to be rightly reproved is extremely beneficial. Think carefully about what He says in 2 Timothy 3:16, *"All Scripture inspired of God is profitable … for reproof…."*

In the previous section of this chapter, the words "appropriate" or "appropriately" were used several times with some explanation of what appropriate reproof is. One of the most important aspects of "appropriate" reproof is that it will always be biblically based. Helpful reproof will be given in kindness, and it will also always be biblically directed and derived. It's the Scriptures that are profitable for reproof, not your opinions or preferences, or those of anyone else. The only reproof that is really worth giving or receiving is reproof that comes from the Bible.

What people think is wrong, what people think needs to be changed, how people think you should improve, is relatively unimportant, and usually unhelpful. Not so with God's reproof. If God says we're thinking or living wrongly, we are. If God says there is something in our lives that should be changed, it should be changed. His reproof is always accurate and it is always helpful when heeded. Even God's negatives are given for positive purposes.

What this means is that whenever we read, study, or hear the Bible being expounded we ought to be praying, "O, God, show me what I'm doing or thinking that's wrong. Show me where I'm in error. Show me where I'm failing." Some people want to be entertained or made to feel good when they read, study, or hear the Bible taught. That's all they want when they expose themselves to the Bible. They don't want to be convicted; they don't want to be reproved; they don't want their sins to be exposed; they don't want to be challenged to change. That's why they get very little out of the Bible. That's why their lives don't change through biblical teaching. That's why they don't like the Bible. That's why many people say the Bible is dry, boring, or uninteresting. They approach Scripture with the wrong motivation, and thus they get little out of it.

IT'S THE SCRIPTURES THAT ARE PROFITABLE FOR REPROOF, NOT YOUR OPINIONS OR PREFERENCES, OR THOSE OF ANYONE ELSE.

For example, as fathers, we ought to come to the Bible to be shown how we're failing as fathers. We ought to come saying, "O, God show me how I can be a better father. Show me where I am failing." Concerning every aspect of our lives we ought to approach the Scripture with the attitude, "O God, use Your Word to show me my sin, to expose it to me, to search me and convict me, to show me where I'm wrong and how I need to change."

The Bible is profitable for reproof. And, since none of us is perfect and since reproof is one of the ways to help us to grow and improve, all of us ought to welcome the right kind of reproof.

Remember, since none of us is in heaven where we will be totally changed and perfected, as long as we're in this world there will always be room for growth. So let us say with the psalmist, "Come on righteous people, come on Lord, reprove me, show me where I'm wrong and I will regard it as oil on my head" (Psalm 141:5; 139:23-24).

AS LONG AS WE'RE IN THIS WORLD THERE WILL ALWAYS BE ROOM FOR GROWTH.

QUESTIONS FOR DISCUSSION

1. Describe the nature and comprehensiveness of the teaching found in Scripture. What are some things about which the Bible teaches us?

_____

_____

2. According to Psalm 119 what are some of the characteristics of the teaching found in the Bible?

_____

_____

3. In what ways does Psalm 119 extol the value of the teaching of God's Word? What are some of the things that this psalm indicates paying attention to the teaching of the Bible will do for us?

_____

_____

4. What was the psalmist's attitude toward the Word of God?

_____

_____

5. Why is the fact that the teaching we have in the Bible is inspired by God such a wonderful and valuable benefit to Christians? What are the practical implications of this truth for believers?

_____

_____

6. Summarize the illustration and the point of the illustration about the secular psychology course where the issue of values was discussed.

_____

_____

7. Summarize some of the reasons given in this chapter about the value of reproof in our lives. Why is the right kind of reproof profitable for us?

_____

_____

8. What was the point of the story in Luke 16 of the rich man?

_____

_____

9. Summarize the teachings about reproof found in Psalm 141:5.

_____

_____

10. Describe some of the features of "appropriate" reproof.

_____

_____

11. What implications does the teaching about the profitability of reproof have for us as we personally study or listen to God's Word being preached?

_____

_____

PERSONAL RESPONSE

1. Do you regularly come as a student to the Word? How long has it been since God really taught you?

_____

_____

2. What are the most important things He has taught you in the last week? In the last two weeks?

_____

_____

3. Is it your practice to come regularly to have God reprove you through the Bible? Are you open to reproof? Do you seek it?

_____

_____

4. Were you reproved through this chapter about your attitude toward the Bible? About your use of the Bible? In what ways?

_____

_____

5. In what other ways have you recently been reproved by God's Word? What passages has He used to do the reproving?

_____

_____

6. How do you react when someone reproves you with God's Word? Do you view reproof the way the psalmist did in Psalm 141:5?

_____

_____

7. What difference would a Psalm 141:5 attitude toward reproof make in your life?

_____

_____

8. Describe the last time someone reproved you. What was it about? What passages of Scripture were used? How did you respond?

_____

_____

9. What were the most important lessons you learned from this chapter? In what ways were you challenged in your Christian life?

_____

_____

CHAPTER 6

FULLY TRAINED AND EQUIPPED

I have not departed from the command of His lips; I have treasured the words of His mouth more than my necessary food (Job 23:12). How sweet are Thy words to my taste! Yes, sweeter than honey to my mouth! From Thy precepts I get understanding (Psalm 119:104). I have inherited Thy testimonies forever, for they are the joy of my heart (Psalm 119:111). The law of Thy mouth is better to me than thousands of gold and silver pieces (Psalm 119:72). O how I love Thy law! It is my meditation all the day (Psalm 119:97). Thy testimonies also are my delight; they are my counselors (Psalm 119:24). I have more insight than all my teachers, for Thy testimonies are my meditation (Psalm 119:99). Thy words were found and I ate them, and Thy words became for me a joy and the delight of my heart (Jeremiah 15:16).

These few selected statements from Scripture describe the way past believers viewed the value of God's Word in their lives. For Job, God's Word was more valuable than the food he ate at meal times. For the psalmist it was refreshingly delicious; it was his source of understanding; it was his chief source of joy and delight; it was more valuable than vast sums of wealth; it was his chief source of counsel and insight. For him God's Word was so valuable that he regularly spent long periods of time thinking about it, memorizing it, meditating on it, seeking to understand and apply it. For Jeremiah, it was so valuable that he consumed it, devoured it, digested it, and found it to be a source of refreshment, renewal, incredible joy, and delight.

These men understood, through personal experience, that God's Word is one of the greatest gifts that God could ever give to man. They knew the truth that the apostle was proclaiming in 2 Timothy 3:14-17. All of them would have heartily endorsed Paul's statement about the usefulness and profitability of the Scriptures. And so it should be with every believer. According to these men and the apostle Paul, the person who has, understands, and applies God's Word is truly a blessed person.

Thus far in our consideration of Paul's grand statement in 2 Timothy 3:14-17 about the Scriptures, we have noted three of the primary ways in which the Scriptures are useful: (1) they are profitable because they are able to make us wise unto salvation; (2) they are profitable because they are able to teach us the most important lessons in life; (3) they are useful in that they are able to appropriately and accurately reprove us.

In this chapter, we move on to note two other ways in which Paul indicates the Scriptures are profitable for us as believers. In particular, we're going to see that God has given us the Scriptures to correct and train us.

IT IS PROFITABLE FOR CORRECTION

The words *"all Scripture is inspired of God and profitable…for correction"* call our attention to the fourth way in which the Bible is profitable for us. The Greek word translated here as "correction" literally means somebody who's been knocked down – someone who is lying flat on the ground. And that's what often happens when we read the Word of God. The Word of God levels us. It knocks us down.

THE GREEK WORD TRANSLATED HERE AS "CORRECTION" LITERALLY MEANS SOMEBODY WHO'S BEEN KNOCKED DOWN.

Have you ever been knocked down by the Bible in that your sense of self-righteousness has been destroyed? As you have read or heard God's Word being preached, have you ever been convicted of your sinfulness? Have you experienced the reproving ministry of the Scriptures in a painful and discomforting way? Has the inspired Word of God caused you to see various areas in which you've been failing miserably, and have you been devastated by that awareness? Have you ever come to that place as you've read the Word of God, not just before you became a Christian, but since you've been a Christian?

Through the reproving, convicting ministry of the Bible have you been caused to cry out as Paul did in Romans 7: *"Wretched man that I am! Who will set me free me from this body of death?"* (Romans 7:24). Can you identify with Isaiah, who as a believer, was so convicted of his sinfulness that he cried out, *"Woe is me, for I am ruined!…I am a man of unclean lips"?* (Isaiah 6:5).

HAVE YOU EVER BEEN KNOCKED DOWN BY THE BIBLE IN THAT YOUR SENSE OF SELF-RIGHTEOUSNESS HAS BEEN DESTROYED?

When these men made these statements they were already believers. At the time they became believers they had already known something of the experience of the character named Christian as author John Bunyan describes him in the first chapter of *The Pilgrim's Progress*. As Christian read the Bible he saw himself dressed in rags, unfit for entrance into heaven. As he continued to read, he developed an oppressive burden on his back and began to weep and tremble. The burden, of course, was the burden of the conviction of sin, the weeping and trembling were the result of his understanding of how greatly he had sinned against God. It was as he read the Bible that he was reproved, shown how wicked and wrong he had been. That was the effect that the Word of God had on him.

So it was with Isaiah, Paul and every other person who becomes a believer as the Holy Spirit brings them to salvation. By God's law comes the knowledge of sin and by God's law comes the knowledge of the greatness of that sin (Romans 3:20). *"I would not have come to know sin except through the law"* are the words of Paul (Romans 7:7). God's Word reproved Paul and made him understand his need of forgiveness. The convicting ministry of God's Word doesn't stop at salvation. It continues throughout our lives as believers.

As we look at ourselves in the light of God's holiness and His revealed standards, we see how much wickedness and sin still remains in us. We recognize that our motives have not always been godly. We become aware that we still experience selfishness, pride, and unbelief; that our thoughts are not always pure; that our words are not always wholesome and God-honoring; that the way we relate to people isn't always loving; that we don't always love God with all our hearts, souls, minds and strength. We become aware that there is much room for improvement in our lives, because we don't always respond to difficulties and problems in a biblical way. As we read and study the Scriptures, the Holy Spirit makes us aware of how wrong we are in many areas of our lives and causes us to turn to the Lord for help in dealing with the sin in our lives.

By the Word, the Spirit reproves us and knocks us down, and as we have seen, that is profitable. But thank God that's not all the Spirit does with the Word. According to 2 Timothy 3:16, He uses the same Bible to correct us. He first uses it to show us how we're wrong and how we need to change, then He uses it to show us how to make things right. The Greek word translated "correct" literally means to stand somebody up on his feet and get him headed in the right direction.

In the Bible, God gives us His standards and tells us how we ought to think and live, and what we ought to believe. God comes and shows us, through His Word, that we don't believe as we ought to believe, that we don't live as we ought to live. As a result we are leveled, knocked flat, proven guilty. Then, as we continue to study and read the Word of God, God says, "Now that you know

THE GREEK WORD TRANSLATED "CORRECT" LITERALLY MEANS TO STAND SOMEBODY UP ON HIS FEET AND GET HIM HEADED IN THE RIGHT DIRECTION.

how wrong you've been, I'm going to tell you how to get it straightened out. I'm going to tell you how to solve your problems, how to deal with them."

This means that when we read and study the Bible we should do so with the attitude that we are looking for and will find everything we need to know about how to make what's wrong in our lives right – about how to be corrected. All the areas of life for which the Bible gives us corrective information include the spiritual, emotional, attitudinal, relational, occupational, mental, aspirational, volitional areas of life, and our relationship with God, people, and our environment.

The Bible is God's solution book. It contains everything we need for life and for godliness (2 Peter 1:3-4). It can make us adequate and fully prepared for every good work (2 Timothy 3:17). It can provide the medicine for every one of our spiritual ills. It can provide the answers to all of life's most important questions. For every time the Word exposes our sinful errors, it gives us a Divine directive which tells us how to correct our problems. For every negative there is a positive. The Bible was given not only to tell us what our problems are and why we have them; it was given to tell us what do about our problems and how to make them right.

In explaining the meaning of the word "correction," Jay Adams has written:

> The Word of God wounds, but it also binds up; it cuts out the soul's cancer, and then it heals the soul (See Isaiah 30:26.)....That is the idea behind the Greek word apanorthosis....It is the sense of "standing something up" or "making something to stand again." In modern Greek it has come to mean "redress, reparation, rectifying"....The Word of God has the positive power of rectifying what has gone wrong. It is able to set straight what has been knocked off base or out of line....The Bible boldly claims to supply what is necessary to help one change any attitudes or behaviors out of accord with God's will....The Bible helps us get out of the messes into which we fall....[10]

Having been a Christian for more than five decades, I can look back on many difficult situations that I have faced in life and remember mistakes that I have made, sins I have committed. As I have faced God's Word, I have been frequently reproved about how I have handled situations wrongly in my marriage, family, ministry, personal life, and my relationships with others.

THE BIBLE WAS GIVEN TO TELL US WHAT DO ABOUT OUR PROBLEMS AND HOW TO MAKE THEM RIGHT.

Having been involved in Christian ministry for over forty years, I have been called on to help people who have sinned grievously, who have created horrible messes by the things they have done or said or by the things they have not done or said, who have developed patterns of thinking, attitudes, feeling, and living that have brought great distress and heartache to them and other people.

As I have been confronted with my own sins and have been called upon to help people experiencing great difficulties, my absolute conviction that I will never face a situation in my own life, or in my ministry to others, for which the Scriptures will not provide all of the corrective information that is needed, has been incredibly encouraging. As I confront the problems in my own life or seek to help others with difficulties in theirs, I may not know exactly what God want us to do to make the wrongs right. But I know that somewhere in the Bible there is all the corrective information I need. That produces confidence rather than fear. That causes me to search the Scriptures more diligently rather than turning to extra-biblical sources for solutions.

Reflecting once more on John Bunyan's great allegory, *Pilgrim's Progress*, we see this great truth of the corrective value of Scripture played out again and again. According to Bunyan, it was the reproving Word that produced Christian's misery over his sin before he became a Christian. But, it was also the Word that God used to relieve Christian's misery. As he sought help, Evangelist told him to keep his eyes on the light and that the light would lead him to the resolution of his misery. When Bunyan spoke of the light, he was referring to God's Word, which Psalm 119:105 declares is a "lamp to our feet, and a light to our path." He was, in effect, saying that the same instrument that exposed the need provides the solution to the problem.

Later in the book, when Christian finds himself in the clutches of Giant Despair and is so miserable that he even contemplates suicide, the Word of God was the primary means by which he was delivered from his depressive problem. When he encountered intense spiritual warfare in the valley of humiliation, the sword of the Spirit (which is the Word of God) was the primary means by which he overcame during this time of intense struggle. Again and again throughout *Pilgrim's Progress*, Christian found help for handling and solving the difficulties he faced in life by reflecting on the truths of God's Word. For Bunyan, the Bible, inspired by God, was profitable for reproof and correction. He was absolutely convinced that through God and His Word we can find all the corrective information we need to handle any problems that come our way in life.

SOMEWHERE IN THE BIBLE THERE IS ALL THE CORRECTIVE INFORMATION WE NEED.

That is how it should be with us as we face our difficulties in life. We should be coming to the Bible with the confidence that it contains all the corrective information to straighten out the difficulties that we have in every aspect of life. Is that your attitude as you face the problems in your life? Is that the kind of confidence you have in the Scriptures? It should be, because most assuredly, "all Scripture is inspired of God and is profitable for teaching, reproof and correction…."

IT IS PROFITABLE FOR TRAINING IN RIGHTEOUSNESS

Continuing in his description of the profitability of Scripture, Paul wanted us to know that beyond all these things, God's Word is also profitable for training in righteousness. This aspect of the practical value of Scripture goes far beyond anything he has said thus far. To know that God's Word is profitable for salvation, for teaching, for reproof, and for correction is wonderfully encouraging. It's great to know what we should do and think; it's great to know for certain how and why we're wrong; it's great to know what we should do to make the wrong right. But it is even greater to be trained in righteousness.

THEY GIVE UP BECAUSE THEY DON'T UNDERSTAND THAT CHANGE IS A PROCESS, THAT REAL CHANGE USUALLY HAPPENS AS A RESULT OF TRAINING.

It's possible for people to read the Word and see that what they are doing is wrong. It's possible for them to even see what they ought to do to make it right. It's possible for them to say, "I need to change. I know what I should do" and then actually try to do it. But even with all that, it's still possible for them to give up before they really do change. Often this happens because they don't understand that change is a process, that real change usually happens as a result of training.

What often happens is this: People gain some understanding of what they're doing that's wrong (sinful, unbiblical). They are convicted. They are given instruction about what to "put off" and "put on," what needs to be displaced and what they should replace it with. They decide to do it. On day number one they try and fail more than they succeed. They then become somewhat discouraged and begin to wonder if they can really change. Once they had made the decision, they were expecting change to come quickly and easily. They don't understand that change is difficult and will require continuous effort.

Maybe they had decided they were going to be more calm and patient. Maybe they had decided they were going to pray more, or speak more sweetly to other people, or control their emotions more, or be less materialistic, less competitive, less selfish, less envious, less discontented, less critical, less fearsome, or less worried.

Now they've come to the end of the first day after they made their decision and they realize they have really blown it. They didn't expect it to be this way. They're somewhat discouraged, but they decide they'll try again tomorrow. They say to themselves and the Lord, "Tomorrow I'm going to really try. Tomorrow I'm going to be different." They get up the next day, pray about it, and go out to be different; but as the day goes on they find themselves slipping back into the same old patterns.

Within a short period of time of deciding, trying, and then failing, they begin to think that there is no use trying because they are just going to fail anyway. They know what they are doing or thinking or desiring is wrong, but they start wondering if they can ever really be different. Then they begin to say to themselves, and others, such things as: "I can't change. I can't be any different. That's the way I am. I was born that way. If God had just made me stronger then I'd be different. I've tried to do it God's way, but it doesn't work. I'm this way because this is the way my mother or father were. I guess it was something I inherited. Other people are doing it, so it can't be that bad. I'm not as bad as other people are. I'm just an emotionally, mentally, physically weak person, that's why I don't change. I lack willpower. Others have more strength than I do, that's why they're different. If only my situation were different then I wouldn't be this way. I have these problems and can't handle them better because of my background, because of past abuse, etc., etc. I may do some things wrong, but I do a lot of things right. Maybe what I'm doing or thinking isn't right, but then it's no worse than what Abraham or David or Noah or Peter did. Nobody's perfect. If other people had a husband like mine, or a wife like mine, or children like mine, or parents like mine, or a boss like mine, or physical problems like mine, they would be just as bad as I am, probably worse."

According to Paul, who is really writing God's truth, real change is possible for any Christian. We can replace any sinful pattern of life with a righteous one. We can be trained in righteousness. Righteousness means doing it rightly, and doing it rightly is doing it God's way, the biblical way. Training means several things: it means doing something over and over again – repetition; it means that it will involve a struggle, that it will be difficult; it will require effort, discipline, commitment, and determination.

REAL CHANGE IS POSSIBLE FOR ANY CHRISTIAN.

THE PURPOSE OF TRAINING IS TO MAKE THAT WHICH IS DIFFICULT EASIER, THAT WHICH IS UNNATURAL NATURAL.

WHEN PROPERLY USED, THE BIBLE CHANGES OUR HABITS AND PATTERNS.

The purpose of training is to make that which is difficult easier, that which is unnatural natural, to develop new habits and patterns so that we regularly and almost without deliberate thought or choice, do things in a right way. The instrument God uses to train us is the Word of God. Scripture is profitable for training in righteousness. Real, Godly, biblical change can happen. New patterns of living, thinking, feeling, and relating, can be developed, but they will only be developed through training. Moreover, they will only be developed as we consistently use the Word of God in the way and for the purpose God has prescribed. Regularly and diligently (2 Timothy 2:15; Psalm 119:9, 11; Acts 20:32; Psalm 19:1-11; Psalm 1:2-3; Joshua 1:9), we must come to the Word to be made wise unto salvation in the sense of becoming like Jesus, to be taught, to be reproved, to be corrected, and to be trained.

The Bible when properly used, when meditated on, when applied to our lives, trains us. It changes our habits and patterns. You don't usually change long-standing, habitual was patterns of thinking, living, behaving, acting, reacting, or feeling in a day or two days or three days or even four days. It will usually require continuous effort and struggle for a period of time.

To illustrate this truth, try this simple little exercise. Put your hands together and without thinking about it, intertwine your fingers. Which thumb do you find on top? When I intertwine my fingers and look down, I find that I have my right thumb on the top. When I switch my thumbs and put the left thumb on the top and the right thumb under it, it feels strange. It feels out of place. Why? Because for more than six decades of my life when I intertwine my fingers I've been automatically putting my right thumb on top of my left thumb. Intertwining my fingers in this way has become a habit and a pattern with me.

Now suppose for some reason I wanted to change that pattern. I'd say to myself, "From now on, I will put my left thumb on top of my right thumb." And suppose I would do just that today. Initially doing it would feel a little weird. I could then say, "Ah, what's the use? I can never change the way I put my hands together." But suppose instead I decided to continue. When I did it tomorrow, it would still feel a bit strange. It would probably still feel a bit strange on the third day. But suppose I would keep on practicing. I'd have to concentrate, but I could do it. Suppose day after day, week after week, I continued to practice putting my left thumb on top of my right thumb. What would happen? Eventually, the time would come when it would be natural for me to put my hands together that way. You can change patterns, but it takes training.

That silly example illustrates the method by which Christians indwelt by the Spirit of God can change unrighteous patterns into righteous patterns – by training, by diligence, by consistency, by practice, and by perseverance. And how do Christians train? Christians train as they continue to apply themselves to the Word of God, as on a daily basis, they come to the Word to be taught, reproved, and corrected. They train as they get up from their study of the Word or as they go out from the preaching of the Word to immediately put it into practice on Monday and keep putting it into practice on Tuesday, Wednesday, Thursday, Friday, and Saturday, and for the rest of their lives.

Those who want to change are convicted about something before God. They see what they should do correct it. Then on a daily basis they consistently apply themselves to work on changing in the area they want to change. They consistently ask God for help. When they do this on a daily basis, they find that within eight to twelve weeks of daily practice, doing it the righteous, godly way starts to become easier.

It usually takes time to change, but most of us quit trying too quickly. We say, "It's so hard. It's so difficult. It can't be done." Yes, it is hard. We're changing patterns. We're changing habits. Habits and patterns don't change easily, but they do change if we're willing to be trained by the Word of God.

What's the result of all of it? Verse 17 tells us, as we are saved through the Word of God; as we are reproved by the Word of God; as we are corrected by the Word of God; and as we are trained by the Word of God we become adequate, complete, mature. We grow up; our lives take on meaning and fulfillment. We accomplish something. Life is really worthwhile.

Years ago Alfred Adler, a disciple of Freud's, taught that within the bosom of every human being is a desire to accomplish something in life. He said that people are miserable and unhappy because they have a sense of inferiority. They don't think they are accomplishing anything. They don't see themselves achieving anything.

Alfred Adler was wrong about most things. He was wrong about how a person goes about gaining a sense of achievement. He was wrong in making that the ultimate goal of life. But he was right in the sense that God is an achiever. God is a producer. My Father works. Because we are made in the image of God, we will find contentment and satisfaction only as we have a productive life. The

WITHIN EIGHT TO TWELVE WEEKS OF DAILY PRACTICE, DOING IT THE RIGHTEOUS, GODLY WAY STARTS TO BECOME EASIER.

MOST OF US QUIT TRYING TOO QUICKLY.

greatest satisfaction comes out of having a life that is productive in honoring and glorifying God.

BECAUSE WE ARE MADE IN THE IMAGE OF GOD, WE WILL FIND CONTENTMENT AND SATISFACTION ONLY AS WE HAVE A PRODUCTIVE LIFE.

How can you have that kind of fulfilling life? That life where you know you are accomplishing something? You can find that kind of life as you are made wise unto salvation; as you are taught; as you are reproved; as you are corrected; and as you are trained by the Word of God. The inevitable result of experiencing these things through God's profitable Word will be godly success, accomplishment, and achievement. You will become adequate as a father. You will become adequate as a wife. You will become adequate as a mother. You will become adequate as a husband. You will become adequate as a young person. You will have a sense of satisfaction, achievement, and security because of what the Word of God is doing in your life. You will, in the words of 2 Timothy 3:17, be equipped for every good work. Everything we need to know to have a life of godliness, a life of productivity, a life that brings glory to God and is good for us and other people is found in this book.

HOW LONG HAS IT BEEN SINCE YOU REALLY FOUND SOME SOLUTIONS TO A VERY PRACTICAL PROBLEM IN THE WORD OF GOD?

As we end this chapter, ask yourself these questions: What's your view of God's Word? Do you look upon the Bible in the way that Paul describes it in 2 Timothy 3:14-17? Do you come to the Bible wanting God to do those things in your life and expecting Him to do them? Do you come with some excitement and confidence? Do you come to the Bible to be made wise unto salvation, to be made more like Jesus? Do you expect God to use His Word in that way in your life? Do you regularly come as a student to the Word to have God teach you what He wants you to know? How long has it been since God really taught you? Is it your practice to come regularly to have God reprove you through the Bible? Are you open to reproof? Do you seek it? Were you reproved through this chapter about your attitude toward the Bible? About your use of the Bible? How long has it been since you really found some solutions to a very practical problem in the Word of God?

YOU WILL ONLY EXPERIENCE THESE BENEFITS AS YOU USE IT AND USE IT PROPERLY.

Well, that's why God gave it. "All Scripture is inspired by God and profitable for teaching, for reproof, for correction, for training in righteousness." It is profitable in all these ways. But you will only experience these benefits as you use it and use it properly.

QUESTIONS FOR DISCUSSION

1. What does the word "correction" signify?

_____

_____

2. Why do we need to be corrected?

_____

_____

3. Why is correction so valuable?

_____

_____

4. Describe how Bunyan regarded the Bible and illustrated that belief in Pilgrim's Progress?

_____

_____

5. What encouragement does this fact have for us personally and in our personal ministeres?

_____

_____

6. Why is the fact that the Bible is profitable for "training in righteousness" such a wonderful truth for Christians?

_____

_____

7. What does the word "training" signify about change and solving life's problems?

_____

_____

8. How does the concept of training explain why some people don't change? Describe what happens in some people's lives when they are reproved and

_____

corrected that explains why they don't change. What wrong concept of change do they have?

_____

_____

9. What is involved in the process of training?

_____

_____

10. What is the purpose of training?

_____

_____

11. What promise does 2 Timothy 3:17 hold for those who use the Word of God in the way and for the purpose described in 2 Timothy 3:14-16?

_____

_____

PERSONAL RESPONSE

1. Describe some of the problems in your life to which you have found the solutions, the corrective information, in God's Word.

_____

_____

2. When you are struggling with a problem in your life, marriage, family, relationships what is your usual way of responding to it?

_____

_____

3. Describe a time when you had a problem and what you did in response to that problem.

_____

_____

4. Describe a time in your life when you have turned to another biblically wise, godly person for help to find God's solution to a problem in your life.

_____

_____

5. Do you know what it is to come to God's Word to be trained? Is that your attitude toward the Scripture? Do you want to be, and pray that you will be, trained by the Word? What are you presently doing to make this desire a reality in your life? In specific ways, how are you using the Bible to train yourself?

_____

_____

6. In what areas of your life do you need more training from God's Word?

_____

_____

7. In what areas of life is God working on training you right now?

_____

_____

CHAPTER 7

How to Overcome Giants

Everybody loves the story of David and Goliath. Perhaps it's so popular because of its happy ending: Teenage shepherd boy defeats evil giant. But did you ever notice how pitifully this triumphant story begins?

God's people were scared silly. Can you picture it? The men of Israel, the great soldiers of the land, were shaking at the sight of one giant. The author of 1 Samuel describes the scene: *All the men of Israel, when they saw the man, fled from him and were dreadfully afraid* (1 Samuel 17:24). These boys were petrified.

Into this anxious group of cowardly men walked a boy named David. He was an unlikely hero, not trained in the art of war, not even a soldier. The only reason he was there at all was because he had come to check up on his older brothers. Yet he was absolutely confident that he could defeat Goliath. His brothers thought he was full of himself. The king thought he was crazy. But still David persevered and ended up shocking the world by slaying the great giant with a couple of stones and a slingshot.

Most think of David as the first of the great underdogs, but he knew better. He knew the reason he was so courageous. It's recorded in 1 Samuel 17:45-48:

> Then David said to the Philistine, "You come to me with a sword, spear, and a javelin, but I come to you in the name of the Lord of hosts, the God of the armies of Israel, whom you have taunted. This day the Lord will deliver you up into my hands, and I will strike you down and remove your head from you. And I will give the dead bodies of the army of the Philistines this day to the birds of the sky and the wild beasts of the earth, that all the earth may know that there is a God in Israel, and that all this assembly may know that the Lord does not deliver by sword or by spear, for the battle is the Lord's and He will give you into our hands."

David simply acted on what every soldier in the Israelite army should have already known. God had promised Israel, *"When you go out to battle against your enemies, and see horses and chariots and people more numerous than you, do not be*

EVERYBODY LOVES THE STORY OF DAVID AND GOLIATH. BUT DID YOU EVER NOTICE HOW PITIFULLY THIS TRIUMPHANT STORY BEGINS?

afraid of them; for the Lord your God is with you.... Do not let your heart faint, do not be afraid, and do not tremble or be terrified because of them; for the Lord your God is He who goes with you, to fight for you against your enemies, to save you" (Deuteronomy 20:1-4).

OVERCOMING GIANTS

Do you see the great mistake the Israelite soldiers made? They were thinking just like the Philistines. They were looking at the situation from the exact same perspective – as if God didn't exist. The Israelites failed to recognize that the resources for battle available to the people of the world are nothing in comparison with the resources available to the people of God.

What's a giant, or a javelin, or a spear in comparison with the One Who rules over the entire universe? The people of God don't need to be intimidated by the giants of the world. David understood this. The Philistines depended on a giant. David relied on God. That's why he was able to demonstrate such great strength. He realized that if God is on your side, even if the entire world is against you, you are in the majority!

Don't be too quick to point your finger and shake your head at those Israelite soldiers. Too often our response to the troubles of life looks more like the trembling soldiers than it does that courageous shepherd boy. Too often, we look at life from exactly the same vantage point as the world, thinking only in terms of what we can see rather than on the basis of Who God is. We think victory over life's problems depends on mankind's wisdom or strength instead of on God. So when problems arise, we rely on people and their resources rather than on God and the resources available to us in Christ.

Do you really want to solve life's problems God's way? This is where it begins. Stop thinking like the world. Stop trusting in people. Stop looking to people for the strength and wisdom that only God can provide. *Trust in the Lord with all your heart, and lean not on your own understanding. In all your ways acknowledge Him and He will make your paths straight* (Proverbs 3:5-6).

All too often we depend on people for the help that only God can provide. When tough times come into our lives, we don't even think of turning to Him; instead we anxiously look to other people for support. When we don't find it, we end up sitting on the sidelines, just like those Israelite soldiers. We limp

STOP THINKING LIKE THE WORLD. STOP LOOKING TO PEOPLE FOR THE STRENGTH AND WISDOM ONLY GOD CAN PROVIDE.

around with an inferiority complex because we look to people, rather than God, for strength and deliverance.

God hates that. I know that may seem like strong language, but that's the language Scripture uses. *"Thus says the Lord, 'Cursed is the man who trusts in mankind, And makes flesh his strength, and whose heart turns away from the Lord' "* (Jeremiah 17:5). *"Do not trust in princes, In mortal man, in whom there is no salvation"* (Psalm 146:3). *"Stop regarding man, whose breath of life is in his nostrils, For why should he be esteemed?"* (Isaiah 2:22).

God doesn't want us to trust in anyone or anything other than Him for victory over the problems of life. *"The king is not saved by a mighty army; a warrior is not delivered by great strength. A horse is a false hope for victory; nor does it deliver anyone by its great strength"* (Psalm 33:17). *"The horse is prepared for the day of battle, but victory belongs to the Lord"* (Proverb 21:31).

It's not wrong to "prepare the horse," but it's foolish to trust in it. We make idols out of things that God designed for our good. Imagine someone who wants to build a house trusting in the tools to do it for him. He looks at the hammer and he says, "Go, hammer, go!" He puts his confidence completely in the screwdriver, saying, "Do your magic." Will those tools get up by themselves and build him a house? Of course not! Don't put your trust in the tools. Go find a builder.

We're just as silly when we put our trust and hope in created things rather than in the Creator. Those things are just tools that a sovereign God uses to accomplish His great purpose.

If this seems obvious to you, good. The problem is, all too often God's people fail in just this area. They depend on people and created things instead of the Creator. If you don't believe it, just take a look at the Old Testament. Israel made this mistake over and over again. God wanted His people to learn to depend on Him alone – not only for salvation, but for all things. But God's people keep looking to other people for the help and strength only God can provide.

Honestly, isn't that just like us? Isn't that the way we often respond to troubling circumstances and the problems of life? Don't we often fall back on human ideas and human strategies in times of trouble, rather than first turning to God? "Trust God? Rely on God? Are you crazy? I've got to figure my own way out!" Human

GOD DOESN'T WANT US TO TRUST IN ANYONE OR ANYTHING OTHER THAN HIM FOR VICTORY OVER THE PROBLEMS OF LIFE.

wisdom tells us to look to other people for help; but God's wisdom says look to Him alone.

You are reading a book about how to find God's solutions to life's problems. That's great. But as you work through this book, and begin to make strategies for dealing with the problems in your life, you need to understand that you are absolutely incapable of overcoming your problems on your own. You are excited about changing your life, and that's great. But recognize where you need to start.

You can't change apart from God. You need to depend on Him. Don't look to other people for the strength and wisdom only God can provide. God is the only one worthy of our trust. One of the reasons we are spiritually weak is because we look to the wrong source for strength. Do you wonder why you can't overcome your problems? Perhaps the explanation begins here: You are thinking like the world; you are trusting in people instead of God.

The reason we fail to trust in God is because our view of mankind is too big and our view of God is too small. Iain Murray explains, "All spiritual weakness is ultimately due to poverty of thought about God, and such weakness will persist as long as we suppose that man is the starting point for it's resolution."[11] If we could just gain a right understanding of who God is and who mankind is, we would quickly see how foolish it is to trust in people and how wise it is to trust in God.

THE WISDOM OF TRUSTING GOD ALONE

We should depend upon God completely because He is sovereign and He is good.

Too often we treat the doctrine of the sovereignty of God like it is a taboo subject – just another idea for theologians to debate. But when we ignore God's sovereignty in times of trouble we neglect the very doctrine that will give us strength to overcome.

Our God is in control, and His control extends beyond the major events of the world to even the smallest details. That means we have no reason to fear. Jesus explains in Matthew 10:29-31: *"Are not two sparrows sold for a cent? And yet not one of them will fall to the ground apart from your Father. But the very hairs of your head are all numbered. Therefore do not fear; you are of more value than many sparrows."* To encourage us to be courageous, Jesus points to the sovereignty of God over the most insignificant of events.

Jerry Bridges comments:

> Jesus' words are so familiar to us that we can easily fail to grasp the significance of what he said. The word translated as a "penny" was often used to denote a trifling amount. Yet Jesus said not one of those birds, worth only a trifle, could fall to the ground (i.e., lose its life) without the will and permission of God our Father. But Jesus extends our Father's care to a yet finer detail: "even the very hairs of your head are all numbered." The average human head has about 140,000 hairs. Jesus said that each individual hair is numbered; that is, it has its own identity. The obvious inference is that each hair is important to God. God does not exercise his sovereignty in only a broad way, leaving smaller details of our lives to "chance" or "luck." That is precisely Jesus' point. God our Father, who exercises sovereignty in such minute detail as to control the destiny of a little bird, will certainly exercise his sovereignty to control even the most insignificant details of our lives."[12]

God's sovereignty wouldn't be much comfort however, apart from another equally important biblical truth. God is good. He is morally perfect and infinitely kind. The psalmist wrote, *"The Lord is gracious and merciful; slow to anger and great in lovingkindness. The Lord is good to all, And His mercies over all His works"* (Psalm145:8-9). It's His goodness that makes His sovereignty so precious. God cares about our needs, and He is powerful enough to do something about them! Why don't we trust Him?

THE FOOLISHNESS OF TRUSTING IN MAN

We should depend upon God completely because apart from Him we can do nothing.

One of the reasons we don't depend on God is because we have too small a view of God. Another reason is because we have too high a view of ourselves. A clear understanding of our own abilities will motivate us to be a dependent people. Jesus explained, *"Abide in Me, and I in you. As the branch cannot bear fruit itself, unless it abides in the vine, so neither can you, unless you abide in Me. I am the vine, you are the branches; he who abides in Me and I in him, he bears much fruit; for apart from me you can do nothing"* (John 15:6). Jesus does not say, "Apart from me you

ONE OF THE REASONS WE DON'T DEPEND ON GOD IS BECAUSE WE HAVE TOO HIGH A VIEW OF OURSELVES.

can do most things," or "Apart from me you can do some things," or "Apart from me you can do the little things." No, He says, "Apart from me you can do nothing."

We need to constantly remind ourselves that we are completely dependent on God in every area of our lives. We're dependent on God for our physical needs and our spiritual needs. Jerry Bridges comments:

> It is…difficult however for us to learn our dependence on God in the spiritual realm. A lack of money for food or to make the monthly mortgage payment gets our attention very quickly, and the need is obvious. The money is either available or it isn't. There's no pretending. But we can pretend in the spiritual realm. We can exist for months going through the motions, perhaps even teaching Sunday school, or serving as an elder or a deacon, depending on nothing more than mere natural human resources. The possible extremity of physical circumstances and my very real dependence on God to meet physical needs serves as a daily reminder of my spiritual dependence on Him. If I am dependent in the physical realm, how much more dependent am I in the spiritual realm, where our struggle is not against flesh and blood, but against spiritual forces of evil (Ephesians 6:12)?[13]

You can't solve life's problems apart from Christ, so why even try?

THE DEPENDENT PERSON PRAYS

The proud person is a person of little prayer.

Pride is a blinding kind of sin. This means that the people who are proud generally don't think they are very proud at all. They think that they are dependent on God just fine. But mark this, here is a sure, no-fail, indicator of spiritual pride: The proud person is a person of little prayer. Proud people think have an unbiblical view of God and an unbiblical opinion of themselves, and though they may not admit it, they prove this is true, by failing to pray about all things.

You don't realize how dependent you are on God if you are not a person of prayer! Don't say you are depending on God alone for strength and wisdom to solve your problems if you are not crying out to Him in prayer.

Think about who you are. You are desperate for God's help. Stop trusting in yourself. You can't solve your problems on your own. Oswald Chambers explains:

> During a war many a man prays for the first time in his life. When a person is at his wit's end, it is not a cowardly thing to pray, it is the only way to get in touch with reality. As long as we are self-sufficient and complacent, we don't need to ask God for anything, we won't want Him; it is only when we know we are powerless that we are prepared to listen to Jesus Christ and do what He says.[14]

Jesus says, *"Apart from me, you can do nothing."* We all know enough to nod our heads in agreement when that verse is read, but most of us don't really believe it. We think we can do some things. We don't realize how much we need God. We say we trust in God and depend on Him, but we don't.

How could you truly believe that apart from Christ you can do nothing, and still try to do so many things without prayer? How can you believe that apart from Christ you can do nothing and still try to overcome your problems without continually running to God in prayer?

Charles Spurgeon reminds us:

> God's people by saying, "Let us go speedily to prayer" manifest that they have a sense of their needs, they feel they want much, much that nature can't yield them, they feel their need of grace, their need of quickening, their need of God's help if even those who are saved are to be steadfast, their need of help of the Holy Spirit, that they may grow in grace and glorify God. He who never prays surely does not know his own needs, and how can he be taught by the Lord at all.

Think about who God is. You can pray confidently because you know that God is in control of your circumstances. If God were not sovereign, prayer would be pointless. It would just be another human relaxation technique. But we know that it is much more than that. God is King and in prayer we are able to present our requests to Him. Imagine being able to present your requests to the one who rules over all things! What a privilege! God is not an impotent, weak, deposed ruler who is powerless to help you. He is the Sovereign King of the universe Who does whatever He wishes!

JESUS SAYS, *"APART FROM ME, YOU CAN DO NOTHING."* WE ALL KNOW ENOUGH TO NOD OUR HEADS IN AGREEMENT, BUT MOST OF US DON'T REALLY BELIEVE IT.

IF GOD WERE NOT SOVEREIGN, PRAYER WOULD BE POINTLESS.

God's sovereignty wouldn't be much comfort, however, if He didn't care about our needs and didn't listen to our prayers. Yet time and time again throughout the Scripture, God calls on us to draw near to Him and depend on Him for deliverance. The writer of Hebrews explains, *"We do not have a high priest who cannot sympathize with our weaknesses, but one who has been tempted in all things as we are, yet without sin. Let us therefore draw near with confidence to the throne of grace, that we may receive mercy and may find grace to help in the time of need"* (Hebrews 4:15-16). Imagine that, God calling on you to talk to Him!

These truths may be very familiar to you, but do they make any impact on the way you live? If you are going to solve life's problems, you need to depend on God and demonstrate that dependence through prayer. Sure, sure. You learned that in Sunday school. But take a moment and reflect on the last difficult situation that you experienced. Did God's sovereignty make any impact at all in your attitude in that situation and your prayer life throughout it? Many times believers can recite a great definition of God's sovereignty and goodness, but they fail to see how it connects to their lives and their circumstances. If you truly believe that God is sovereign and that He is good, you will depend on Him completely through prayer.

THE PRIVILEGE OF PRAYER

Think about the privilege you have in prayer. Prayer is a duty, but even more than that, prayer is a demonstration of God's grace. God allows us to draw near to Him in our time of need because He loves to bestow mercy and love on His children. The Sovereign King Who rules over everything in the entire universe calls on you to come close to Him because He longs to help you. What fool would call that a difficult duty? We are a privileged people because God is not only our King, He is also our Father. And a good father loves to help his kids. Jesus explains, *"What man is there among you, when his son shall ask him for a loaf, will give him a stone? Or if he shall ask for a fish, he will not give him a snake, will he? If you then, being evil, know how to give good gifts to your children, how much more shall your heavenly Father give what is good to those who ask Him?"* (Matthew 7:9-11).

WHEN WE FAIL TO TRUST GOD, WHEN WE REFUSE TO DEPEND ON HIM COMPLETELY, WE ARE CALLING HIM A LIAR AND REJECTING HIS WORD.

Lack of prayer demonstrates a lack of trust in the character of God. When I was a child, I used to struggle intensely with fear. My mom would often come to me when I was becoming afraid and ask me, "Does the Scripture say that God is good and that He promises to hear the prayers of His children and do what's best for them?" I knew enough to say that it did. Then she would look at me and ask, "And do you really believe that you are so important that God, Who has kept every single promise that He has ever made for thousands of years, would break His first promise when it comes to you?" She knew how to put me in my place! My mother was right. When we worry, when we fail to trust God, when we refuse to depend on Him completely, we are calling Him a liar and rejecting His Word.

Even our Savior continually expressed His complete dependence on God through prayer. He did not allow the pressures of ministry and the demands of other people to hinder His devotion to prayer. In Luke 5 we find Jesus' ministry exploding: *The news about Him was spreading even farther, and great multitudes were gathering to hear Him and be healed of their sicknesses* (Luke 5:16). And what did Jesus do? Did He use the needs of people and the lack of time as an excuse to be shallow and superficial in His prayer life? No! In the very next verse, we read that *He himself would often slip away to the wilderness and pray* (Luke 5:17). This was not a one-time event. All throughout the gospel of Luke we find Jesus making time for prayer: *"And it came about that while He was praying alone"* (Luke 9:18). *"And some eight days after these sayings, it came about that He took along Peter and John and James, and went up to the mountain to pray"* (Luke 9:28). *"And it came about that while He was praying in a certain place"* (Luke 11:1).

JESUS PRAYED BEFORE HE MADE MAJOR DECISIONS....HOW MUCH MORE SHOULD WE PRAY BEFORE WE MAKE ANY DECISION!

Did you catch the phrase, *"And it came about..."*? Sometimes we neglect prayer because we feel like we aren't doing anything. But here we see just the opposite happening. Jesus went out to pray, and things "came about!" Significant teaching times and ministry opportunities often centered around those occasions when He went out to pray. Jesus prayed before He made major decisions. It's interesting to note what Luke tells us happened right before Jesus chose the twelve disciples: *"It was at this time that He went off to the mountain to pray, and He spent the whole night in prayer to God"* (Luke 6:12). If Jesus, the Son of God, devoted a whole night to prayer before making this significant decision, how much more should we pray before we make any decision! Jesus cried out to God in times of trouble.

Many times in difficult situations we turn away from the very Person to Whom we should be running. Not Jesus! In the Garden of Gethsemane, knowing the agony of the cross was quickly approaching, what was Jesus doing? Mark tells us *He went a little beyond, and fell to the ground, and began to pray that if it were possible, the hour might pass Him by* (Mark 14:36). Jesus depended on God alone for strength and deliverance in every area of His life!

Paul demonstrated his dependence on God through prayer. Read through his letters to the churches, and you'll quickly see how devoted he was to prayer. He told the Corinthians that he always thanked God for them; the Ephesians, that he made mention of them in his prayers; the Philippians, that he prayed for their spiritual growth; the Colossians, that he did not cease to pray for them; and the Thessalonians, that he and his ministry team cried out to God for them continually. Reading how much time Paul devoted to praying for the churches makes you wonder how he had time to do anything else. Why would an important, intelligent, capable, busy man like Paul spend so much time praying? He recognized his complete dependence on God. *"What then is Apollos? And what is Paul? Servants through whom you believed, even as the Lord gave opportunity to each one. I planted, Apollos watered, but God was causing the growth. So then neither the one who plants nor the one who waters is anything, but God who causes the growth"* (1 Corinthians 3:5-6).

Paul didn't only pray for the churches; he asked them to pray for him! He wrote in 2 Thessalonians 3:1, *"Finally, brethren, pray for us that the word of the Lord may spread rapidly and be glorified, just as it did also with you."* Paul was a seasoned warrior for Christ, a man of tremendous intellect and abilities – the Thessalonians were a relatively new church full of new converts. Yet the great apostle Paul pled with these young believers to devote themselves to praying for him! Why? Because the apostle Paul needed God's help to accomplish anything of true spiritual value.

Learn to depend on God like this and you will become a person of great strength. Think of Shadrach, Meshach and Abednego, three Israelite refugees who stood before the great and powerful King Nebuchadnezzar. They alone refused to worship the idol the king had established. The Bible says that the king was filled with rage, and threatened them saying, *"But if you will not worship, you will immediately be cast into the midst of a furnace of blazing fire; and what god is there who can deliver you out of my hands?"* What would you have done in their place, three of you against an entire nation, with a fire waiting for you if you refused.

These men stood strong because of their complete reliance on God.

> *O Nebuchadnezzar, we do not need to give you an answer concerning this matter. If it be so, our God whom we serve is able to deliver us from the furnace of blazing fire; and He will deliver us out of your hand, O king. But*

even if He does not, let it be known to you, O king, that we are not going to serve your gods or worship the golden image that you have set up (Daniel 13:16-18).

"We trust God, whether He brings us through the fire or allows us to perish," they told the king! Don't think their attitude of dependence on God began that day. They were able to stand strong in the midst of a most difficult trial because they had learned to remain dependent during much smaller ones.

You must stop thinking about life and your problems in the same way the world does. You will never be able to solve life's problems God's way until you stop placing your confidence in people to do what only God can; and start depending on Him through prayer.

Since you have come this far in this study, you are probably not an atheist. (*God's Solutions to Life's Problems* probably isn't too enticing a title for someone who professes not to believe in God!) But I wonder, are you a "practical" atheist?

ARE YOU A PRACTICAL ATHEIST?

Practical atheists are people who profess to believe in God but live as if God doesn't exist. They go to church, say their prayers, and look religious, but in the day-to-day matters of life they don't depend on God. They live their lives with little thought of their need for God.

THEY LIVE THEIR LIVES WITH LITTLE THOUGHT OF THEIR NEED FOR GOD.

James describes these people this way: *"Come now, you who say, 'Today or tomorrow, we shall go to such and such a city, and spend a year there, and engage in business and make a profit.' Yet you do not know what your life will be like tomorrow. You are just a vapor that appears for a little while and then vanishes away. Instead you ought to say, 'If the Lord wills, we shall live and also do this or that.' But as it is, you boast in your arrogance, all such boasting is evil"* (James 4:13-16). The problem with these people is not that they make plans, but that they make those plans without any reference to God. Their problem is not so much what they do say, as what they don't say. They may believe in God, but when it comes to their everyday life, they don't rely on Him. They act like they have the power in and of themselves to do whatever they want. They pretend they have some control over their lives. They are "practical" atheists.

Unfortunately, many believers are "practical" atheists when it comes to solving life's problems. Just like the person in James, when problems arise, they make plans, they set goals, and they strive to change. But they do so trusting in their own strength. They do not completely rely on God. And again, just like the person in James, their boasting is arrogance – and all such boasting is evil.

It's all too easy in our day and age to forget how much we need God. When we are in a difficult financial situation, we don't run to Him in prayer; we look to credit cards, money in our bank accounts, or friends and family for help. When we are experiencing problems in our lives and our relationships, we don't run back to Scripture and to the promises of God for strength and direction; instead we turn to psychologists, psychotherapists, and self-help books to reveal a path we should follow. It's possible for us to go weeks with little thought of our need for God.

This should not be. The thesis of this chapter is very simple: *If you are going to solve life's problems God's way you need to completely rely on Him.* You can't be a "practical" atheist and be a triumphant Christian. It's not wrong for you to make plans. It's not wrong for you to work hard at changing and overcoming your problems. But mark this – it is wrong if you are attempting to do so without an attitude of complete dependence on God. You will continually be frustrated in your attempts to solve your problems if you are not relying completely and totally on God alone.

Everything and everyone else will fail you, but not God. George Mueller once explained:

> They that trust in the Lord shall never be confounded. Some who helped for a while may fall asleep in Jesus, others may grow cold in the service of the Lord, others may be as desirous as ever to help, but have no longer the means – were we to lean upon man, we would surely be confounded; but in the leaning upon the living God alone, we are beyond disappointment, and beyond being forsaken because of death, or want of means, or want of love, or because of the claims of other work. How precious to have learned in any measure to stand with God alone in the world and yet to be happy, and to know that surely no good thing shall be withheld from us whilst we walk uprightly.[15]

YOU CAN'T BE A "PRACTICAL" ATHEIST AND BE A TRIUMPHANT CHRISTIAN.

QUESTIONS FOR DISCUSSION

1. Why was David courageous? Why were the Israelite soldiers so fearful?

_____

_____

2. What mistake did the Israelite soldiers make?

_____

_____

3. What does it mean to depend on God? Be specific.

_____

_____

4. Give several reasons it is foolish to put your hope in created things rather than the Creator.

_____

_____

5. What did Iain Murray mean when he wrote, "All spiritual weakness is ultimately due to poverty of thought about God, and such weakness will persist as long as we suppose that man is the starting point for its resolution?"

_____

_____

6. Give several reasons we can and should depend on God.

_____

_____

7. What difference should God's sovereignty make in our lives? Be specific.

_____

_____

8. Why should a clear understanding of our own abilities motivate us to be dependent people?

_____

_____

9. What are some reasons it is difficult to remember our dependence on God in the spiritual realm?

_____

_____

10. What is one indicator of spiritual pride?

_____

_____

11. Why is prayer so important?

_____

_____

12. What does a lack of prayer demonstrate?

_____

_____

13. What is a practical atheist? What does it "look like" to be a practical atheist?

_____

_____

PERSONAL RESPONSE

1. Is there a situation in your life in which you are dreading the giants of the world? What is it? Why are you fearful?

_____

_____

_____

_____

2. What does it mean to depend on God alone? (Go beyond the cliché.) Why is this important? What does it have to do with solving life's problems?

_____

_____

3. In whom or what are you tempted to trust rather than God? To whom do you turn first when you have a problem?

_____

_____

4. Does God's sovereignty make any difference in your life? Explain specifically how it made a difference in your life this past week.

_____

_____

5. What would be different about the way you lived if you were a more dependent person?

_____

_____

6. What are some examples of ways people don't rely on God? Be specific.

_____

_____

7. What difference will the truths of this chapter make in your life?

_____

_____

CHAPTER 8

FIRST OF ALL, PRAY

As I read the apostle Paul's first letter to Timothy, his son in the faith, I never cease to be impressed by the instructions he gave in 1 Timothy 2:1. I am impressed by these words because of the context in which they are found, and because given Timothy's circumstances, Paul's counsel is quite different from the counsel most of today's so-called experts would give to someone facing the things Timothy was facing.

In 1 Timothy chapter one, Paul described some of the serious challenges and problems Timothy was experiencing. Prior to writing this epistle, Paul had been used of God to establish the church in the city of Ephesus. When he left for other ministries, he commissioned Timothy to stay on to supervise the development of the church in Ephesus. In chapter 1 he reminded Timothy of his responsibilities, informed him about certain challenges and difficulties he would experience, and told him of problems he would face and of men who would seek to mislead the people Timothy was overseeing. Paul made it clear that Timothy's ministry there would not be a picnic, it would not be a bed of roses, it would not be an easy task. He informed Timothy that he was going to be involved in a fight; he charged him to fight the good fight and diligently keep the faith and a good conscience.

> PAUL'S COUNSEL TO TIMOTHY IS QUITE DIFFERENT FROM THE COUNSEL MOST OF TODAY'S SO-CALLED EXPERTS WOULD GIVE TO SOMEONE.

"Timothy," Paul implied, "you are going to face many problems in your own life and in your ministry. You're going to be tempted to give up the faith; you're going to be tempted to lower your standards; you're going to be tempted to compromise, to become weary in well doing." In other words, Paul was telling Timothy that as he lived and ministered, he, Timothy, was going to be confronted by gigantic problems.

WHEN YOU FACE DIFFICULT PROBLEMS, MAKE PRAYER A PRIORITY

Then came the impressive words of 1 Timothy 2:1 in which Paul described what Timothy must do if he were not going to be overwhelmed by the difficulties Paul had described. What was it Timothy had to do? *"First of all, then,*

GIVEN TIMOTHY'S PROBLEMS, THESE WORDS ARE IMPRESSIVE, EVEN SURPRISING — ALMOST SHOCKING.

HE WANTED TIMOTHY TO KNOW THAT NOTHING IS MORE IMPORTANT THAN, OR EVEN AS IMPORTANT AS, PRAYER.

I urge that entreaties and prayers, petitions and thanksgivings be made...." Given Timothy's problems, these words are impressive, even surprising – almost shocking. As mentioned previously, these words are impressive to me because they are not what many people who are facing serious problems are usually told. And if the counsel people with problems receive does include a suggestion about prayer, prayer isn't usually mentioned as the most important thing they are to do. They aren't told to pray first of all; to put it at the top of their priority list when it comes to solving their problems. Yet that's precisely what Paul told Timothy to do. It's also what he told us to do when facing problems. Throughout the epistle, Paul gave a variety of instructions about how to prevent and resolve problems, but he wanted Timothy to know that nothing is more important than, or even as important as, prayer. That is impressive and challenging!

BIBLICAL EXAMPLES OF PEOPLE WHO, WHEN FACING DIFFICULT PROBLEMS, MADE PRAYER A PRIORITY

In 2 Chronicles 20, Jehoshophat, king of Judah, found himself and the nation he governed facing a very serious problem. A coalition of other nations comprising a "great multitude" of soldiers came to wage war against Jehshophat. Jehosophat's initial response to this problem was fear, but his second response was prayer. Others might have advised him to quickly call a cabinet meeting, to assess his military resources, to devise plans and strategies for resisting and overcoming the enemy. None of these things would have been wrong in and of themselves. In fact, at the appropriate time they would have been the wise thing to do.

But Jehoshophat knew that if the problem they were facing was to be solved there was something more important than any of these things. Scripture indicates that before Jehoshophat did anything else he *"turned his attention to seek the Lord."* More than that, he encouraged others to do the same. Scripture indicates that when they heard of the problems that confronted them *"Judah gathered together to seek help from the Lord; they even came from all the cities of Judah to seek the Lord"* (2 Chronicles 20:1-4). Long before Paul ever wrote 1 Timothy 2:1, Jehoshophat believed that when we are confronted by problems, our response should be to give prayer priority.

Acts 4 describes a time when the early church was confronted with some serious problems. *"The priests and the captain of the temple guard, and the Sadducees came upon them, being greatly disturbed because they were teaching the people and proclaiming in Jesus the resurrection of the dead. And they laid hands on them, and put them in jail....*" After carefully discussing what they should do, these religious leaders, who also had political power, decided to warn and threaten them to cease from their teaching ministries. Scripture says *they commanded them not to speak or teach at all in the name of Jesus.* Then, not knowing what else to do because they had "*no basis on which they might punish them on account of the people, because they* (the people) *were all glorifying God,*" they threatened them and temporarily released them (Acts 5:1-21).

As indicated by what they had just done to Jesus (putting Him to death) and what they would later do in flogging and even putting to death some of the early Christians (See Acts 5:40; Acts 12:1-2.), these religious political leaders were very distressed and willing to do almost anything to stifle the growth and impact of the early church. So when the disciples were warned and threatened to never again teach about Jesus, they knew the possible consequences of disobedience. They knew they had a huge problem.

Their response to this problem is very interesting. First, "*they went to their own companions, and reported all that the chief priests and elders had said to them.*" Second "*they lifted up their voice to God in one accord....*" When confronted with a life-threatening, church-threatening problem, the early Christians didn't wring their hands in despair. They didn't allow their fears or anger to control them. They didn't question God's wisdom, power, or love. They didn't call a committee meeting and discuss strategy. They didn't act rashly or irresponsibly. Rather, they did what Paul indicated we ought to do when facing problems in our lives. They made prayer a priority in their lives.

In keeping with Paul's admonition in 1 Timothy 2:1, these biblical examples illustrate the importance of making prayer a priority when facing problems in life. Paul and the people in these passages prayed "*first of all*" because they were absolutely convinced that "*the effectual fervent prayer of a righteous man avails much*" (James 5:16). They prayed "*first of all*" because they were convinced that many times we have not because we ask not (James 4:2). They prayed "*first of all*" because they knew, believed, and practiced the truth of Psalm 50:15, "*Call upon me in the day of trouble and I will deliver you and you will glorify me.*" They prayed "*first of all*" because they knew, believed, and rejoiced in the truth of Matthew 7:11, which declares that our heavenly Father is eager to give good things to those who ask Him.

DON'T CALL A COMMITTEE MEETING, CALL A PRAYER MEETING

CONTEMPORARY STATEMENTS ABOUT THE PRIORITY OF PRAYER

ALL CHRISTIAN VICTORY "IS WON, IN SECRET, BEFOREHAND BY PRAYER."

Paul and these people would have totally agreed with S.D. Gordon who wrote that all Christian victory "is won, in secret, beforehand by prayer. Service is merely picking up the results, claiming the victory already won. Prayer is striking the winning blow at the concealed enemy. Service is gathering up the results of that blow among the men we see and touch."[16]

Similarly, they would have said a hearty amen to the statement of John Piper. "It is true for individuals and churches. No prayer, no power....If we are not vigilant [in prayer], we will be ensnared by temptation. Our defense and offense is an active, persistent, earnest, believing prayer force."[17]

They would have affirmed the words of Richard Newton who stated that "the principal cause of *our* leanness and unfruitfulness is due to an unaccountable backwardness to pray...Prayer and patience and faith are never disappointed.....When I can find my heart dissolved in prayer, everything else is comparatively easy."[18]

Note carefully several of the phrases found in these quotes that relate to the matter of solving life's problems. S.D. Gordon reminds us that in prayer we strike the winning blow at the concealed enemy. John Piper asserts that without prayer we are impotent to face our problems and will be overcome by them. Richard Newton would have us know that we experience leanness and unfruitfulness because we don't pray aright and that when we do pray aright everything else (which would certainly include facing and solving the problems of life) is "comparatively easy."

PRAYER PRINCIPLES FOR SOLVING LIFE'S PROBLEMS THROUGH PRAYER

What role does prayer play in solving life's problems? A crucial role! But will any old kind of prayer get the job done? No. It has to be the kind of prayer that Paul describes in Philippians 4:6-7. This great text summarizes for us some of the key factors involved in effective prayer, the kind of prayer that is required for overcoming life's problems. In it, Paul provided some answers to several important questions about the what, when, where, how, and why of effective prayer. *"In everything,"* Paul wrote, *"by prayer and supplication with thanksgiving, let your requests be made known to God. And the peace of God, which surpasses all comprehension, shall guard your hearts and your minds in Christ Jesus"* (Philippians 4:6-7).

THE *WHAT* OF EFFECTIVE PROBLEM-SOLVING PRAYER

What should we pray about? The answer is "everything." Looking at the larger context of the entire book of Philippians, "everything" would include all the problems and issues Paul has previously mentioned. Because of limited space in this chapter, we will not be able to fully explore the breadth of the "everything" from previous chapters of the book, much less from the rest of the Bible. We will, however, mention a few things from the book of Philippians by way of example.

Going back to chapter 1, we see that "everything" should include praying for an increase of love, a love that is wise and discerning (Philippians 1:9). Sometimes we have a problem loving other people, perhaps members of our own family or church. Perhaps we have problems loving some neighbors or people at work or school. With some people, it's easier to be bitter and unloving than loving. At times, we really do care for people. We do want to help them, but our love isn't very wise or discerning. We want to love them, but we don't know the best and most productive way of showing that love to them. What would Paul tell us to do when we face a problem like this? Paul would say *"in everything by prayer"* is an important part of solving this problem (Philippians 1:9).

"Everything" should also include the problem of making wise decisions (Philippians 1:10; 4:6). As we go through life, we are constantly confronted by circumstances where we must make choices. We must make choices about the use of our time, money, talents, which opportunities we will accept, which person we will help, and the best way to help them. None of the choices before us may necessarily be wrong in themselves. The question under consideration is not, "Which of the choices is good and which is evil?" Instead, the question we must answer is, "Which of these choices is really the best, the most excellent one?" What would Paul tell us to do when we face a problem like this? Paul would say *"in everything by prayer"* is an important part of solving this problem.

"Everything" should include the problem of maintaining a consistent life of integrity, honesty; a life free from hypocrisy, guile and compromise in the midst

WHAT SHOULD WE PRAY ABOUT? THE ANSWER IS "EVERYTHING."

WE SHOULD PRAY ABOUT LOVE.

WE SHOULD PRAY ABOUT MAKING WISE DECISIONS.

WE SHOULD PRAY ABOUT MAINTAINING INTEGRITY.

WE SHOULD PRAY ABOUT BEARING FRUIT.

WE SHOULD PRAY ABOUT OVERCOMING SELF.

WE SHOULD PRAY ABOUT UNDERSTANDING CIRCUMSTANCES.

of the routine pressures and temptations that bombard us in this world (Philippians 1:10; 4:6). When we're constantly being pressured to conform to the world's standards and way of living, when others oppose the standards of Scripture, live for themselves, do what pleases them, and have no concern for what pleases God, when they mock the things we hold dear, remaining sincere and blameless in the midst of this present evil world is a constant challenge. What would Paul tell us to do when we face a problem like this? Paul would say *"in everything by prayer"* is an important part of solving this problem.

"Everything" should include the challenge of being spiritually productive, of being filled with the fruit of righteousness (Philippians 1:11; 4:6). It would include the challenge of being righteous internally and externally, in our hearts, our actions, and our speech, and seeing that kind of righteousness as something that is really worthwhile while others around us believe this kind of lifestyle is foolishness. "Everything" would include the challenge of believing that living a righteous life and being a righteous person will bear fruit; that it will make you a truly productive and useful person; that God will cause your righteous life to make an impact on others. What would Paul tell us to do when we face a problem like this? Paul would say *"in everything by prayer"* is an important part of solving this problem.

"Everything" should include overcoming the problem of our own selfishness and self-centeredness; of our tendency to live for ourselves, for our own glory; of our tendency to live to please people, to want to impress people with our own greatness; the tendency to make our own advancement the main goal of our lives, the "be all" and "end all" of our existence (Philippians 1:11; 4:6). It would include the tendency to make decisions on the basis of how it will benefit us and promote our own advancement. It would include overcoming the practice of being opportunistic or manipulative in our relationships with people, seeking first our own kingdom, wanting to control people. What would Paul tell us to do when we face a problem like this? Paul would say *"in everything by prayer"* is an important part of solving this problem.

"Everything" should include the problem of understanding why God allows unpleasant things to happen to people who are serving Christ faithfully (Philippians 1:12-14; 4:6). It would include the temptation to become discouraged or fearful or filled with doubts when things occur that don't seem to make sense, that seem to be a hindrance to the cause of Christ. It would include handling the problem of seeing how certain circumstances fit into the *"all things working together for good"* of Romans 8:28. What would Paul tell us to do when we face a problem like this? Paul would say *"in everything by prayer"* is an important part of solving this problem.

"Everything" should include the grief that comes from seeing selfishness, pride, malice, rudeness, inconsiderateness, cruelty, jealousy, or envy in the lives of professing Christians manifested toward other Christians (Philippians 1:14-18; 2:3-4; 4:6). It would include responding in a godly fashion when certain Christian leaders take advantage of other believers, when they seem to gloat and rejoice over the difficulties that other Christians encounter. What would Paul tell us to do when we face a problem like this? Paul would say *"in everything by prayer"* is an important part of solving this problem.

We should pray about grief.

"Everything" would include personally handling the problems of opposition, mistreatment, suffering, persecution, mockery, ridicule, and abuse that come to us from other people primarily because we have taken a stand for Christ (Philippians 1:27-29; 4:6). What would Paul tell us to do when we face a problem like this? Paul would say *"in everything by prayer"* is an important part of solving this problem.

We should pray about divisiveness.

"Everything" should include facing the problem of divisiveness, schisms, and lack of harmony and unity among people in our local churches, our families, and the church at large (Philippians 1:27; 2:1-4; 4:6). What would Paul tell us to do when we face a problem like this? Paul would say *"in everything by prayer"* is an important part of solving this problem.

"Everything" would include handling the problem of a lack of Christlikeness in yourself or others; handling the problem of a lack of compassion and affection, hard-heartedness (Philippians 2:1-8; 4:6). What would Paul tell us to do when we face a problem like this? Paul would say *"in everything by prayer"* is an important part of solving this problem.

"Everything" should include overcoming the problem of grumbling, murmuring, complaining, argumentativeness, and contentiousness (Philippians 2:14-15; 4:6). What would Paul tell us to do when we face a problem like this? Paul would say *"in everything by prayer"* is an important part of solving this problem.

We should pray about our attitude.

WE SHOULD PRAY ABOUT STANDING FIRM.

Understanding the "everything" of Philippians 4:6 by looking at the previous chapters of Philippians helps us grasp a bit of the role that prayer should play in facing and solving life's problems God's way. Our understanding of the meaning of Paul's "everything" is even further expanded by the more immediate context in which it is found. The "everything" of this verse would include praying that God would help us fulfill all of the commands of the preceding verses in chapter 4.

Standing firm in the Lord is a problem we often encounter (Philippians 4:1, 6). We are prone to allow ourselves to be pushed around, to be inconsistent, to begin well and then quit, to fall down rather than stand, to cave in under pressure, to be led astray by the clever and seemingly persuasive arguments of unbiblical teachers and teachings. Standing firm is a problem. What would Paul tell us to do when we face problems like these? Paul would say *"in everything by prayer"* is an important part of solving these problems.

Let's face it, the command to rejoice in the Lord always is a command that is difficult to obey (Philippians 4:4, 6). At those times when unpleasant things happen to us, when our cherished expectations and desires are not fulfilled, when we encounter difficult circumstances, when people we count on are uncooperative and unappreciative, when pain and hardship become our constant companion, "rejoicing always" seems to be an impossible dream. We tend to tell ourselves that perhaps we can rejoice occasionally, maybe even frequently. But always? You've got to be kidding. It's impossible. It's beyond what any human being can do.

How would Paul respond to this kind of thinking? In all likelihood he'd say, "You're right. It is impossible for you, but it's not impossible for God. So make it a matter of prayer. *'In everything by prayer'* is an important part of receiving strength to fulfill this command."

WE SHOULD PRAY ABOUT DEVELOPING PATIENCE.

Then there's the matter of developing a forbearing spirit toward all men (Philippians 4:5-6). That seems almost as difficult to develop and sustain as rejoicing always. "You mean," we ask Paul, "God wants us to be patient, forbearing, unruffled, gentle, and slow to anger with all men and at all times? Come on, Paul, get real. There are some people with whom it's pretty easy for me to be forbearing and gentle. There are some people who are just nice people, and I usually find it easy to get along with them. Oh, there may be times when I'm tempted to be impatient with them, but not often. But you didn't say, 'Be forbearing with some people,' nor did you say, 'Be forbearing some of the time.' You said, 'all men' and you implied 'at all times.' I guess that means even when they don't agree or even when they aren't appreciative or even when they do things more slowly than I would like or even when they forget to do things they said they would do. It seems like you're saying, 'Be forbearing even then.' Is that what you mean?"

How would Paul respond to that line of questions? He would affirm the accuracy of the speaker's interpretation of what he meant in Philippians 4:5. Then he would go on to say, "You're right. It is impossible for you to always be forbearing with all people, but it's not impossible for God. So make it a matter of prayer. *'In everything by prayer'* is an important element of receiving strength to fulfill this command."

WE SHOULD PRAY ABOUT FEAR AND WORRY.

"Everything" should include all the circumstances or situations that tempt us to worry or become anxious. Paul began Philippians 4:6 with another amazing, almost unbelievable command. He wrote that we should *"be anxious for nothing...."* He then followed that command with another command, *"but in everything by prayer...."* In other words, Paul was saying that the right kind of prayer is part of the antidote to the problem of worry or anxiety. Scripture makes it clear that as we go through life, we are going to encounter many potentially fearful, uncertain, dangerous, or threatening circumstances over which we have no control and for which we don't have the personal resources to overcome or handle. Yet even though Paul knew what we will face and our personal weaknesses and inadequacies, he still told us that there is never an occasion, circumstance, or problem about which we should worry or be anxious. Again, some of us are inclined to say, "Come on, get real. You're telling us to do something we simply don't have the strength to do."

And again, Paul would respond, "You're right. I know you can't fulfill this command on your own. I can't either. In fact no sinful human being can. Fulfilling this command requires the recognition that in and of yourself you can't overcome worry. It requires that you recognize your own inability and that when you are tempted to become anxious, you turn to God and seek His help. The issue is not whether or not you can overcome anxiety on your own, but whether or not God has the power to help you. And I assure you, He does. To overcome, you must realize that *'In everything by prayer'* is part of the solution to the problem of fear and worry."

NO PROBLEM WE FACE IN LIFE — NO CIRCUMSTANCE OR SITUATION — WHICH WILL EVER CONFRONT US IS NOT INCLUDED IN THE "EVERYTHING."

IF IT WERE A CRIME TO MAKE PRAYER A PRIORITY — WOULD THERE BE ENOUGH EVIDENCE TO CONVICT YOU?

THE PERSON WHO JUST GOES THROUGH THE MOTIONS OF PRAYER "SHOULD NOT EXPECT TO RECEIVE ANYTHING FROM THE LORD."

The "everything" of this text means just what it says; it means everything. It goes far beyond anything we've described thus far. There is no problem we face in life – no circumstance or situation – which will ever confront us that is not included in the "everything" of Philippians 4:6. In every difficult situation or circumstance, with every problem we encounter, Paul would say to us what he said to Timothy, "First of all, pray."

Can you honestly say that you agree with Paul about the priority of prayer? Not just in theory. Do you agree with him in practice? Does the way you respond to the challenges of life prove that you have the same conviction about prayer that Paul had? Do you pray first? Do you really believe that prayer is a crucial, top-of-the-list priority in your life and ministry? That prayer is one of the most important things you can do to handle problems?

If making prayer a priority was a crime, is there enough evidence from your life to convict you? Or would your problem-solving practice demonstrate that for you, prayer is more a last-resort matter rather than a first-resort issue? Would your problem-solving practice reflect the idea that when all else fails, try prayer? Would your prayer practice demonstrate that for you prayer is more of a formality, a practice in which you go through the motions – a practice in which you say your prayers, but don't really think that prayer is all that important, productive, or worthwhile? If prayer is a last resort or a mere formality for you, the Scripture would remind you that your prayers are worthless, because it is *"the effectual fervent prayer of a righteous man that avails much"* (James 5:16). and the person who just goes through the motions of prayer *"should not expect to receive anything from the Lord"* (James 1:6-7).

THE *WHEN* AND *WHERE* OF EFFECTIVE PROBLEM-SOLVING PRAYER

Solving our problems God's way includes more than knowing what to pray about. It also includes knowing when and where to pray. Once again, part of the answer to the when and where of effective problem-solving prayer is found in the words "in everything." To say that we are to pray about everything certainly implies that there is never a time or place when prayer is inappropriate.

In these words, Paul was certainly implying that prayer should be a lifestyle for Christians. It was for Paul. Scattered throughout the New Testament are numerous statements that indicate that prayer was a part of Paul's lifestyle. Earlier in his letter to the Philippians, Paul had told the them he was *"always offering prayer"* for them (1:4). When writing to the Colossians, Paul informed them that he was always praying for them (1:4) and that he never ceased to pray for them (1:9). To the Thessalonians, he stated that he was always making mention of them in his prayers (1 Thessalonians 1:2-3; 2 Thessalonians 1:11). To the Ephesians and Philemon, he made similar statements (Ephesians 1:15-16; Philemon 4). To Timothy, he wrote the same thing, but then added that he prayed for him *"night and day"* (2 Timothy 1:3).

Luke, who knew Paul well because he had spent much time with him on his missionary journeys, gave us some interesting insights into the prayer life of Paul. For example, he recorded the fact that prayer was part of Paul's life from the time of his conversion (9:11). He also indicated that Paul prayed when he ordained elders in the churches he founded (14:23); that he prayed at midnight after he had been flogged with many blows and put in prison (16:23-25); that he prayed during an elders meeting and when he was about to depart from them (20:36); that he prayed in the temple (22:17); and that he prayed in the home of one of the leading men on the island of Malta.

To understand how much a part of Paul's lifestyle prayer was, it is important to realize that many of the statements indicating that he was always praying for people were referring to times when he was under house arrest and chained to someone who was guarding him night and day. When Paul entered into his prayer closet to pray, it had to be in his own heart. He couldn't get away from his guard. He was constantly in the presence of someone, constantly under observation. But prayer was so important to Paul that he didn't allow this to hinder him. Wherever he was, whomever he was with, whenever it was, Paul prayed. One can only imagine the powerful impact the content and continuity of Paul's prayers must have had on his guards as they watched him and listened to him pray. Paul not only told others to pray "in everything;" he actually did it himself. He prayed anywhere and everywhere; at any time and all the time. As far as Paul was concerned, there was no place and no time when prayer was inappropriate.

No wonder that although Paul faced unbelievable pressures and problems (beyond anything that most – or all – of us have ever or will ever experience), he was able to stand firm, rejoice constantly, be forbearing and patient with all men, overcome anxiety and worry, love his enemies, make wise decisions, and

THERE IS NEVER A TIME OR PLACE WHEN PRAYER IS INAPPROPRIATE.

WHEREVER HE WAS, WHOMEVER HE WAS WITH, WHENEVER IT WAS, PAUL PRAYED.

respond in a godly way to horrible mistreatment, danger, threats, persecution, and suffering. Paul's exemplary, godly life in the face of severe distress simply cannot be understood apart from understanding that prayer was a part of his lifestyle.

He not only exhorted others to *"pray without ceasing"* (1 Thessalonians 5:17), he personally prayed without ceasing. He not only instructed others to *"devote yourselves to prayer, keeping alert in it…"* (Colossians 4:2), he was personally devoted to prayer. He not only commanded others to *"be instant in prayer"* (Romans 12:12), he personally was instant in prayer. He not only admonished others to pray in every place (1 Timothy 2:8), he prayed in every place. He not only told Timothy to respond to his challenges with prayer and to make prayer a priority in his life and ministry (1 Timothy 2:1), he personally made prayer a priority in his own life and ministry.

For Paul, prayer was a whenever and wherever issue. It was as natural for him to pray as it was for him to breathe. Wherever he went, he breathed. Whenever it was – morning, noon, evening, all through the night – he breathed. In like fashion, as far as Paul was concerned there was no time or place that he considered prayer inappropriate or unnecessary.

PRAYER IS AS IMPORTANT TO LIFE AS BREATHING.

It should be the same with us. Prayer (communicating with God) should be a lifestyle for us. Our attitude should be that we need God's help at all times and that prayer is as important as breathing. We know we can't live without breathing, but do we really know and believe that we can't really live spiritually without praying?

The question is: Do we think of and practice prayer in any way that resembles the prayer practice of the apostle Paul? Is there enough evidence from your daily life to prove that you do? Is prayer your lifestyle?

THE *HOW* OF EFFECTIVE PROBLEM-SOLVING PRAYER

Thus far we've noted the what, when, and where of the effective problem-solving practice of prayer described by Paul in Philippians 4:6. But there's more. He also had something to say about the "how" of effective problem-solving prayer. To get the full impact of what he taught, we need to carefully note and fully understand the different words he used to describe this important activity.

IN EVERYTHING BY PRAYER

In the original language, *proseucho*, the word translated "prayer," includes the idea of worship. Jesus used this word when he described the temple as a "house of prayer" (Matthew 21:13; Mark 11:17; Luke 19:46). Luke used this word when he described the conversion of Lydia that took place by a river which was the "place of prayer" (Acts 16:14). It carries with it the idea of worshipful prayer.

Worshipful prayer is what Jehoshophat did in 2 Chronicles 20 when he faced a great problem. As noted earlier, when Jehoshophat received news about a great multitude of armies coming against him, he immediately went to pray. What kind of prayer did he pray? He prayed worshipfully. He began with an acknowledgement of God's majesty, glory, and sovereignty. He mentioned the fact that God is the God in the heavens, that He is the Ruler over the kingdoms of the nations, that power and might are in His hands and that no one can stand before Him. He then went on to review the fact that God drove the Canaanites out of the land and gave it to the Israelites. What was he doing? He was worshipping (2 Chronicles 20:1-8).

Worshipful prayer is what Nehemiah did when he faced the challenge of going back to Jerusalem and supervising a large construction project on behalf of the people of God. When he began this project, he was without adequate expertise or resources. Nehemiah had never been to a university where he had been trained as a structural engineer. Nor did he have the financial resources to purchase the necessary materials. Yet he was convinced that rebuilding the walls was his responsibility. So what did he do? "First of all pray." How did he pray? He prayed worshipfully. He began his prayer by acknowledging that God is the Lord God of heaven, the great and awesome God, the One Who preserves loving-kindness and mercy. His prayer didn't begin on a low note describing the magnitude of the problem he was facing. It didn't begin with moaning and groaning and complaining and begging. It began on a high note as he reminded himself about God's greatness, His worthiness. It began with worship and praise.

IN EVERYTHING BY PRAYER AND SUPPLICATION

The word "supplication" suggests at least two ideas about effective problem-solving prayer. First, it suggests the idea of earnestness or seriousness. In real

> IN THE ORIGINAL LANGUAGE, THE WORD TRANSLATED "PRAYER" INCLUDES THE IDEA OF WORSHIP.

prayer, you are not merely mouthing words or going through the motions. Real prayer is "fervent" prayer (James 5:16). It's the kind of praying that Epaphras did. Paul wrote that Epaphras was *"always laboring earnestly … in his prayers"* (Colossians 4:12). It's the kind of praying that Jesus did when he was here on this earth. Hebrews tells us that *"in the days of His flesh, He offered up… supplications with loud crying and tears …"* (5:7).

REAL PRAYER IS "FERVENT" PRAYER.

Epaphras didn't play at prayer; he labored. And he didn't merely labor; he labored earnestly. Jesus didn't merely offer up supplications; He offered up supplications with loud crying and tears. In other words, these individuals were fervent and earnest, deadly serious in their prayers. Their prayers availed much; they accomplished much. The book of Hebrews distinctly tells us that as Jesus offered up these earnest supplications, *"He was heard."* It also seems to indicate that His earnest supplications were an indication of His piety, His devoutness, His worshipful, God-centered attitude (5:7).

The word "supplication" also indicates the importance of humility in effective problem-solving prayer. This word was used to describe what a beggar would do. A beggar doesn't ask you to give him something because he deserves it or because he has earned it. He asks you to give him something out of your mercy and because he needs it. True beggars are humble people.

REALIZE THAT YOU ARE NOTHING, HAVE NOTHING, CAN DO NOTHING, AND STAND IN NEED OF ALL THINGS.

Praying with supplication means that you come to God realizing that God doesn't owe anything to you; that you're not asking Him to do something because you merit His help; that you come to God as one who is "poor in spirit" (Matthew 5:3). It means you come to God with the realization that you are nothing, have nothing, can do nothing, and stand in need of all things.

It means you come to God with the attitude of the publican described in Luke 18:13. Luke tells us that this man "stood afar off" (depicting a sense of unworthiness); that he "hung his head" (depicting humility); that he "beat on his breast" (depicting earnestness) and that he "asked for mercy" (depicting a sense of unworthiness, earnestness and humility). This supplicant wasn't demanding or parading his own merit. He acknowledged that if God helped him it would be because he had a need and God chose to be merciful. He recognized that God was under no obligation to do anything for Him and that if He chose not to do anything He would be completely just in doing so.

In Everything by Prayer and Supplication with Thanksgiving

The words "with thanksgiving" also suggest two ideas about effective problem solving prayer. First, they suggest an idea that is directly related to the previous understanding of what it means to be a supplicant. Anyone who has the attitude of a supplicant, who recognizes that whatever he receives is pure mercy, will be thankful for what he receives. It's more than he has a right to hope for or to expect. How then could he not be thankful for it?

Luke 17 records the story of ten lepers who came to Jesus for healing. Jesus healed all of them, but only one returned to give thanks. This man did so because he was grateful, because he knew Jesus had done something for him that he didn't deserve. The others took their healing for granted. They asked, but when granted their request they didn't return to express gratitude. In failing to do so, they indicated a lack of appreciation for the great gift they had been given. Perhaps they also indicated that they really didn't have the attitude of a supplicant. True supplicants give thanks when they receive what they ask for because they know that what they receive is entirely due to the mercy of God.

The words "with thanksgiving" also suggest the idea of faith. It may be that Paul is suggesting that at the time we offer our prayers and supplications, we should do so "with thanksgiving." When we offer our prayers and supplications, we should be thankful for the privilege of making our requests known to God, for the privilege of bringing our petitions to Him and knowing that He hears us. Could anything be more encouraging than the realization that the God Who made the heavens and earth, the God Who is so huge that the heavens can't contain Him, the God Who is awesome in His being, the God Who is eternal, immortal, omniscient, omnipotent, and omnipresent, the God before Whom all men shall appear and give an account, actually is available to us and has ears that are open to our cry? He has invited us to pour out our hearts before Him, and He has assured us that He will be a refuge for us (Psalm 62:8; 1 Peter 3:12).

When we offer our prayers and supplications, we should be thankful because we know that *"if we ask anything according to His will, He hears us. And if we know that He hears us in whatever we ask, we know that we have the requests which we have asked of Him"* (1 John 5:14-15). We should be thankful in advance because we know that if we're making supplication for anything He has promised, our requests will be granted. We know this because our God who cannot lie has said

TRUE SUPPLICANTS GIVE THANKS WHEN THEY RECEIVE WHAT THEY ASK FOR BECAUSE THEY KNOW THAT WHAT THEY RECEIVE IS ENTIRELY DUE TO THE MERCY OF GOD.

THE WORDS "WITH THANKSGIVING" ALSO SUGGEST THE IDEA OF FAITH.

that *"as many as may be the promises of God, in Him (Christ) they are yes..."* (2 Corinthians 1:20). We can be thankful ahead of time when we pray according to His promises because His Word assures us that He has given to us His great and magnificent promises in order that by them we might become partakers of the divine nature and escape the corruption that is in the world (2 Peter 1:4). When we pray according to the promises of God, our faith in the God of the promises and in the promises of God causes us to be thankful in advance of their fulfillment.

Thankfulness, then, is another key factor in the kind of prayer that is a part of solving life's problems God's way. Just any old kind of prayer won't do. No, it must be worshipful prayer, earnest, humble, and thankful prayer. This is the kind of prayer that helps us be *"more than conquerors in Christ Jesus."* This is the kind of prayer that makes us overcomers rather than those who are overcome.

THE *WHY* OF EFFECTIVCE PROBLEM-SOLVING PRAYER

In considering what Philippians 4:6 teaches about effective problem-solving prayer, it is important to note that it, along with many other biblical texts about prayer, is in the form of a command. They are in the imperative mood. In other words, in this text God is not merely giving a word of advice, making a suggestion that we can take or leave at will. He's not saying, "Here's an idea. Why don't you try it?" No, He's giving us a mandate that we must obey if we claim Him as Lord. And since the Bible teaches that *"sin is a transgression of the law"* (I John 3:4), our failure to make prayer a part of our habitual response to the problems of life is flat-out disobedience to, or rebellion against, God. If we fail to obey this command, we are just like the people to whom Jesus said, *"Why do you call me Lord, Lord and do not the things I say?"* (Luke 6:40). So, one answer to the question "Why pray?" is that we should pray because our Lord commands us to do it.

A second reason suggested by our text as to why we should pray is contained in the word "but." "Be anxious for nothing, but...." Surely what Paul says on the other side of the word "but" contains part of His divinely revealed antidote to the very serious, debilitating problem of worry. If you were to ask Paul the question, "Why should we pray in the way you prescribed in Philippians 4:6?" a part of his answer would be, "Do it because it is part of God's way of solving your problems." In other words, pray because through prayer you are enlisting

JUST ANY OLD KIND OF PRAYER WON'T DO. NO, IT MUST BE WORSHIPFUL PRAYER, EARNEST AND HUMBLE PRAYER AND THANKFUL PRAYER.

WHY PRAY? BECAUSE OUR LORD COMMANDS US TO DO IT.

the help of God; pray because it is part of God's program for avoiding defeat and being a winner in the struggles and difficulties of life.

This thought that prayer is a channel through which we receive the power and help of God is reinforced by what follows the word "and" in verse 7. The word "and" connects what is about to be said to what has just been said. In verse 7, Paul is saying, "If you pray in the way I've suggested in verse 6, you will experience the opposite of anxiety, you will experience the *peace of God which surpasses all comprehension* and Christ Jesus will guard your hearts and minds from worry."

In this great passage, Paul makes it clear that the right kind of prayer is an absolutely essential aspect of solving the problem of anxiety. Many other passages of Scripture clearly teach that the prayer principle Paul applies specifically to the problem of worry is fundamentally important for solving all of the problems of life. Solving the problem of worry is but one example of the kinds of problems for which the right kind of praying is a crucial factor. When writing to Timothy (1 Timothy 2:1) and to the Philippians, Paul highlights the importance of prayer in effectively solving the problems of life.

Do you want to know what it means to be an overcomer? Do you want to know what it means to be more than a conqueror? Well then, you must know, believe, and practice the truths taught by Paul in Philippians 4:6. Along with the other factors described in other chapters of this book, it's part of the process of growing more and more into the image of Christ.

QUESTIONS FOR DISCUSSION

1. What is impressive about the words of Paul in 1 Timothy 2:1?

_____

_____

2. In what way is the Jehoshophat account in 2 Chronicles 20 an example of someone who did what Paul commanded in 1 Timothy 2:1? Describe the circumstances.

_____

_____

3. In what way is the Acts 4 account an example of people who did what Paul commanded in 1 Timothy 2:1? Describe the circumstances.

_____

_____

4. According to S.D. Gordon, when and where is Christian victory won?

_____

_____

5. What did John Piper say happens when Christians don't pray?

_____

_____

6. What did Richard Newton say is the principal cause of our leanness and unfruitfulness?

_____

_____

7. From the context of the book of Philippians explain what the "everything " of Philippians 4:6 would include.

_____

_____

8. Explain what Philippians 4:6 indicates about the when and where of our praying.

_____

_____

9. What is meant by the statement "prayer should be a lifestyle for the believer"?

_____

_____

10. Using Scripture, explain how Paul's own life was an example of this kind of praying.

_____

_____

11. Why does the fact that Paul was in prison when he made many of these statements about prayer make them so impressive?

_____

_____

12. What words in Philippians 4:6 are used to tell us how to pray?

_____

_____

13. Explain what each of these words teaches us about effective problem-solving prayer.

_____

_____

14. What does Paul mean when he says we should pray "with thanksgiving?"

_____

_____

15. What do Philippians 4:6-7 teach about why we should pray? Explain the two reasons for prayer found in this text.

_____

_____

PERSONAL RESPONSE

1. Given the problems that Timothy was facing, what might people today counsel Timothy to do "first of all?"

_____

_____

2. Before reading this chapter, what would you have told Timothy to do "first of all?" Be honest!

_____

_____

3. If you had been in Jehoshophat's situation or in the situation of the Christians in Acts 4, what would you have been tempted to do "first of all?"

_____

_____

4. Can you honestly say that when you are confronted with a big problem you consider prayer to be the most important thing you should do to resolve it? Give some illustrations of what you did when faced with problems in your life.

_____

_____

5. What do you personally think of the statements about prayer made by Gordon, Piper, and Newton? Why do you think that way about these statements?

_____

_____

6. Does your life and prayer practice demonstrate that you pray about "everything?"

_____

_____

7. What would it look like if prayer were a lifestyle for you? What would that mean in your actual practice?

_____

_____

8. Are there times when and places where you fail to pray or would hesitate to pray?

_____

_____

9. How is it possible for a Christian to "pray without ceasing?"

_____

_____

10. Was there anything about Paul's prayer practice, even while chained to another person, that was convicting or challenging to you? What? Why?

_____

_____

11. Was there anything in the discussion of the how of praying that was especially challenging or convicting to you in your prayer life?

_____

_____

12. Was there anything about the example of Epaphras in Colossians 4:12 or Jesus in Hebrews 5:7 that was especially challenging or convicting to you?

_____

_____

13. What does a failure to make prayer a lifestyle indicate about a person?

_____

_____

14. Do you agree that a failure to pray in the way Paul prescribes is a sin? Why or why not?

_____

_____

15. What is your personal response to the teachings of this chapter?

_____

_____

CHAPTER 9

How's Your Hearing?

What would you think if I told you I wanted to become physically strong, but I stubbornly refused to eat? What if I said becoming strong was a top priority in my life, but I thought eating was a waste of time?

You'd probably think I was a little nuts; that I wouldn't stand a chance; that if I refuse to eat I soon wouldn't even have the strength to work out; that if I didn't eat I was going to become weak.

This point is so basic, you wouldn't even think it needs to be said. Most authors of body-building manuals don't sense the need to spend a chapter on the importance of eating, because we all know it before we even pick up the book.

That same principle is true spiritually. You can't become spiritually strong apart from a steady diet of God's Word. Yet one of the reasons many people can't overcome their problems is just this basic: They refuse to feed themselves God's Word.

Although we may not need to be told that to become physically strong we need to eat, we desperately need to be reminded that if we are going to become spiritually strong, we need to be well-fed first. Our churches are full of weak, malnourished Christians who claim they want to become strong but never seem to get there. The reason? They are starving spiritually. The sad thing is, most of them are doing it to themselves. They are spiritual anorexics.

Just take a look at the lackadaisical attitude believers often have toward the preaching of God's Word. Many view preaching as a "take it or leave it" matter. They don't view careful listening as an urgent task. If they make it to church, they make it; if they miss, they miss. If the pastor is interesting, they'll listen; if they're tired, they'll fall asleep. They don't eagerly anticipate the preaching of God's Word. Instead, they just try to endure it, hoping their pastor gets finished in time for them to see the beginning of the big game. They view the sermon as a good opportunity to think about what they have to do when they get home, or at the office in the next week. They don't think about the message until the

THIS POINT IS SO BASIC, YOU WOULDN'T EVEN THINK IT NEEDS TO BE SAID.

YOU CAN'T BECOME SPIRITUALLY STRONG APART FROM A STEADY DIET OF GOD'S WORD.

OUR CHURCHES ARE FULL OF WEAK, MALNOURISHED CHRISTIANS WHO CLAIM THEY WANT TO BECOME STRONG BUT NEVER SEEM TO GET THERE.

pastor starts to preach, and they don't think about it again after the sermon is completed.

Yet the Bible makes it clear that preaching is one of the primary means by which the Holy Spirit promotes spiritual growth in the life of the believer. Therefore, saying you want to become strong spiritually and refusing to properly listen to God's Word is as foolish as saying you want to become strong physically and refusing to eat.

Paul considered the preaching of God's Word an essential tool for promoting spiritual maturity – which means that he considered properly listening to God's Word a basic requirement for spiritual growth. It's pretty amazing how often he stressed just this point to both Timothy and Titus. In the pastoral epistles, he instructed his two young protégés on the absolute essentials of a biblical ministry. Over and over again, he reminded them: Preach and teach the Word.

Fill in the missing words in the following verses:

1 Timothy 1:5: *The goal of_____is love from a pure heart and a good conscience and a sincere faith.*

1 Timothy 4:6: _____ *you will be a good servant of the Christ Jesus, constantly nourished on the words of the faith and of the sound doctrine which you have been following.*

1 Timothy 4:13: *Until I come, _____, to exhortation and teaching.*

1 Timothy 4:16: *Pay close attention to yourself _____; persevere in these things; for as you do this you will ensure salvation both for yourself and for those who hear you.*

1 Timothy 5:17: *Let the elders who rule well be considered worthy of double honor, especially those_____ _____.*

1 Timothy 6:2: _____ *these principles.*

REFUSING TO PROPERLY LISTEN TO GOD'S WORD IS AS FOOLISH AS REFUSING TO EAT.

2 Timothy 2:2: *The things which you have heard from me in the presence of many witnesses,*_____.

2 Timothy 2:15: *Be diligent to present yourself approved to God as a workman who does not need to be ashamed,*_____

_____.

2 Timothy 4:1-2: *I solemnly charge you in the presence of God who is to judge the living and the dead, and by His appearing and His kingdom,*_____,

*be ready in season and out of season;*_____

_____.

Titus 1:9: *He tells Titus to appoint elders who hold fast the faithful word which is in accordance with the teaching, that he may be able*_____

_____.

Titus 2:1: *As for you,*_____

_____.

Titus 2:15: *These*_____

_____. *Let no one disregard you.*

Titus 3:8: *This is a trustworthy statement and concerning these things*_____

_____, *so that those who have believed*_____

_____. *These things are good and profitable for men.*

Do you think Paul was trying to make a statement? Time and time again he said, "You've got to preach the Word!" He wasn't stuttering. He wasn't repeatedly reminding Timothy and Titus of this because he had nothing else to say and had to fill up the page. He considered the preaching of God's Word a task of utmost importance. If Timothy and Titus failed to preach God's Word, God's people would suffer.

PERHAPS YOU'RE STILL WONDERING WHAT ALL THIS HAS TO DO WITH YOU.

You may agree, but perhaps you're still wondering what it all this has to do with you. Paul said pastors need to preach, great, but you're not a pastor. So why do you need to know this?

If Paul considered it absolutely vital for pastors to preach, that implies that he considered it absolutely essential that God's people listen! Paul didn't urge

Timothy and Titus to preach God's Word because he thought they needed something to do. He didn't think to himself, "Well, let's see. What can they do when the people get together on Sundays? I need something that will fill up some time. Oh, I've got it. Why don't they teach the Word? Yeah, that's it. That would be a good filler." No, he told them to preach God's Word because he knew believers desperately need to hear it!

Are we making too much of this? Can it really be that important? It can. It is. You will never reach your full potential for Christ until you learn to properly listen to God's Word. If you saw a middle-aged man acting like a baby, you would think something was wrong. Yet our churches are full of men and women who have been Christians for years and years and are still acting like spiritual babies. Something is wrong. They aren't feeding on God's Word.

YOU NEED TO PLACE A TOP PRIORITY ON LISTENING TO GOD'S WORD.

You need to place a top priority on listening to God's Word because it is God's Word. *"All Scripture is inspired by God...."* God speaks to us through His Word. The pastor's job is not to say what he thinks about this or that, but to expound the Scripture so we can hear what God says. He's to speak for God, and he does so when he faithfully proclaims the message of the Scriptures. As Jay Adams explains, "Hearing preachers who preach His Word is hearing Christ; rejecting preachers who preach His Word is rejecting Christ."[19] We don't come to church to hear the opinions of a man. We've got enough opinions in the editorial section of the newspaper. We come to church to hear a man faithfully proclaim the Word of God.

WE'VE GOT ENOUGH OPINIONS IN THE EDITORIAL SECTION OF THE NEWSPAPER. WE COME TO CHURCH TO HEAR A MAN FAITHFULLY PROCLAIM THE WORD OF GOD.

That should excite us. If I told you to go to such and such a place at such and such a time and you will be able to hear God speak, wouldn't that get your blood pumping? If it doesn't, I don't know what will. When a man faithfully expounds and proclaims God's Word, God is speaking to us. In theory we know that should be thrilling. But in practice we all too often place a very small value on hearing God's Word proclaimed. Would you rather hear a message from the Creator of the universe, or see a movie, watch TV, or go out to dinner? The answer's obvious. Or is it?

Sometimes we don't get excited about listening to God's Word because our pastors have failed us. Dr. MacArthur writes:

> Sadly, some of the most careless handlers of Scriptures are those whose responsibility it is to teach. The sloppy theology that comes from many

contemporary pulpits is shocking. Can the church afford to countenance leaders who approach their calling with a lackadaisical recklessness? Certainly not. Imagine the practical implications if teachers of mathematics or chemistry were as slapdash as some who handled the Word of God. Would you want to be served by a pharmacist, for example, who used the "best guess" method of filling prescriptions? Or would you take your business to an architect who worked mostly with approximations? Or would you allow a surgeon to operate on you with a table knife instead of a scalpel? The sad truth is that society would quickly grind to a halt if most professions approached their work the way many Bible teachers do.[20]

Hold your pastor's preaching up to high standards. Be as the Bereans, searching the Word daily to see if what they say is so (Acts 17:11). Psychological insights and funny stories won't feed God's people the truth they need to be strong. Pastors who exchange God's Word for man-made ideas should be ashamed of all the harm they are bringing on God's people.

It's not always the pastor's fault we aren't excited about hearing God's Word. Many times we aren't excited because we don't care enough about what God has to say! It's a hard truth, yet if I don't listen to you when you are speaking to me, what am I saying about my feelings for you? Either I'm deaf, or I don't really care much about you. If I cared about you, I would care about what you have to say. In the same way, you can say all you want that you love God and you really care about Him, but if you continually refuse to carefully listen to Him speak, all your talk is just that – talk!

You need to place a top priority on listening to God's Word, because the world we live in is full of lies. The Scriptures are true, and God has given us the Bible to be a "light for our path and a lamp for our feet" enabling us to see clearly in a very dark world.

Imagine trying to cross a field filled with live land mines. It's dark outside and you don't have any idea where the mines are located. You'd be terrified for your life. But now picture that you have a flashlight and a map telling where all the mines are. If you just keep your flashlight on and follow the path the map lays out, you'll make it across just fine. What kind of fool, after receiving the flashlight and map, would turn the light off and throw the map away? You'd never do that, because you would know that by doing so, you put your life in

SADLY, SOME OF THE MOST CARELESS HANDLERS OF SCRIPTURES ARE THOSE WHOSE RESPONSIBILITY IT IS TO TEACH.

SOCIETY WOULD QUICKLY GRIND TO A HALT IF MOST PROFESSIONS APPROACHED THEIR WORK THE WAY MANY BIBLE TEACHERS DO.

SEARCH THE WORD DAILY TO SEE IF WHAT THEY SAY IS SO.

PASTORS WHO EXCHANGE GOD'S WORD FOR MAN-MADE IDEAS SHOULD BE ASHAMED OF ALL THE HARM THEY ARE BRINGING ON GOD'S PEOPLE.

MANY TIMES WE AREN'T EXCITED BECAUSE WE DON'T CARE ENOUGH ABOUT WHAT GOD HAS TO SAY!

IMAGINE TRYING TO CROSS A MINE FIELD IN THE DARK. WHAT KIND OF FOOL WOULD TURN OFF THE LIGHT AND THROW AWAY THE MAP?

THE WORLD IS NOT NEUTRAL TOWARD TRUTH. IT IS AGAINST IT.

SATAN'S GREAT GOAL IS TO LEAD SINNERS AWAY FROM THE TRUTH.

great danger. Yet that's just what you do when you ignore the Scriptures and fail to listen to good preaching of God's Word. You turn out the light, throw away the map, and grope about in the darkness.

If you don't value the Word of God, you place yourself in great spiritual danger. The world is not neutral toward truth. It is against it. Jesus calls Satan the "father of lies" (John 8:44). Satan has been attempting to deceive men since the Garden of Eden, and he's such an effective liar that John tells us he's deceived the whole world (Rev.12:9).

Satan's great goal is to lead sinners away from the truth and into greater and greater wickedness through deception. Why? Because he's evil. That's his nature. He's a liar. To accomplish this, he's developed this whole world-system full of intricate, detailed, elaborate lies. Paul explained this in 2 Corinthians 10:4-5, *"The weapons of our warfare are not carnal but mighty in God for pulling down strongholds...."* A stronghold is a fortress, a place where people hide when attacked. These strongholds are *"arguments and every high thing that exalts itself against the knowledge of God."*

Satan has sold the world this great big set of lies, and people, when confronted with the truth, often run back to those satanic deceptions and hide in those "strongholds" to avoid having to submit to the truth. God's Word pulls down those strongholds.

The devil doesn't want us to listen to the Word because he knows it will expose his lies. He does everything he can to stop us from listening to the truth.

J.I. Packer explains:

> If I were the devil, ... one of my first aims would be to stop people from digging into the Bible. Knowing that it is the Word of God, teaching men to know and love and serve the God of the Word I should do all I could to surround it with the spiritual equivalent of pits, thorn hedges and man traps, to frighten people off. With smug conceit, no doubt as if receiving a compliment I would acknowledge that Jonathan Edwards had me pegged when he wrote, "The devil never would attempt to create in persons a love for that divine word which God has given to be the great and standing rule...The devil has always shown a mortal spite and hatred towards that holy book the Bible; he has done all in his

power to extinguish that light…He is engaged against the Bible, and he hates every word in it…." How would I attempt to stop people from digging into the Bible? Well, I should try to distract all pastors from preaching and teaching the Bible, and spread the feeling that to study this ancient book directly is a burdensome extra which modern Christians can forgo without loss. I should broadcast doubts about the truth and relevance and good sense and straightforwardness of the Bible, and if any insisted on reading it I should lure them into assuming that the benefit of the practice lies in the noble and tranquil feelings evoked by it rather than noting what the Scripture actually says. At all costs I should want to keep them from using their minds in a disciplined way to get the measure of its message.[21]

The point is: We live in a dangerous world. This world is not a playground; it's a battleground. We are constantly hearing lies. Men all around us have completely given themselves over to the lies that Satan has invented. To survive, we must continually hear the truth. We need to have our minds continually renewed by the Word of God. If they aren't, we're going to start believing lies before we know it. It's just that simple.

Error destroys; truth transforms. Believing Satan's lies always has serious consequences. I've met with and counseled so many people who have ruined their lives by believing falsehoods. Many of their problems could easily have been avoided or solved if they had just thought biblically about their situation and acted in obedience to the truth. But time and time again, they failed to listen to God's Word.

You need to place a top priority on listening to God's Word, because to fail to do so is disobedience. You are not only insulting God by refusing to hear His Word, you are also disobeying Him. Dr. Adams explains that hearing God's Word is an ethical issue. When Jesus says, *"Whoever has ears, let him hear"* (Matt.13:9) and repeats the same expression at the conclusion to each of the letters to the seven churches in Revelation (chapters 2-3), He thereby strongly indicates that He expects His people to pay attention to what He says….These strong words about listening, you will note, are aimed not at the preacher but at those who listen to him. Again and again, in all sorts of forms, the command goes forth from God's Word: "Listen; listen carefully, so that your life may be affected by what you hear and the message will cause you to become fruitful." But that is not all. At the conclusion of the Sermon on the Mount, the point of

> THIS WORLD IS NOT A PLAYGROUND; IT'S A BATTLEGROUND. TO SURVIVE, WE MUST CONTINUALLY HEAR THE TRUTH.

> ONE REASON GOD SO FREQUENTLY REMINDS US TO LISTEN IS BECAUSE WE SO OFTEN FAIL TO DO IT.

the motivational parable of the two foundations is not, as some suppose, to trust Christ as Savior…but to hear and obey His words. (Matt.7:24)[22]

You're thinking this is obvious. You're well aware that when God speaks you ought to listen. But are you? One reason God so frequently reminds us to listen is because we so often fail to do it. Open up your Bible to the Old Testament and you'll find this is the story of Israel. God told Jeremiah, *"This is what I commanded them say, 'Obey my voice, and I will be your God, and you will be my people; and you will walk in all the way which I command you, that it may be well with you. Yet they did not obey or incline their ear, but walked in their own counsels and in the stubbornness of their evil heart, and went backward and not forward…This is the nation that did not obey the voice of the Lord their God or accept correction; truth has perished and has been cut off from their mouth"* (Jeremiah 7:23-24, 28). And again in Jeremiah 11, *"I solemnly warned your fathers in the day that I brought them up from the land of Egypt, even to this day, warning persistently, saying, 'Listen to My voice.' Yet they did not obey or incline their ear, but walked, each one, in the stubbornness of his evil heart…"* (verses 11:7-8). God spoke, but His people wouldn't listen.

PEOPLE IGNORE GOD BECAUSE THEY JUST DON'T LIKE WHAT HE HAS TO SAY.

It's ridiculous and completely irrational to ignore God when He speaks. But many times people do so because they just don't like what He has to say. That's what God says about His people in Isaiah 30:9-10: *"This is a rebellious people, false sons, sons who refuse to listen to the instruction of the Lord, who say to seers, 'You must not see visions,' and to the prophets, 'You must not prophesy to us what is right, speak to us pleasant words, prophesy illusions, get out of the way, turn aside from the path, let us hear no more about the Holy One of Israel…."* In other words, we don't want the truth; just tell us what we want to hear!

MANY TIMES PEOPLE AREN'T REALLY CONCERNED WITH WHAT IS TRUE OR NOT TRUE, BUT WITH WHAT MAKES THEM FEEL GOOD.

We face the same temptation today. That's why Paul warned Timothy, *"The time will come when they will not endure sound doctrine; but wanting to have their ears tickled, they will accumulate for themselves teachers in accordance with their own desires; and will turn away their ears from the truth and will turn aside to myths"* (2 Timothy 4:3-4). People don't like hearing the truth because it conflicts with their desires. So they turn from truth-tellers to men who tell them what they want to hear. This way they can pretend they are listening to God when in reality they are listening to themselves.

Understand this: You are going to face the temptation to ignore God because what He says doesn't match what you want. You need to evaluate your heart.

Are you failing to listen to the truth because of your sinful desires? Are you willing to submit to God's Word even when it tells you things that are difficult for you to accept because they are not in accordance with your desires?

What I've found is that many times people aren't really concerned with what is true or not true, but with what makes them feel good. They reject biblical counsel and stop listening to God's Word because it is too hard. Instead, they go out and find counsel they like better. They are like King Ahab, who hated the prophet of God because, *"He does not prophecy good concerning me, but evil...."* (1 Kings 22:7)

The problem is: Whenever we fail to listen to God, we are not only disobeying Him, we are hurting ourselves! That's why God cries out to us and says, *"Now therefore, O sons, listen to me, For blessed are they who keep my ways. Heed instruction and be wise, and do not neglect it. Blessed is the man who listens to me, watching daily at my gates, waiting at my doorposts. For he who finds me finds life, and obtains favor from the Lord. But he who sins against me injures himself; All those who hate me love death"* (Proverbs 8:32-36). Reject God's counsel and die.

You need to place a top priority on listening to God's Word because God uses the preaching of Scripture to transform us. The purpose of preaching is not to fill our minds with random Bible trivia so that we can impress our friends. Preaching is a God-given tool God uses to help us grow and become more like Christ.

Paul was very clear about this. *"We proclaim Him, admonishing every man and teaching every man with all wisdom that we may present every man complete in Christ"* (Colossians 1:28). He was saying, "This is the goal of my ministry; this is why I teach; this is why I correct; this is why I proclaim; this is why I instruct. I want to see Christians become mature in Christ!"

We need preaching, teaching, and admonishing if we are going to become mature in Christ. John Calvin explains:

> Who is it that by nature will not desire his happiness and his salvation? And where could we find it but in the Holy Scriptures....Woe to us if we will not listen to God when He speaks with us, seeing that He asks nothing but our advantage. He does not seek His own profit, for what need has He of it? We are likewise reminded not to read the Holy

THE PURPOSE OF PREACHING IS NOT TO FILL OUR MINDS WITH RANDOM BIBLE TRIVIA SO THAT WE CAN IMPRESS OUR FRIENDS.

Scriptures so as to gratify our fancies, or to draw from it useless questions. Why? Because it is profitable for salvation. Thus, when I expound the Holy Scriptures, I must be guided by this consideration, that those who hear me receive profit from the doctrine which I teach that they may be edified....If I do not have that desire...I am a sacrilegious person, profaning the Word of God. On the other hand, they who read no scripture, or who come to the sermon to listen, if they are in search of some foolish speculation, if they come to take here their amusement, are guilty of having profaned a thing so holy..[23]

THEY SAY THEY WANT TO KNOW GOD, BUT THEN DENY IT WITH THEIR DEEDS.

Calvin made two important points. First to leaders: When you preach, remember that God's Word is meant to edify His saints. If you preach and forget that you are to build up the saints by doing so, you are perverting the purpose of God's Word. Second, to the congregation: When we come together as a church, don't come just to go through the ritual. Don't sit through the preaching just to get it over with. Instead, there should be an aching within your hearts. "God, I want to know You. I want to learn something from this that I can take and apply to my life. God, I know that You have appointed the faithful teaching of Your trustworthy Word not just to fill my head with all sorts of information but to change my life. So I am here this morning and God, I want to know how You want to transform me. Give me the truth!"

If you say that you want to become strong and you go out and buy a weight bench, but then just let it sit there in your basement, is that weight bench going to help you? Of course not! But many Christians are like that when it comes to their relationship with God. They profess with their mouths they want to know God, but they deny it with their deeds. "I want to know God," yawn, yawn, "but I'm not going to study God's Word, and I don't really care if I hear it proclaimed every Sunday. Why make such a big deal about preaching? Who really cares if the pastor is preaching the Word or not?"

ARE YOU WONDERING WHY YOU AREN'T ABLE TO SOLVE LIFE'S PROBLEMS? IT COULD BE THAT YOU AREN'T REALLY LISTENING!

That's like a person saying he's really hungry but when dinner is laid out before him he says, "No thanks, I guess I'll wait." If you're hungry, you eat! When we fail to do so, we are insulting God, we are disobeying Him, and we are hurting ourselves. That's what He told the Israelites, *"So I spoke to you, but you would not listen. Instead you rebelled against the command of the Lord, and acted presumptuously and went up into the hill country. And the Amorites who lived in that hill country came out against you, and chased you as bees do, and crushed you from Seir to Hormah. Then you returned and wept before the Lord, but the Lord will not listen to your voice, nor give ear to you"* (Deuteronomy 1:43-45).

Don't say you want to know God if you are continually neglecting and rejecting the very means He has given you to come to know Him better. Don't say you want to become strong unless you are willing to use the means He has given for producing strength.

Are you wondering why you aren't able to solve life's problems? It could be that you aren't really listening!

Maybe you're thinking it sounds easy. "Just listen to preaching? I can do that." Be aware that God is very specific about the way in which He wants you to listen. Just showing up and sitting there will not do. You need to prepare your heart to receive God's Word. James wrote, *"Therefore putting aside all filthiness and all that remains of wickedness, in humility receive the word implanted which is able to save your souls"* (James 1:21). Peter explained: *"Therefore, putting aside all malice and all guile and hypocrisy and envy and all slander, like newborn babes, long for the pure milk of the word, that by it you may grow in respect to salvation..."* (author paraphrase). You're not going to desire the Word and you're not going to be able to properly listen to the Word unless you first repent of your sins.

Jay Adams explains:

> Learning is a moral-spiritual matter. The Holy Spirit is involved in communicating truth. He enables you to 'welcome' it and assimilate it into daily life...But it is also true that a Christian out of fellowship with God simply is not in a state of mind to receive or act upon the truth. He must first repent of the sin that stands between God and himself. God is not a cosmic vending machine from whom we may mechanically obtain what we want when we want it by pressing the right buttons. He is a person. We must be in proper relationship to Him in order to benefit from His Word.[24]

You need to realize that the end of the sermon is really just the beginning. God doesn't want us to merely hear His Word, He wants us to obey it. You're not listening the way God desires if you are not seeking to implement the truth of His Word into your life. As James commands, *"Prove yourselves doers of the Word, and not merely hearers who delude themselves"* (James 1:22). Don't deceive yourself. Don't think that just because you know when to nod in church it means you're living in obedience to the truth you affirm. Make it your goal to listen to obey. Ask God to show you the areas in your life that need to be changed. Think hard about what the message has to do with your life. It may help you to ask yourself these four questions at the end of every sermon:

LEARNING IS A MORAL-SPIRITUAL MATTER.

THE END OF THE SERMON IS REALLY JUST THE BEGINNING.

- What did the passage say?
- What did the passage mean?
- How does the passage apply?
- How am I going to change as a result?

Yes, it will be hard work, but it will be worth it. If every believer would just take one biblical principle from every sermon he hears and apply it to his life, the church would be transformed in a matter of months. The world wouldn't be able to recognize us!

How is your spiritual diet? Are you feeding on the truth, or are you malnourished? For your own spiritual good, for the good of your family, and for the good of the church, make a great effort to become a good listener.

Some men and women will work seventy- and eighty-hour work weeks in order to make money. Others exercise for hours every day in order to get in good physical shape. The truth is, most people are willing to work hard at things that are important to them.

Is your soul important to you? If it is, then you can't afford to be lazy when it comes to listening to God speak! To find God's solutions to life's problems, you need to start carefully and prayerfully listening to biblical preaching.

> MOST PEOPLE ARE WILLING TO WORK HARD AT THINGS THAT ARE IMPORTANT TO THEM. IS YOUR SOUL IMPORTANT TO YOU?

QUESTIONS FOR DISCUSSION

1. Why are many believers so spiritually weak?

_____

_____

2. Why is saying you want to become strong and refusing to listen to God's Word foolish? Support your answer with Scripture.

_____

_____

3. Why did Paul urge Timothy and Titus to preach God's Word?

_____

_____

4. Give several reasons we ought to make listening to God's Word a priority.

_____

_____

5. What are some specific ways we ought to prepare ourselves to listen to God's Word?

_____

_____

6. What are several reasons people don't get more excited about hearing God's Word?

_____

_____

7. Why does God so frequently remind us to listen?

_____

_____

8. Why do people stop listening to God's Word?

_____

_____

9. When we fail to listen to God, what are we doing? Support your answer with Scripture.

_____

_____

10. What does Calvin's statement, "God will have His people edified and He has appointed His Word for that purpose…" mean? What difference should knowing that make in how you listen to preaching?

_____

_____

11. What kind of listening does God desire? Be specific.

_____

_____

12. How should you prepare your heart to listen? Support your answer with Scripture.

_____

_____

13. What does Jay Adams mean when he writes: "Learning is a moral-spiritual matter…?" What difference should knowing that make on how you listen to preaching?

_____

_____

14. What does this statement mean: "The end of the sermon is really just the beginning…?"

_____

_____

PERSONAL RESPONSE

1. What is your attitude toward preaching?

_____

_____

On a scale of 1 to 10, how excited are you to hear God's Word?

_____

2. Which excites you more – hearing God's Word or going to a movie? What kinds of sacrifices do you make to listen to God's Word? What excuses do you use to get out of hearing God's Word?

_____

_____

3. If someone asked you, "Why listen to a lecture on Sunday mornings?" How would you answer?

_____

_____

4. What was your pastor's sermon about last week? What specific changes have you made as a result of listening to it?

_____

_____

5. How have you changed in the last year as a result of listening to the Word? Be specific.

_____

_____

6. Do you have a game plan for becoming an effective listener to God's Word? What is it?

_____

_____

7. Could you tell if your pastor wasn't preaching the Word, but his own opinions? Have you spotted error recently?

8. Read 1 Peter 2:1-3. Do you desire the Word the way a baby desires milk? If not, do you need to repent of the qualities he describes in verse 1?

_____

_____

9. How is your spiritual diet? Are you malnourished? If so, what are you doing about it?

_____

_____

CHAPTER 10

WHATEVER HAPPENED TO THE HOLY SPIRIT?

On his third missionary journey, as described in Acts 19, the apostle Paul came to the city of Ephesus where he met some people who claimed to be disciples of Jesus Christ. When he met these people, he asked them a very interesting question. It's interesting because as far as the biblical record is concerned, the apostle Paul didn't usually begin his association with professing Christians or anyone else in the manner he did with these people.

What was the question? *"Did you receive the Holy Spirit when you believed?"* Why did Paul ask them this question? Scripture doesn't tell us; perhaps he observed something in their lives or conversations that caused him to wonder about the issue his question raised. Paul knew how important the Holy Spirit is in the lives of believers, and there probably was something about these people that caused him to wonder if they had received or understood who He is and what He can do in the lives of Christians. Perhaps Paul saw something in the way they spoke – what they talked about; the way they related to other people; the way they faced their problems; the way they did their work; the way they worshipped; the way they used their time and money – that made him think something was lacking in their lives. He probably saw little evidence among them to convince him that they were indwelt by the Holy Spirit.

So he asked them the question. And how did they answer? They said, *"We have not seen or heard whether there is a Holy Spirit."* Imagine that! These professing believers were totally ignorant of the existence and ministry of the Holy Spirit. Obviously, then, they were not benefiting from His ministry; they were not accessing the blessings Scripture promises through the indwelling presence of the Spirit of God.

I've often wondered if Paul were to return today whether he would begin his association with many of us with the same question. I suspect that as Paul observed the lives and conversations of many present-day professing disciples he might be inclined to ask us the same question. Paul believed that the

PERHAPS PAUL OBSERVED SOMETHING IN THEIR LIVES OR CONVERSATIONS THAT MADE HIM THINK SOMETHING WAS LACKING IN THEIR LIVES.

presence of the Holy Spirit in the lives of people should make an incredible difference in the way they live their lives and face their problems. Unfortunately, the way many professing Christians live their lives and handle the inevitable problems they experience isn't that much different from the way non-Christians do.

If Paul were to ask us the same question he asked the Ephesians, most of us wouldn't say we have never heard of the Holy Spirit. We'd probably say we believe He is the third member of the holy Trinity. We'd probably say He is God and that He had something to do with the birth of Christ and with the production of holy Scripture. We might even indicate that He had something to do with our becoming Christians, and even that He has something to do with us living the Christian life.

But, apart from these generalities, many Christians have very little understanding of the crucial role the Holy Spirit is to play in our daily lives. The way they live their lives proves that they are woefully ignorant of the fantastic resource we have in the Holy Spirit. They talk like unbelievers. They live like unbelievers. They respond to pressures and difficulties like unbelievers. If they are true believers, they have the wonderful resource of the Holy Spirit, but they live as though they have nothing more than unbelievers have. Like the Collyer brothers, mentioned in chapter 4 of this book, many Christians live like paupers even though they have tremendous wealth.

In his book, *Our Sufficiency in Christ*, John MacArthur describes our present-day situation in this way:

> The Holy Spirit's ministry … is one of the wonderful resources Christ has made available to all who know Him. The apostle Paul wrote, "We have received, not the spirit of the world, but the Spirit who is from God, that we might know the things freely given to us by God" (I Corinthians 2:12). All spiritual wisdom and resources come from the Holy Spirit. We may simply turn to Him if we want to know the truth about ourselves and the solutions to our problems. Tragically, the current neglect of the Spirit's ministries has greatly crippled many Christians' willingness and ability to do so….Now the Holy Spirit's ministries as outlined in the holy book seem to have been de-emphasized almost to the point of neglect.[25]

PAUL BELIEVED THAT THE PRESENCE OF THE HOLY SPIRIT IN THE LIVES OF PEOPLE SHOULD MAKE AN INCREDIBLE DIFFERENCE IN THE WAY THEY LIVE THEIR LIVES AND FACE THEIR PROBLEMS.

MANY CHRISTIANS HAVE VERY LITTLE UNDERSTANDING OF THE CRUCIAL ROLE THE HOLY SPIRIT IS TO PLAY IN OUR DAILY LIVES.

In this statement, John MacArthur calls our attention to several things about the Holy Spirit. First, he indicates that the biblical ministry of the Holy Spirit is tragically neglected. Second, he notes that all spiritual wisdom and resources for understanding ourselves, our problems, and the solutions to them comes from Him. Third, the neglect of the Holy Spirit's ministries has greatly crippled the lives of many Christians. And fourth, the resources that believers have in the Holy Spirit are not available to unbelievers. In other words, we as Christians have resources for understanding and resolving our problems that non-Christians do not have.

"Whatever happened to the Holy Spirit?" is an extremely important question for us to ask and answer. In our day, among professing Christians, His ministry is often either neglected or misrepresented. And as John MacArthur has said, this neglect has a crippling effect on our lives as Christians. This neglect goes a long way in helping us understand why so many Christians are living life on a sub-par level, why they are being overcome by the problems of life rather than being overcomers.

The title of this book is *God's Solutions to Life's Problems*. In this book we are describing the essential elements for fulfilling and experiencing what the title suggests. Everything we have studied is extremely important in discovering and implementing those solutions. Nothing, however, is more important in realizing the purpose of this book than properly understanding and accessing the ministry of the Holy Spirit. To solve life's problems God's way, we must not neglect or misunderstand the role of the Holy Spirit. You simply cannot really know, implement, or benefit from God's solutions apart from His ministry.

Obviously, we cannot fully describe the Holy Spirit's ministry in one chapter. To think we could do this would be like thinking we could pour the ocean into a teacup. Suffice it to say, we will highlight some of His important functions and seek to clarify the role He must play in solving life's problems God's way. In addition to that, we will explain they way in which believers can access the important ministries of the Holy Spirit in a practical way.

THE ROLE OF THE HOLY SPIRIT IN THE LIVES OF CHRISTIANS

According to Scripture, the Holy Spirit Who indwells every believer (Romans 8:9; John 14:17) enables us to resist and overcome the desires and deeds of the

CHRISTIANS HAVE RESOURCES FOR UNDERSTANDING AND RESOLVING OUR PROBLEMS THAT NON-CHRISTIANS DO NOT HAVE.

TO SOLVE LIFE'S PROBLEMS GOD'S WAY, WE MUST NOT NEGLECT OR MISUNDERSTAND THE ROLE OF THE HOLY SPIRIT.

flesh. The Bible describes our manner of life prior to becoming Christians this way: We *"walked* [conducted our lives] *according to the course of this world, according to the prince of the power of the air* [Satan], *of the spirit who is now working in the sons of disobedience* [all unbelievers]. *Among them we too* [those of us who have become Christians] *all formerly lived in the lusts* [desires] *of our flesh, indulging the desires of the flesh and of the mind..."* (Ephesians 2:2-3).

What's involved in living in or according to the lusts and desires of the flesh? To walk according to the flesh is to walk in opposition to the Spirit (Galatians 5:17). It's to live in conformity to the world's standards rather than God's; it's to live in the way Satan wants you to live, in conformity to his desires rather than God's; it's to live a life that is hostile to God; it's to have your mind set on what you want rather than what God wants; it's to focus mainly on satisfying yourself rather than on pleasing God (Romans 8:5-13). Sinclair Ferguson describes what it means to live in the lusts of the flesh this way: "The characteristics of life in the flesh include self-absorption, self reliance and indulgence, dependence on outward ceremony and ritual instead of their spiritual reality, and clinging to the shadow rather than their fulfillment in Christ."[26]

When we become Christians, God makes us new creatures in Christ Jesus and causes old things (i.e., living a life dominated by Satan and selfish desires – by the flesh) to pass away and all things to become new (i.e., new desires, a new way of thinking and living, new standards, new power, new potential for godliness (2 Corinthians 5:17). When God saves us, He washes (cleans us up, clears out the debris) and renews us by the Holy Spirit (Titus 3:5,6); the flesh (selfish and self-centered life orientation) with its ruling passions and desires is crucified (Galatians 5:24). We receive *"a new self, which in the likeness of God has been created in righteous and holiness of the truth"* (Ephesians 4:24), and as Peter puts it, we receive a new nature and are therefore enabled to escape the corruption that is in the world through fleshly desires (2 Peter 1:4). All of this becomes our portion because of our identification, our union with Christ. Because of this we can now walk in newness of life; we don't have to be controlled and ruled by our sinful desires (Romans 6:1-14).

Nevertheless, though we are really new, and therefore have tremendous potential for living a new kind of life, the Bible makes it clear that old, deeply ingrained, sinful, selfish patterns of thinking, desiring, and living continue to try to hinder us. Peter reminds us that though we are Christians we still struggle with fleshly desires that are waging war against the soul (1 Peter 2:11). James is referring to the same phenomenon when he speaks of the fact that our pleasures or desires are waging war in our members (James 4:1). On a practical, experiential, day-by-day level, these sinful patterns continue to plague us and must be put to death (Romans 8:13; Colossians 3:5-9) or they will cause all kinds of difficulties in our lives. They will manifest themselves in *immorality, impurity, passion, evil desire, greed, idolatry, anger, wrath, malice, slander, abusive speech and deceitfulness*" (Colossians 3:5-9).

Unless we constantly work at putting them to death these "holdovers" from what we were before we became Christians will promote the *deeds of the flesh*" (Galatians 5:19-21), and we will find ourselves living and doing things that are contrary to the will of God. The war with our sin and sinful patterns has been won through our identification with Christ and the implanting of a new nature, but these "holdover patterns" continue to fight guerilla warfare. They continue to "war against the soul."

THE WAR WITH OUR SIN AND SINFUL PATTERNS HAS BEEN WON, BUT "HOLDOVER PATTERNS" CONTINUE TO FIGHT GUERILLA WARFARE.

The great Puritan theologian, John Owen, explains it this way:

> There are yet in them [Christians] inclinations and dispositions to sin, proceeding from the remainders of a contrary habitual principle. This the Scripture calls the "flesh," "lust," the "sin that dwells in us," "the body of death"….This yet continues in them, inclining them unto evil and all that is so, according to the power and efficacy that is remaining unto its varying degrees… although we are renewed again into the image of God really and truly (yet not absolutely, nor perfectly, but only in part), we have yet remaining in us a contrary principle or ignorance of sin, which we must always conflict withal, Galatians 5:16-17.[27]

Sinclair Ferguson puts it this way:

> Christ dwells in the heart [of a Christian] through faith (Ephesians 3:17). Yet sin also dwells within. True, the situation is not that of two equal powers opposing one another. Grace is reigning through righteousness! We are not "in" the flesh, but "in" the Spirit. But for that reason the tension and conflict are all the more bitter and urgent. There is a radical and deep-seated conflict situation … that should never be played down. To do so would incline us either to fall into incipient perfectionism (the flesh has no energy in me), or to have an inadequate view of salvation (failing to realize that, by the Spirit, the Lord Jesus indwells us as the hope of glory).[28]

Paul's words in Romans 7 indicate that these "holdovers" from our pre-Christian life can be powerful. In that passage, he vividly described his struggles with indwelling patterns of sin in his life. He acknowledged that though he wanted to always do good, he didn't always do it. He joyfully concurred with the law of God, but he honestly acknowledged that he sometimes did the things he hated. Furthermore, he said that when this happened it was because his sinful patterns, the "holdovers" from his pre-Christian life were still trying to dominate him (Romans 7:14-23).

So, Paul wanted us to know that even though we're Christians, we are still involved in a battle – a battle with "the lusts of the flesh." A battle that is too much for us; a battle in which we need divine assistance if we're going to win. Paul knew this well, so he frequently wrote about the solution to this problem. To win this battle, he told the Galatians, *"walk in the Spirit."* Then he wrote that if they would walk in the Spirit they would *"not carry out the desires of the flesh"* (Galatians 5:16). To the Roman Christians, he said, *"The law of the Spirit of life in Christ Jesus has set you free from the law* (i.e., controlling power) *of sin and death," "If the Spirit of Him who raised Jesus from the dead lives in you, He who raised Christ Jesus from the dead will also give life to your mortal bodies through His Spirit who indwells you. So, then, brethren, we are under obligation, not to the flesh, to live according to the flesh – for if you are living according to the flesh, you must die, but if by the Spirit, you are putting to death the deeds of the body, you will live"* (Romans 8:10-13).

Note in these passages the contrast between the flesh and the Spirit. Paul was saying that the flesh still harasses us, but the good news is that we are not under obligation to the flesh. No longer are we obliged to be controlled by the flesh. We can overcome; we can win this battle. Why is this true? Why can we win this battle? We can win this battle because the Spirit of God lives in us, and through His power we can put to death the desires and deeds of the flesh. In no uncertain terms, Paul indicated we must put to death the deeds of the flesh. But more than that, he asserted that we can put them to death "by the Spirit." The Holy Spirit is our main source of power in this battle. If we avail ourselves of His ministry and walk in the Spirit, we will win. Conversely, these passages indicate that we will lose this battle if we fail to walk in the Spirit. According to Paul, there is no alternative. It is an either/or proposition: Either walk by the Spirit and overcome, or walk in the flesh and lose.

In reference to this ongoing battle and the means of victory, John Owen wrote:

We are not able of ourselves, without the especial aid, assistance of the Spirit of God, in any measure or degree to free ourselves from this pollution *(the pollution, defilement and controlling power of sin)*. It is true, it is frequently prescribed unto us as our duty, - we are commanded to "wash ourselves," to cleanse ourselves from sin;"…but to suppose that…we have the power of ourselves to do this, is to make the cross of Jesus Christ of none effect….Of ourselves, therefore, we are not able, by any endeavors of our own, nor ways of finding out, to cleanse ourselves from the defilement of sin….Until His Spirit is formed in us,…we cannot perform any one act that is spiritually good, nor any one act of vital obedience.[29]

In these words, Owen emphasizes our own innate inability to overcome the lusts of the flesh, but he also implies that with the help of the Holy Spirit we can have victory. And what he implies in this place, he clearly states in another place:

> "The Holy Ghost…doth work, effect and create in us a new, holy, spiritual, vital principle of grace…which he cherisheth, preserveth, increaseth and strengtheneth continually, by effectual supplies of grace from Jesus Christ, disposing, inclining, and enabling the whole soul unto all ways, acts and duties of holiness, whereby we live to God, opposing, resisting, and finally conquering, whatever is opposite and contrary thereunto.[30]

In his book on spiritual warfare, Jay Adams quotes Philip Brooks who says that if we are going to experience victory in our lives we must struggle to know who our true enemy is. "The enemy, known by many code names, is what they call in espionage terminology a 'mole' – someone who has penetrated deeply into the very vitals of every Christian. And that enemy is the flesh. You are your worst enemy…." Adams then asserts that "success or failure in the war within depends on whether or not a Christian avails himself of the help of the Holy Spirit….Victory in the various battles we fight depends on availing yourself of the Holy Spirit's power."[31]

Scripture could not state our dilemma and the solution to it more clearly. We have a major problem, a problem that can only be solved through the power of the Holy Spirit. *"Walk in the Spirit and you will not fulfill the lusts the flesh"* (Galatians 5:16). Those are great words, filled with all kinds of hope as we face the problems of life, but to benefit from them we must go farther and clarify

THE ENEMY, KNOWN BY MANY CODE NAMES, IS WHAT THEY CALL IN ESPIONAGE TERMINOLOGY A "MOLE."

what it actually means to walk in the Spirit. I agree with Jay Adams who wrote, "But to say that [i.e., that victory is possible through the Holy Spirit] is, if nothing more is said, purely nebulous, or at best mystical."[32] To get the full benefit out of these words and make them really practical, we must answer the question: What does it mean to walk in the Spirit? What is Paul really telling us to do?

WHAT DOES IT MEAN TO WALK IN THE SPIRIT?

Clearly, the mood of the Greek verb translated "walking" contradicts the idea that victory for Christians means that we do nothing, that we become inactive or passive, that we just sit around and wait for the Holy Spirit to do it all. Many people have mistakenly understood that this kind of behavior (or non-behavior) is the way to victory. But this text can't mean that we have no responsibility; that we should just "let go and let God." Paul couldn't have meant this because the verb that Paul used is in the imperative mood, meaning, of course, that we must get up and do something. It isn't something that someone else does for us; it is something we must personally do.

Moreover, the verb is in the present or continuous tense, meaning that whatever he is telling us to do is to be a habit with us. Walking in the Spirit is to be our lifestyle, something we do every day and every moment, now and throughout the rest of our lives. Victory comes as we develop the lifestyle of walking in the Spirit.

WALKING IN THE SPIRIT IS SYNONYMOUS WITH BEING "LED BY THE SPIRIT."

In the context of Galatians 5, walking in the Spirit is synonymous with being *"led by the Spirit"* (Galatians 5:18). As we look at the context of both of these (walking and being led) we discover that the Spirit leads us to put off the desires and deeds of the flesh, to put off boastfulness, argumentativeness, one-upmanship, envy, attempting to be saved through legalism/works, selfishness, inconsiderateness, and even cruelty toward other people (Galatians 5:1-26). Walking in and being led by the Spirit involves standing firm in the faith; believing that we are saved by faith alone by grace alone; being considerate and loving toward other people; developing a life filled with love, joy, peace, patience, kindness, goodness, faithfulness, gentleness and self control; allowing the desires of the Spirit, rather than our own passions and desires, to be our main concern; seeking to restore people who are caught in any trespass; bearing the burdens of others; sharing with those who faithfully teach us; sowing to the Spirit; continuing to do good to other people and glorying in the cross of Christ (Galatians 5:1-6, 16).

Being led by the Spirit and walking in the Spirit involve relying on the Holy Spirit, trusting the Holy Spirit's judgment and insights, and trusting the Holy Spirit for power to do what He calls on us to do. Moment by moment, day after day, all through our lives, whenever it is or wherever it is, we must consciously and joyfully rely on the Holy Spirit for everything we need to do His will and accomplish His purposes for our lives. Earlier in this epistle, Paul admonished the Galatians with this question: *"Are you so foolish? Having begun by the Spirit, are you now being perfected by the flesh?…Does He then who provides you with the Spirit…do it by the works of the law, or by the hearing of faith?"* (Galatians 3:3, 5).

Paul challenged these professing Christians to think biblically and realistically. He charged them with foolishness. In effect, he was saying that they were thinking unbiblically and unrealistically. How? Every true Christian knows and believes that God saves us by grace alone through faith alone; they also know that they are Christians because of the work of the Spirit of God. True, they repented and believed, but they know that faith and repentance are gifts of God brought to us and worked in us by the Spirit of God. They know, as Paul indicates in this passage and Galatians 5:25, that we owe our spiritual lives to the Spirit.

At the beginning of their spiritual lives, these Galatian believers knew they owed it all to the Spirit of God. In Paul's words, they had *"begun by the Spirit."* Here, however, he indicated they had ceased to rely on the Holy Spirit to complete (perfect) the work and had turned to trusting in the flesh. *"This,"* said Paul, *"is foolishness. You relied on the Spirit's enabling at the beginning of your Christian life. You ought to do the same throughout every aspect of the Christians life. And failure to do this doesn't make sense"* (Galatians 3:3).

Walking in the Spirit involves relying completely on the Spirit for every aspect of the Christian life even as we relied on Him at the beginning of our Christian lives. It means believing, as Paul did, that we need to be constantly strengthened by the Spirit in the inner man if we're going to live the way God wants us to live, overcoming the desires and deeds of the flesh and producing, instead, the fruit of the Spirit.

Walking in the Spirit means living in the consciousness of His personal presence in us and with us. It involves trusting His judgment and insights, i.e., trusting that what He says is absolutely true and righteous altogether. Walking in the Spirit means that we will allow His thoughts and perspectives to dominate our

WALKING IN THE SPIRIT MEANS LIVING IN THE CONSCIOUSNESS OF HIS PERSONAL PRESENCE IN US AND WITH US.

thoughts. It means that we will fill our minds with His Word so that His thoughts will be our thoughts, His standards will become our standards, His work will become our work, His will will become our will, His desires will become our desires.

It means that you will memorize God's Word, meditate on God's Word, believe God's Word, and live by God's Word. It means that since the Bible is the Spirit's book, you will *"let God's Word richly dwell within you,"* so that you can with all wisdom (wisdom derived from the Word) teach and counsel others (Colossians 3:16).

Walking in the Spirit means you will think much about Jesus because the Spirit has come to glorify Christ (John 16:14). Walking in the Spirit means walking thought by thought, decision by decision, act by act under the Spirit's control. It means yielding every step to the Spirit's control and being willing to allow Him to be the leader in all of your thoughts, decisions, and actions.

Walking in the Spirit means trusting the credibility of Holy Spirit, that He will do what He has said He will do. Included among the many things the Spirit said He would and could do for us in His Word are the following things: help us in our weaknesses (Romans 8:26; 2 Timothy 1:7); empower us for witnessing and other acts of service (Acts 1:8; 1 Corinthians 12:7); convict us of sin (John 16:8-9); produce in us His fruit (Galatians 5:22-23); make us holy and conform us to the image of Christ (1 Corinthians 6:11; 2 Corinthians 3:18); enable us to put to death the desires and deeds of the flesh (Romans 8:13; Galatians 5:16); set us free from the control of sin (Romans 8:2-4); seal, preserve, and authenticate us (Ephesians 4:30); enable us to love and think properly (Romans 5:4: 2 Timothy 1:7); help us have a greater understanding and experience of the love of God (Ephesians 3:16-18); produce unity and harmony (Ephesians 4:3; Philippians 2:1-2; 2 Corinthians 13:14); enable us to understand, receive, and live out God's Word (1 Corinthians 2:14-16).

Walking in the Spirit and being led by the Holy Spirit mean that you will be willing to do what the Spirit tells you in His Word to do. If He says, *"Put on the Lord Jesus Christ, and make no provision for the flesh to fulfill the lusts thereof"* (Romans 13:14), it means you will obey. If He says to you as a husband, "Love your wife as Christ loved the Church. Give yourself up for her. Seek to help her in the process of sanctification. Nourish and cherish her, honor her, live with her in an understanding way," walking in the Spirit means you will rely on Him

WALKING IN THE SPIRIT MEANS WALKING THOUGHT BY THOUGHT, DECISION BY DECISION, ACT BY ACT UNDER THE SPIRIT'S CONTROL.

WALKING IN THE SPIRIT MEANS TRUSTING THAT HE WILL DO WHAT HE HAS SAID HE WILL DO.

to give you the strength to do it and move out in obedience to actually do it (Ephesians 5:25-29; 1 Peter 3:7). If He says to you as a wife, "Submit yourself to your own husband as to the Lord. Be his helper. Show respect to him," walking in the Spirit means you will rely on Him to give you the strength to do it and move out in obedience to actually do it (Ephesians 5:22-24, 33; 1 Peter 3:1-6). Walking in the Spirit means that you will take all of His commands found in His Word seriously because they express His desires, and it means that you will rely on Him to give you the strength to do it and move out in obedience to actually do it (Ephesians 5:25-29).

In his comments on walking in the Spirit, John MacArthur writes:

> Among other things, walking implies progress, going from where one is to where he ought to be. As a believer submits to the Spirit's control, he moves forward in his spiritual life. Step by step the Spirit moves him from where he is toward where God wants him to be. So while it is the Spirit who is the source of all holy living, it is the believer who is commanded to walk....The power for Christian living is entirely from the Holy Spirit, just as the power of salvation is entirely in Jesus Christ....The Christian is not to sit on the sidelines, as it were, and simply watch the Holy Spirit do battle for him. He is called to consider himself "to be dead to sin, but alive to God in Christ Jesus," to refuse to "let sin reign in (his) mortal body," to resist presenting "the members of (his) body to sin as instruments of unrighteousness" and rather to present them "as instruments of righteousness to God" (Romans 6:11-13)....The believer who is led by the Holy Spirit must be willing to go where the Spirit guides him and do what the Spirit leads him to do.[33]

As all of us know by experience and from the Bible, living in a godly and victorious manner in this present evil world is a challenge. We are constantly being confronted with problems and challenges. Unfortunately, the biggest problem we have has to do with what Jay Adams calls the "mole" within or what the Bible calls "the flesh." Until the day we die, we will struggle with the conflict between "the flesh" and "the Spirit." That's the bad news. The good news, however, is that we can overcome. There is hope. There is victory. God has a solution for this problem, and a major part of that solution is found in the ministry of the Holy Spirit. "Walk in the Spirit and you will not fulfill the lusts of the flesh" is a rock-solid directive containing a rock-solid, take-it-to-the-bank promise. Believe it, obey it, and move forward into a life of joy and victory.

IT MEANS THAT YOU WILL BE WILLING TO DO WHAT THE SPIRIT TELLS YOU IN HIS WORD TO DO.

QUESTIONS FOR DISCUSSION

1. Why did Paul ask the Ephesians who claimed to be disciples of Christ the question, "Did you receive the Holy Spirit when you believed"?

_____

_____

2. What did John MacArthur indicate is the present-day attitude and regard for the Holy Spirit and His ministry among many Christians today?

_____

_____

3. Why does he think this way? Do you agree or disagree with him?

_____

_____

4. Why is the question, "Whatever happened to the Holy Spirit?" an extremely important question for us today?

_____

_____

5. What does Ephesians 2:1-3 indicate about the way we lived before becoming Christians?

_____

_____

6. What does it mean to live "according to the lusts of the flesh"?

_____

_____

7. What happens to us when we become Christians? What changes take place? What does it mean to become "new creatures in Christ"?

_____

_____

8. What does the phrase "holdovers" indicate about us after we've become Christians?

_____

_____

9. What did Sinclair Ferguson mean when he said that after becoming Christians we do not have two equal powers in us which are opposing one another?

_____

_____

10. What does Paul's testimony in Romans 7 teach us about the nature of the Christian life?

_____

_____

11. What did Paul mean when he wrote in Romans 8 that we are not under obligation to the flesh?

_____

_____

12. What was Jay Adams referring to when he wrote that we have a "mole" in us?

_____

_____

13. What is being taught by the fact that the verb translated "walk" in Galatians 5:16 is in the imperative mood?

_____

_____

14. What is being taught by the fact that the verb translated "walk" in Galatians 5:16 is in the present tense?

_____

_____

15. Why did Paul call the Galatians "foolish?"

_____

_____

16. Explain in practical terms what it means to "walk in the Spirit."

_____

_____

PERSONAL RESPONSE

1. When some people think of the Holy Spirit, they think of Him as an impersonal force. From what you have read in this chapter, what indicates to you that the Holy Spirit is a person?

_____

_____

2. What is there about your life that would cause people to know that you are indwelt by the Holy Spirit?

_____

_____

3. Why do you think the Holy Spirit and His ministries are so badly neglected or misrepresented today?

_____

_____

4. How has this neglect of the Holy Spirit crippled many Christians today? Has this neglect affected you? How?

_____

_____

5. Reflecting on the description found in this chapter of what it means to live according to the flesh, evaluate your own life on each of the statements and rate yourself in terms of (4) I never live this way; (3) I seldom live this way; (2) I sometimes live this way; (1) I often live this way.

_____

_____

6. What evidences are there in your life that demonstrate you are a new creature and that you are indwelt by the Holy Spirit?

_____

_____

7. In what situations do you find the conflict between the flesh and the Spirit most intense (when, with what or with whom, where)?

_____

_____

8. What can you do to promote an increase in the "walking in the Spirit" aspect of your life? What is necessary for a person to obey the command of Galatians 5:16?

_____

_____

9. What is required for you to put to death the deeds and desires of the flesh? What must you do?

_____

_____

10. What challenges have you received through this chapter? What new insights have you gained that are of practical value to you in your Christian life?

_____

_____

CHAPTER 11

WHAT'S THE DIAGNOSIS?

Kevin had problems and he knew it. He was angry, depressed, and miserable. Only twenty-three years old, he was already burned out on life. He sat in my office, shoulders hunched over and head hung low, as he explained he had been feeling this way for as long as he could remember.

At first he had turned to drugs and alcohol. But after discovering they only made his problems worse, he went to Narcotics Anonymous. He got a little relief, but eventually, he realized he was just as miserable off of drugs as he was on them.

What frustrated Kevin most was that he had no idea what his problem really was: He had a good job, good friends, a wonderful fiancée, and a great future — everything a man could want. Even so, he was filled with anger, struggled with thoughts of suicide, and was tired of the constant battle. Sitting dejectedly across the desk from me, he wanted to know the answer to this burning question: "Pastor, what's my problem? Why do I do the things I do?"

It didn't surprise me that Kevin was confused. He was a non-Christian, had never studied the Bible, and had only come to me as a last resort. What does surprise and sadden me is that so many professing Christians are just as confused. In fact, some are in worse shape than Kevin. Kevin knew the world didn't have an explanation for his problems, yet many Christians seem to think it does. Believers are bombarded by a multitude of conflicting explanations from a variety of so-called experts as to the cause of man's problems. In the midst of this raging sea of opinions, many professing believers have become distracted from the rock-solid truth of God's Word.

The results are tragic. A doctor must make a proper diagnosis of his patient in order to prescribe the correct treatment. If he is unable to diagnose the problem, or even worse, if he makes an incorrect diagnosis, he'll never be able to give the right prescription. The same is true spiritually.

KEVIN KNEW THE WORLD DIDN'T HAVE AN EXPLANATION FOR HIS PROBLEMS.

You'll never be able to solve your problems until you understand what your problem really is. And you'll never understand what your problem really is until you reject the world's diagnosis and submit to God's. Wrong diagnosis, wrong prescription, no solution!

WHO ME?

You may have seen the T-shirt that reads, "I can't help it if I'm a JERK, I'm having my MID-LIFE CRISIS!" It seems as though everyone these days has some kind of label that not only describes their particular sin, but excuses it as well. In his book, *A Nation of Victims,* Charles Sykes writes:

> Something extraordinary is happening in American society. Crisscrossed by invisible trip wires of emotional, racial, sexual and psychological grievance, American life is increasingly characterized by the plaintive insistence, "I am a victim." The victimization of America is remarkably egalitarian. From the addicts of the South Bronx to the self-styled emotional road-kills of Manhattan's Upper East Side the mantra of victims is the same: "I am not responsible. It's not my fault."[34]

Men and women place the blame for their poor attitudes and behavior on any number of different things. Anyone and everyone is at fault except themselves. Parents are a favorite target. Some people blame the educational system. Others are a bit more sophisticated and claim that they can't obey God until their needs have been met. There are those who say that they have an addiction and therefore cannot be held morally responsible for their behavior.

Recently, I spoke with a young woman who shared with me that before she became a Christian she thought she had multiple personality disorder. She had even named her various "personalities." When she did something wrong, she would just say, "Oh that wasn't me, that was one of my other personalities. Don't blame me, blame her." Others blame society as a whole. Charles Colson notes:

> In recent decades popular political and social beliefs have all but erased the reality of personal sin from our national consciousness. Take for example the passionately advanced argument that society, not the individual is responsible for the evil in our midst: individuals commit crimes because they are forced to, not because they choose to. Poverty, racial oppression, slums, hunger – these are the real culprits; the

YOU'LL NEVER BE ABLE TO SOLVE YOUR PROBLEMS UNTIL YOU UNDERSTAND WHAT YOUR PROBLEM REALLY IS.

AMERICAN LIFE IS INCREASINGLY CHARACTERIZED BY THE PLAINTIVE INSISTENCE, "I AM A VICTIM."

wrongdoer is in reality, the victim. President Lyndon Johnson's attorney general, Ramsey Clark summed up that viewpoint, asserting that poverty is the cause of crime…"[35]

Whether you blame your parents, your education, your unfulfilled needs, your personalities, or society, you are saying the same thing: "Don't look at me. I'm not responsible for my behavior." Americans have bought into this way of thinking, hook, line, and sinker.

Aaron Wildasky calculates that if you add up all the groups in the United States who claim to be oppressed victims, their number amounts to 374% of the population. Charles Sykes explains:

> The National Anthem has become the whine. Increasingly, Americans act as if they had received a lifelong release from misfortune and personal responsibility. As the British Economist notes, "If you lose your job you can sue for the mental distress of being fired. If you drive drunk and crash you can sue somebody for failing to warn you to stop drinking. There is always somebody else to blame."[36]

This modern onslaught of clever excuses for sinful attitudes and behavior has had a terrible impact on the church. Professing believers are now trying to reclaim their "inner child," boost their self-esteem, conquer their co-dependency, and find satisfaction for unmet longings. Psychotherapy has replaced biblical counseling; group therapy has replaced discipleship; recovery has replaced repentance; addictions have replaced ungodly habits; and the list goes on. People are no longer sinful, they're "dysfunctional;" they're no longer selfish idolaters, they're victims of a "personality disorder." Evangelical Christians rush into an ocean of psycho-heresy devoid of power and bereft of Divine solutions.

Dr. John MacArthur notes:

> There is no denying that psychology has made incredible inroads into evangelical culture over the past twenty-five years. The influence of psychology is reflected in the kinds of sermons that are being preached from evangelical pulpits, in the kind of counseling that is being offered over the radio airwaves, in the proliferation of psychologists who cater primarily to evangelical Christians, and in the books that are being offered by many evangelical publishers.[37]

AMERICANS HAVE BOUGHT INTO THIS WAY OF THINKING, HOOK, LINE AND SINKER.

PSYCHOTHERAPY HAS REPLACED BIBLICAL COUNSELING; GROUP THERAPY HAS REPLACED DISCIPLESHIP.

It's not surprising that people try to find excuses for their unbiblical attitudes and actions. Mankind has been doing it since the Garden of Eden (Genesis 3:1-16). It's almost instinctive. Go to any elementary school playground and you'll find that blaming others for one's actions begins very early in life. You don't need to teach children to do that. This explanation is attractive because it absolves us from guilt.

THIS EXPLANATION IS ATTRACTIVE BECAUSE IT ABSOLVES US FROM GUILT.

We can't be held responsible for our behavior if our problems are entirely due to external conditions! But this particular theory falls far short of accurately explaining the real cause of mankind's problems. Even unbelievers acknowledge this. Alan Ehrenhalt wrote:

> Back when Lester Maddox was governor of Georgia, in the late 1960's, there was a riot at the state prison. Reporters asked him what he planned to do about the conditions that caused the trouble. Maddox rejected the entire premise of the question. "There's nothing wrong with our prison system," he said. "We just don't have a very good class of prisoners anymore."
>
> I've told that story to quite a few audiences, and it always gets a laugh. What I never go on to admit is that in all honesty I think there's a kernel of wisdom in it. Prison inmates are entitled to decent food and shelter, and when they don't get it sometimes they cause trouble. But sometimes they cause trouble because they are troublemakers. That's why they are there. This isn't just a point about the correctional system….If in our distaste for blaming the victim, we treat public institutions as the automatic culprit of first resort, there are many…problems in 21st century America we will never understand.[38]

Story

He's right.

Logic alone tells us that mankind's problems are not entirely caused by external conditions. If man's problems are due to poor parenting, why do so many with great parents do so poorly? If man's problems are due to economic conditions, why do the wealthy commit suicide? If man's problems are ultimately due to our circumstances, how is it that so many who have had to endure difficult circumstances have succeeded?

LOGIC ALONE TELLS US THAT MANKIND'S PROBLEMS ARE NOT ENTIRELY CAUSED BY EXTERNAL CONDITIONS.

Your environment does matter, but it does not matter absolutely. Martyn Lloyd Jones explains:

The attempt to explain the ills of life in terms of any or all of these external conditions will break down hopelessly in the face of facts whether negative or positive. We are not so foolish as to say that they do not count at all. What we deny is that they are the controlling factor and therefore of prime importance. We further reject such an explanation on the grounds that is an insult to man in any state or condition to suggest that he is entirely and utterly dependent on his external condition.[39]

The Bible makes it clear that you are never forced to sin. You must not put the blame for your actions and your attitude on your circumstances, on others, or on anything else. It falls squarely on your shoulders. Paul wrote in 2 Corinthians 5:10, *"We must all appear before the judgment seat of Christ, that each one may be recompensed for his deeds in the body, according to what he has done, whether good or bad."* When we stand before God, He's not going to accept excuses.

WHEN WE STAND BEFORE GOD, HE'S NOT GOING TO ACCEPT EXCUSES.

READ

At first you might not like to hear that because it means you are responsible, but you should rejoice because it also means there's hope! You don't have to be a victim. But you think, "You don't know my circumstances." You're right. I don't. But God does; and He says, *"No temptation has overtaken you but such as is common to man; and God is faithful who will not allow you to be tempted beyond what you are able, but with the temptation will provide the way of escape also that you may be able to endure it"* (1 Corinthians 10:13). Paul was telling you that you don't have to fall to temptation. Therefore, if you say that you're a victim – that you had to sin because of your parents or your economic conditions or your circumstances – you're calling God a liar. He says that you can overcome.

But it gets better. The Bible not only says that difficult circumstances can't force you to sin. It also says that God can use them for your good. James wrote, *"Consider it all joy my brethren when you encounter various trials."* He didn't write, "It's okay if you sin when you have difficult times. I understand if you're depressed because your circumstances are so difficult, or your parents were so cruel." No, James says, "Believer, you are to look at those circumstances and you are to think – ALL JOY!" Why? Because God uses difficult circumstances to produce godly character. Adversity isn't always a bad thing. How can you be a victim if God designed that difficult circumstance for your good?

GOD USES DIFFICULT CIRCUMSTANCES TO PRODUCE GODLY CHARACTER.

LET'S GET PHYSICAL

SOME SAY THERE'S NO SUCH THING AS SIN, ONLY DISEASE.

Others offer a slightly different explanation for the cause of mankind's problems. They suggest that every problem that people have is a physical problem. There's no such thing as sin, only disease. Dr. Ed Welch, in his excellent book, *Blame it on the Brain,* tells the story of a prominent politician who was holding a televised press conference. He had taken a hard anti-drug stance, but was recently caught in the act of buying and using illegal drugs himself.

> It was all on tape. How was he going to get out of it this time? As he was moving toward the podium, a reporter called out, "Why did you do it? Why did you lie all these years?" His response was immediate. "I didn't do it," he said. "My brain was messed up. It was my brain that did it. My disease did it." There wasn't a hint of remorse – only indignation that someone would ask him such a question....To my surprise no one was laughing. His answer seemed to satisfy everyone present....[40]

Dr. Stanton Peele notes:

> Americans are increasingly likely to attribute their own and others behavior to innate biological causes....Just about every week now, we read new headlines about the genetic basis for...homosexuality, intelligence, or obesity. In previous years, these stories were about the genes for alcoholism, schizophrenia, and manic depression. Such news stories may lead us to believe our lives are being revolutionized by genetic discoveries. We may be on the verge of reversing and eliminating mental illness for example. In addition, many believe, we can identify the causes of criminality, personality, and other basic human foibles and traits.[41]

Their point is this: You're not a sinner; you're sick. You're not responsible for your sin; you have a disease.

This is why it is very common to see advertisements in magazines and on television promoting drugs that allegedly make the angry kind, the depressed happy, and the timid brave. If you're sick you need a pill, not Scripture!

More and more, Christians are becoming interested in the use of drugs (such as Prozac, Ritalin, and Paxil) because of the supposed dramatic effect they are having on human behavior. They think that through these drugs they finally have hope to overcome the spiritual battles they have fought for years. One writer asks, "Can it be that a pill can do what the Holy Spirit or human will could not?" Some people are relying heavily on drugs to give them a quality of life, a spiritual experience that salvation, the Holy Spirit, the Scriptures, the biblical means of grace could not give. The same article tells us that a few weeks after taking Prozac one woman exclaimed, "I felt like living again. And I began to experience God like never before."[42]

For others, these pills are producing doubts about the validity, importance and effectiveness of Christianity. Yet, in the same article, a man named Carlos Ramirez, who found relief through medication, stated that his drive to deal with his sins was lowered. His relief through medication had caused him to ask himself, "Why am I a Christian?' I now realize that before Zoloft, much of my motivation to follow Christ was a desperation to feel good about myself. But if I can now feel good without God, why follow Him?"[43]

Have scientists finally discovered the true answer to man's problems through medication or hormone and chemical replacement? Do we now know why people do what they do? Before you accept the prescription, you should take a step back and look at the diagnosis. For one thing, it's important to understand that many of the claims we hear are unproven. There is a lot of hype about medical breakthroughs that is just that – hype. One writer illustrates:

> In the late 1980's genes for schizophrenia and manic depression were identified with great fanfare by teams of geneticists. Both claims have now been definitively disproven. Yet while the original announcements were heralded on television news programs and front pages of newspapers around the country, most people were unaware of their refutations....[44]

In fact, as Dr. Gary Almy, a psychiatrist himself, writes:

> With few exceptions, the practice of psychiatry continues to be subjective and irrational. Contrary to what the public is allowed to believe, no disease called depression, manic-depression, or schizophrenia has ever been discovered, and no rational treatment for

MORE AND MORE, CHRISTIANS ARE BECOMING INTERESTED IN THE USE OF DRUGS.

A LOT OF HYPE ABOUT MEDICAL BREAKTHROUGHS, IS JUST THAT — HYPE.

these disorders has ever been devised or proven to be effective. Science understands little about the function of the brain and even less about how the various psychiatric medications affect the brain. Neuroscience can regularly claim to be on the verge of complete understanding of human consciousness and can regularly display colorful scans of human brains in the process of various types of human thought. However, any humility combined with honesty in these scientists should cause them to admit that they have barely scratched the surface of an organ more complex than we can begin to comprehend.[45]

Dr. Michael Gitlin, an associate professor of psychiatry at UCLA concurs: "Despite a remarkable amount of research over the last twenty-five years…there is still no definitive explanation for any psychiatric disorder…."[46] Even more important, believers must understand that this explanation for mankind's problems is based on a fundamentally different perception than Scripture's regarding the nature of mankind and the cause of mankind's problems.

The use of prescription medicines to treat problems the Bible calls sin is based on an evolutionary, materialistic understanding of man. That's a fancy way of saying they believe man is all body and no soul. One of the results of the widespread acceptance of evolution is a minimization of the importance of the soul. According to Darwin, people do what they do because of the brain; the brain secretes thought like the liver secretes bile. Materialists explain that the brain is like an engine. We can take an engine out of the car, examine all of its parts, and figure out exactly why it does what it does. There is no need to imagine that there is some sort of "spirit" of an engine that causes it to work.

ONE OF THE RESULTS OF THE WIDESPREAD ACCEPTANCE OF EVOLUTION IS A MINIMIZATION OF THE IMPORTANCE OF THE SOUL.

The idea is that if we can just figure out the human brain, then we will be able to explain why we do what we do. Every problem that man has is a physical problem, and to fix those problems, all we need to do is figure out the right medicine to prescribe. Dr. Francis Crick explains, "You and your joys and sorrows, and your memories and ambitions, your personal identity and free will, are in fact, no more than the behavior of a vast assembly of nerve cells and their associated molecules."[47]

Understanding people and their behavior in this materialistic way eliminates the need for thinking that there is some sort of nonphysical soul or spirit, an inner man, that affects and influences people in what they do. At first glance, this idea may sound fairly reasonable. After all, no one has ever seen a soul. If you were to go to a doctor for an operation and he opened you up, he wouldn't see a soul inside. Besides that, people like this idea because, once again, it takes away responsibility for their behavior. You can't help what you do. It's your brain's fault. No one can blame you for what you did; you were born this way. But think carefully about the implications of this understanding of people and their behavior. The implications are profound. If we are all body and no soul:

1. We are no different than the animals.
2. There is no such thing as sin, as defined by the Bible.
3. There is no hope for ever truly overcoming our problems. We are just animals that can talk – and really, that's nothing too special because even parrots can do that.

How can there be sin, when we are biochemically predetermined? What once was called sin is really a disease or a biochemical malfunction. And since it is a disease, there is no real hope for victory. We must just learn to cope.

Turn to Scripture and you find that the Bible presents a radically different view of mankind. People are much more than just physical bodies. They are composite beings, made up of both bodies and souls. That's why Jesus said in Matthew 10:28, *"Do not be afraid of those who can kill the body but cannot kill the soul. Rather be afraid of the one who can destroy both soul and body in hell."* And that's why Paul can say, *"Therefore we do not lose heart, but though our outer man is decaying, yet our inner man is being renewed day by day"* (2 Corinthians 4:16).

TURN TO SCRIPTURE AND YOU FIND THAT THE BIBLE PRESENTS A RADICALLY DIFFERENT VIEW OF MANKIND.

The Bible teaches that it is the immaterial part of man – the soul – not the material part, that is the "mission control center" of a person's being. That's the exact opposite of what these theorists are proposing. They claim that man is completely controlled by his physical makeup. The Bible explains you need to go deeper and look at the heart.

THE BIBLE EXPLAINS YOU NEED TO GO DEEPER AND LOOK AT THE HEART.

The first proof of that is Adam and Eve. They didn't rebel against God because of their environment – it was a perfect paradise. And they didn't rebel against God because of some mental abnormality – God created them and said they were "good." They rebelled against God because of a choice they made deep in their souls. This means we do bad things because of a bad heart. Jesus makes this clear, *"That which proceeds out of the man, that is what defiles the man. For from within, out of the heart of men, proceed evil thoughts, fornications, thefts, murders, adulteries, deeds of coveting and wickedness, as well as deceit, sensuality, envy, slander, pride and foolishness. All these evil things proceed from within and defile the man"* (Mark 7:20-23).

Why do we sin? According to Jesus Who is wisdom personified (Colossians 2:3), we do what we do because of what is going on in our hearts. That's why Proverbs 4:23 tells us, *"Watch over your heart with all diligence, for from it flow the springs of life."* That's why Proverbs 27:19 states that *"the heart of man reflects the man."* That's why Proverbs 23:7 informs us that to really know a person you must know what is going on in their heart. That's why James 1:13 indicates that when we sin we are enticed and carried away by our own lusts.

Ultimately, we behave badly (sinfully, unbiblically) not because of what is happening around us or being done to us. From God's perspective, the difficult circumstances we experience outside us provide the context in which we discover what is going on inside us. The bad stuff comes out because there is bad stuff already in our hearts, because selfish motives and desires are already inside us. We behave in ungodly ways because something is wrong in our souls; in the mission control center of our lives.

SCRIPTURE DOES NOT
IGNORE THE BODY; IT
JUST DOESN'T VIEW IT
AS AN EXCUSE OR
REASON FOR SIN.

According to the Bible, man is made up of both a body and soul. Scripture does not ignore the body; it just doesn't view it as an excuse or reason for sin. Jesus Himself had a human body, yet He was without sin. That means we can control the body, or it can control us. The body can't force us to disobey God. There is a unity between the body and soul. The body needs the soul, and the natural place for the soul to be is with the body. A body without a soul is dead. Even when we are in heaven, our souls are going to be connected to bodies; they'll just be better ones (1 Corinthians 15:40-44).

SINCE THERE IS SUCH
A UNITY BETWEEN THE
BODY AND THE SOUL,
IT IS NOT SURPRISING
THAT THEY HAVE AN
EFFECT ON EACH
OTHER.

Since there is such a unity between the body and the soul, it is not surprising that they have an effect on each other. Spiritual problems have physical side-effects. Anxiety may produce ulcers, stress can cause headaches, and so on. And obedience to God's commands can actually benefit your health (Proverbs12:18; 13:3, 14; 14:30, 16:24; Isaiah 58:10). On the other hand, the body has an impact on the soul. For example, lack of sleep does provide the circumstances in which it is more difficult to obey. It is true that some children do have more energy than others, making it more difficult for them to stay settled in class. And there are organic causes for *some* behavioral problems.

IT IS IMPORTANT TO
REMEMBER THAT THE
BODY IS NOT THE
SOUL AND THE SOUL IS
NOT THE BODY.

To understand ourselves and others, our behavior and the behavior of others, it is important to remember that the body is not the soul and the soul is not the body. This means that there are physical problems, and there are spiritual problems. Spiritual problems can have an effect on a person's physical condition. And a person's physical condition can have an effect on them spiritually; yet they are two distinct issues.

If you have a cold, you can read as many Bible verses as you want, but that won't necessarily help your cold. (Though it certainly will help your attitude while you have the cold!) Likewise, if you are struggling with what the Bible classifies as a spiritual issue, it is foolish to treat it as if it were a physical problem.

The Bible was not written to be a medical textbook for dealing with your physical problems, or to provide some sort of magical protection from the trials and difficulties of life. One of the primary reasons it was written, however, was to help you solve problems caused by your own sin – what it classifies as spiritual problems (2 Timothy 3:16-17). God wrote the Bible to provide you what you need to know to be godly and deal with the problems of life. (Refer to chapters 3 through 6 of this book.)

If God talks about a problem and calls it a sin, we dare not excuse it or relabel it a disease. As we search out Scripture and find that God tells us we are not to worry, we'd better not say, "Well, I have an anxiety disorder." Or if we look at Scripture and learn that certain types of anger are sinful, we must not say, "I have a dysfunction in my brain that allows me to lose my temper."

Men and women fall into sin for several reasons.
1. They have never really been born again. (1 Peter 2:22-23)
2. They are not indwelt by the Spirit Who gives the power to resist and overcome temptation. (Romans 8:10-14)
3. They are ignorant of the Word and don't understand how to change. (Ephesians 5:15-17)
4. They are lazy and unwilling to work. (Proverbs 14:23; Hebrews 12:1-3)
5. They are ensnared by their own evil desires. (James 1:13-15)

But nowhere does the Bible give us an "out," an excuse, for sin (ungodly, unbiblical behavior) based on our physical condition. If you ignore what Scripture has to say about the real cause of your problems, you are never going to be able to truly overcome them. You may find ways to make yourself *feel* well; but you won't *be* well.

IF YOU ARE STRUGGLING WITH WHAT THE BIBLE CLASSIFIES AS A SPIRITUAL ISSUE, IT IS FOOLISH TO TREAT IT AS IF IT WERE A PHYSICAL PROBLEM.

That's the problem with taking drugs to deal with spiritual problems. Drugs only create the illusion of wellness. Medical doctor Robert Smith explains:

> Drugs do improve a person's feelings. Medications do make people feel better, and feeling oriented people function better when they feel better. When people feel better from the use of medications, this is used as an argument to prove there was a chemical imbalance. Their "logic" is that because the person felt better and the performance was better, this proves the presence of a chemical imbalance. In science, two concurrent facts do not prove one causes the other…But that is the kind of quasi-logic being used in the above mentioned argument. It is unknown how the chemicals improve the feelings. The fact that there is no explanation why the feeling is improved, does not change the conclusion of those who believe that the bad feelings are the result of a chemical imbalance. It is theorized that somehow the drugs restore the balance. But there is no proof.[48]

READ ⟶

Suppose you go to a doctor because you have a broken arm. He takes a good long look at it, x-rays it, talks to his staff about it, and then comes back to you and says, "I know exactly what will make you feel better. Here's what we'll do. I'm going to give you a special shot that will numb all the pain." If you agree and the doctor gives you an anesthetic, you may feel better. But are you better? Of course not! Why? Because he never dealt with the real problem – and you will be dependent upon the anesthetic until he does! You will never be able to solve life's problems God's way until you accept His diagnosis.

WHAT'S MY PROBLEM?

"But, you might say, "all this talk about sin sounds too harsh! It's cruel to blame my problems on sin." Is it? Would you rather have us not talk about sin? That sounds cruel to me. If you don't understand sin, you won't understand God's Word. God, the Creator of the world, has revealed Himself in a Book, and you won't understand this Book if you don't understand sin. All this talk of judgment, hell, wrath, law, death, punishment, salvation, justification, propitiation, and redemption makes no sense apart from sin. Deny sin, and you deny the Bible. If you don't understand sin, you won't understand yourself.

If you don't understand sin, you will never understand why you are having the problems you are having. You want to understand why you have the problems you're having in your relationships; why a parent treated you the way they did; why your spouse was unfaithful; why your marriage didn't work; why your children are doing what they're doing; why you aren't satisfied at work; why you're depressed; why you get angry. You can't understand any of that apart from understanding what the Bible has to say about sin! You can't understand why you are miserable; why you feel guilty; why you have no hope. It really comes down to this: If you don't understand what the Bible says about sin, you won't understand yourself, other people, or your world.

Mankind has major problems. There are wars, hatred, abuse, poverty, death, and sickness. Why do we have the problems we have in this world? Many people devote their entire lives to answering this very question. We have activists, scholars, philosophers, and people at the United Nations trying to figure this out. But as long as they ignore sin, they will continually be frustrated in their attempts to solve mankind's problems.

Calling sin sin is not harsh or cruel; it's an act of mercy! It's an act of mercy because there is an answer for sin. God has provided a solution. What is harsh and what is cruel is denying what the Bible says about sin. That's like going to a doctor who, after studying your x-rays and blood tests and seeing you have cancer, comes to you and tells you everything is all right. After all, he doesn't want to hurt your feelings. If you have cancer and need an operation, your feelings ultimately aren't that important. Pretending as though the problem doesn't exist isn't going to help solve it! The only way you have a hope of being cured is if you have an accurate diagnosis.

The same is true spiritually. If you're going to solve life's problem's God's way, you must put away the excuses and labels the world gives you. Instead, accept God's diagnosis, call sin sin, and use God's solution found in His all-sufficient Word. That's the solution we are describing in the chapters of this book.

IF YOU DON'T UNDERSTAND WHAT THE BIBLE SAYS ABOUT SIN, YOU WON'T UNDERSTAND YOURSELF, OTHER PEOPLE, OR YOUR WORLD.

PUT AWAY THE EXCUSES AND LABELS THE WORLD GIVES YOU; ACCEPT GOD'S DIAGNOSIS; CALL SIN SIN.

QUESTIONS FOR DISCUSSION

1. Why is it important that we properly diagnose our problems?

_____

_____

2. What are two popular theories on the source of mankind's problems?

_____

_____

3. Give examples of different things on which people blame their problems.

_____

_____

4. Logically, why can't we blame our sin on others?

_____

_____

5. Biblically, why can't we blame our sin on others? Give specific Scripture references.

_____

_____

6. What point was Dr. Lloyd Jones making when he wrote, "The attempt to explain the ills of life in terms of any or all of these external conditions will break down hopelessly in the face of facts whether negative or positive. We are not so foolish as to say that they do not count at all. What we deny is that they are the controlling factor and therefore of prime importance. We further reject such an explanation on the grounds that it is an insult to man in any state or condition to suggest that he is entirely and utterly dependent on his external condition"?

_____

_____

_____

7. Give three implications of the statement, "You are not a victim."

_____

_____

8. What are some of the problems with the "sin is a sickness" theory?

_____

_____

9. What did Gary Almy mean when he wrote, "With few exceptions, the practice of psychiatry continues to be subjective and irrational. Contrary to what the public is allowed to believe, no disease called depression, manic-depression, or schizophrenia has ever been discovered, and no rational treatment for these disorders has ever been devised or proven to be effective. Science understands little about the function of the brain and even less about how the various psychiatric medications affect the brain. Neuroscience can regularly claim to be on the verge of complete understanding of human consciousness and can regularly display colorful scans of human brains in the process of various types of human thought. However, any humility combined with honesty in these scientists should cause them to admit that they have barely scratched the surface of an organ more complex than we can begin to comprehend"?

_____

_____

10. What is a materialist?

_____

_____

11. Explain the implications of a materialist's view of man.

_____

_____

12. Explain the Bible's teaching on the nature of man. Support your answer with Scripture.

_____

_____

13. Explain what the Bible says about the relationship between the soul and the body.

_____

_____

14. Why is it important to remember that the body and the soul are united?

_____

_____

15. Explain several ways the body can have an effect on the soul, and vice-versa.

_____

_____

16. What are the implications of the fact that the body and soul are distinct?

_____

_____

17. Why do people fall into sin?

_____

_____

18. What's the problem with taking drugs to deal with spiritual problems?

_____

_____

19. Why is it cruel to not talk about sin?

_____

_____

20. Why is it dangerous to deny sin?

_____

_____

21. Why is calling sin sin an act of mercy?

_____

_____

PERSONAL RESPONSE

1. Are you making any excuses for your sin? What excuses have you used in the past?

_____

_____

2. What do you believe is the source of your problems? Explain with Scripture.

_____

_____

3. If someone came to you and said, "I am the way I am because of what my parents did," how would you respond? What Scripture would you use to support your response?

_____

_____

4. What's the problem with relying on prescription drugs to solve your spiritual problems?

_____

_____

5. What specific changes are you going to make as a result of the truths of this chapter?

_____

_____

6. Do you have any questions about what was taught in this chapter? Write them down and go to Scripture to find the answers.

_____

_____

CHAPTER 12

HOW TO KEEP GOING

When I headed back to the gym to begin a regular program of exercise after a long lay off, I quickly remembered why I had stopped in the first place: Exercise isn't easy; it's hard. Very rarely do I smile when I'm running on the treadmill.

But do you know what is even harder than exercising? Continuing to exercise. Everybody can put on the old sweatsuit and go for a walk, but very few continue to do so day after day. Why do some people continue to exercise and others give up? One word: motivation. You can sit on your couch and read all the exercise manuals in the world, but if you are not motivated to exercise, these books are not going to do you any good.

WHY DO SOME PEOPLE CONTINUE TO EXERCISE AND OTHERS GIVE UP? ONE WORD: MOTIVATION.

The same is true spiritually. The Bible tells us, *"Exercise yourself for godliness"* (1 Timothy 4:7). That means that living for Christ and solving life's problems God's way isn't easy. God demands a life of no compromise. Exercising yourself for godliness can be painful and will require great sacrifice.

Most people can put on their Sunday suits and go to church once in a while, but very few continue to push themselves to pursue God day after day after day. When many Christians face difficulties and hardships in the nitty-gritty of life, they are overcome by those problems rather than pressing on to find God's solutions to them. They hit a bump in the road and stop moving forward in their spiritual growth and development. They become perplexed, confused, and overwhelmed by the challenges they face in life. As a result, they stop running or even walking, and start crawling or limping through their Christian lives.

THE BIBLE TELLS US *"EXERCISE YOURSELF FOR GODLINESS."*

Why does this happen? Why do some believers face the challenges and persevere in obedience despite their difficulties, and why do others stop? Why is it that some people keep going until they have experienced victory while others struggle on and never do seem to solve their problems? The solutions are available for all of God's people (1 Corinthians 10:13; 2 Corinthians 9:8), but some don't seem to find them or use them. Why? Some are properly and powerfully motivated, and others are not.

TO SOLVE LIFE'S PROBLEMS GOD'S WAY YOU MUST BE PROPERLY MOTIVATED.

To solve life's problems God's way you must be properly motivated. Reading all the self-help, "how to" books in the world – even if they are filled with biblical principles – won't get the job done unless what motivates you is a biblically-based motivation. In the previous chapters of this book, we've spent a great deal of time talking about what it takes to become a godly person and solve life's problems God's way. But all that information won't do you much good if you don't understand why you should to want to solve life's problems and become a more godly person.

The apostle Paul understood that. As you read his epistles, you find many commands and exhortations about how we should think, speak, act, and live. Included among or previous to these practical admonitions, you will also find Paul reminding us of great doctrinal, theological truths that when rightly understood and applied will provide the power and motivation for obeying those admonitions.

Nowhere do we see this more clearly illustrated than in Titus 2. In the first ten verses of this great chapter, Paul described in specific terms how Christians should live. First he addressed older men about the way they should live, then older women, then younger women, and finally younger men. In this passage, he gave specific admonitions to each age group that would mark them as being very different from the way that most people in the world were living. He called on them to do things, to live in such a way that would be very challenging and difficult.

Paul was a realist; he knew that obeying these commands would not be easy. He knew that the people he was exhorting might raise objections and be reticent to live the way he had prescribed. So he anticipated their objections and (in verses 11-14) provided a powerful answer to the question, "Why should we, and how can we, live this way?"

"WHY SHOULD WE, AND HOW CAN WE, LIVE THIS WAY?"

Note carefully how Paul began and ended this magnificent passage. He began with the word "for" which really means "because." He was saying that we should and can live that way for one reason. What's the reason? Because *the grace of God has appeared* (Titus 2:11), and still further because *our great God and Savior, Christ Jesus…gave Himself for us, that he might redeem us from every lawless deed and purify for Himself a people for His own possession, zealous for good deeds"* (Titus 2:14). If you are going to go forward in the Christian life, you've first got to go back, all the way back to the cross. Christ's work on the cross should motivate you to live for Him in the present. If believers are going to solve life's problems God's way, they must understand the Gospel and be motivated by it.

If you were to ask a group of Christians, "Why did Christ give Himself up for us on the cross?" the answers many people would give would be something like, "He died to take the punishment or pay the penalty for our sins" or "To give us eternal life" or "So that we might be forgiven." Those are good and accurate biblical answers; they are all certainly and gloriously true. Paul wrote, *"When we were still without strength, in due time, Christ died for the ungodly…But God demonstrates His own love toward us, in that while we were still sinners Christ died for us"* (Romans 5:6-8). Jesus Christ, our great God and Savior voluntarily humbled Himself to take on human nature, the form of a bondservant, and become obedient to the point of death so that He might serve as a substitute for those who repent of their sins and put their faith in Him (Philippians 2:5-11; Romans 3:34-25). Why did Christ give Himself up? To bear the penalty of our sins.

But although those answers are true, they are only a partial answer to the question, "Why did Christ give Himself up for us on the cross?" There's more. We need to hear the rest of the story. When you think about Christ and His work, you must be very careful that you get the whole picture. Yes, Christ did come and die on the cross to save us from the penalty of our sins, but, catch this: He did not come and die on the cross to do only that. In fact, if you think of it exclusively in terms of dealing with the penalty of your sins, you cheapen and minimize the great saving work of Christ.

One of the most tragic errors in the church today is a wholesale cheapening of the work of Christ. There are those who say that you can be a Christian without ever following after Christ. They teach that if you so choose, you can accept Jesus as Savior but not as Lord. For them, being a Christian is just a matter of saying a prayer in which you confess your sins and invite Jesus into your heart as Savior. Then, once you've done that, they indicate you can go out and live your life however you want to. It's certainly better if you don't do this, but, even if you do, you can still consider yourself to be a bonafide Christian because you have accepted Jesus Christ as Savior. And in support of this idea, they explain that we are saved by grace and not by works, we're not saved by what we do, but by what Christ has done for us on the cross.

IF YOU ARE GOING TO GO FORWARD IN THE CHRISTIAN LIFE, YOU'VE FIRST GOT TO GO ALL THE WAY BACK TO THE CROSS.

ONE OF THE MOST TRAGIC ERRORS IN THE CHURCH TODAY IS A WHOLESALE CHEAPENING OF THE WORK OF CHRIST.

IF YOU THINK YOU CAN CONSIDER YOURSELF A CHRISTIAN AND STILL LIVE HOWEVER YOU WANT TO LIVE, YOU MISUNDERSTAND WHAT IT MEANS TO CONFESS JESUS AS SAVIOR.

Lifestyle

When people explain salvation and what Christ has done for us in this way, they think they are magnifying the work of Christ and the grace of God. In fact, they are doing a gross injustice to the grace of God and the crucifixion of Christ. This kind of thinking minimizes the greatness of God's grace and the magnitude of the work of Christ on the cross. To say that you can be a Christian and still live a life dominated by selfishness, ungodliness, and disobedience to God is to fail to understand how great the salvation that Christ provides actually is.

Paul's statement in Titus 2:11-14 indicates that if you think you can consider yourself a Christian and still live however you want to live (even in blatant and continual disobedience to God), you misunderstand what it means to confess Jesus as Savior. In this passage, Paul makes it crystal clear that as Savior, Jesus Christ came to save us from the power as well as the penalty of our sin, and that one day, as Savior, He will even save us from the presence of sin. If words mean anything, the words *"our great God and Savior, Christ Jesus…gave Himself for us, that he might redeem us from every lawless deed and purify for Himself a people for His own possession, zealous for good deeds"* must mean this much (Titus 2:14). And to say otherwise is to cheapen and minimize the great saving work of Christ.

Jesus Christ came to save us from the power as well as the penalty of our sin. What should motivate believers to attempt to live their lives and solve their problems God's way? What reason do they have for believing that they can live their lives and solve their problems God's way?

The Gospel of God's saving grace in Christ Jesus. Jesus Christ humbled Himself; became man; lived a perfect life of obedience to God's will; died a terrible, sacrificial death on the cross for sin; rose again from the dead; and ascended into heaven on our behalf (in our stead, for us) so that He could be our Savior saving us from the penalty, power and eventually the presence of sin. Understand the greatness of our Savior and His salvation and you will be motivated and empowered to solve your problems God's way and to strive after the holiness God says you must pursue (Hebrews 12:14).

MOTIVATED BY THE REDEMPTION THE GOSPEL PROVIDES

THE WORD "REDEEM" COMES FROM THE GREEK WORD FOR "RANSOM."

Paul seeks to motivate us to godliness in Titus 2:14, specifically by reminding us that *"Christ Jesus gave Himself for us to redeem us."* We don't use this word "redeem" too often anymore. That's unfortunate because it sums up one of the great purposes of Christ's death. It comes from the Greek word for "ransom." Jesus came to ransom the elect. A ransom is basically a payment of a price. When a child is kidnapped, the parents are usually asked to pay a ransom. What are they doing when they pay that ransom? They are paying a price so that the kidnapped person will be set free. To redeem or ransom someone is to set them free by paying a price.

When Paul said Christ came to "redeem us" he indicated that we were in bondage and that Christ came to set us free by paying a ransom, a price. Paul's words bring to mind the picture of a man standing on the auction block at an ancient slave market. Stolen from or sold by his parents at an early age, he has lived years in years in bondage to a cruel master. And now he stands there on the auction block to be sold like an animal. Someone in the crowd cries out, "I'll take him for 100 denarii." The slave doesn't even lift his head to see who bought him because he knows nothing is going to change. He's just going from one master to another. He's still looking down when his new owner comes up to him and gently says to him, "You are free. You have been ransomed. I paid the price to set you free." If this were to occur, the freed slave would have been ecstatic with joy. Count on it, he would have loved his redeemer! And he would have loved the word "redeemed!"

That's what Paul says Christ has done for us. We were slaves to sin and to Satan, but Christ has ransomed us. He has paid the price to set us free. Knowing how terrible our captivity to sin and Satan was, and knowing that Christ has paid the price to set us free ought to cause us to greatly appreciate and be motivated by our redemption. Unfortunately, many professing believers don't seem to realize the awfulness of the captivity from which Christ has rescued them. As a result, they take their salvation for granted.

Imagine living in a billion-dollar home when someone approaches you and says, "I have come to set you free from this home." How would you respond? Would you be excited? Would you be motivated to express gratitude to that person? Would you commit yourself out of gratitude to live your life to please and serve that person? Probably not!

Now, change the situation and imagine yourself living in absolute squalor, owned by and enslaved to a master who tortured and abused you mercilessly, when someone came, paid an incredible price to redeem you, and set you free.

> CHRIST CAME TO SET US FREE BY PAYING A RANSOM, A PRICE.

> UNFORTUNATELY, MANY PROFESSING BELIEVERS DON'T SEEM TO REALIZE THE AWFULNESS OF THE CAPTIVITY FROM WHICH CHRIST HAS RESCUED THEM.

How would you respond? What would you be motivated to do for that person? Or compare your response to someone who helped you by putting a band-aid on a minor abrasion with the way you would respond to someone who raised you from the dead and gave you a new life. Would your response be the same?

The way you view your condition before salvation makes a big difference in the way you view the worth of your salvation. That's why it's so important for us to realize the truth about our state before God saved us. It wasn't very pleasant. It wasn't as if we were living in a billion-dollar home when Christ redeemed us. It wasn't as if we simply had a scratch on our knee when Christ saved us. No, we were enslaved to a terrible, cruel master; we were dead in our sins (Ephesians 2:1-3). Isaiah described our condition as being mortally sick from the top of our head to the bottom of our feet (Isaiah 1:5-6). Second Timothy 2:26 declares that Satan took us captive to do his will. Romans 3:9 asserts that we were under the control of sin.

THE WAY YOU VIEW YOUR CONDITION BEFORE SALVATION MAKES A BIG DIFFERENCE IN THE WAY YOU VIEW THE WORTH OF YOUR SALVATION.

When many people think of their pre-salvation situation, they may do what some death-row inmates may do just to survive. They may pretend that their situation isn't really serious; that somehow they will escape; that they will not be taken into the death chamber. These people live in some kind of dream world.

According to the Bible, sin makes us view everything, ourselves included, in a crazy way. Ecclesiastes 9:3 states that *the hearts of the sons of men are full of evil and insanity is in their heart....* In other words, God is saying that until we are redeemed, we are under the control of evil. If you are full of something, you are under the control of whatever you are full of. Still further, this text indicates that until Christ sets us free, we lack a sane evaluation of things. To interpret our condition or anything else in a way other than the way God does is insane because God knows only truth; He knows the way things really are. He never makes a mistake. We think we know things accurately, but we really don't.

BEFORE CHRIST REDEEMED US, WE WERE ON DEATH ROW, ENCAGED IN A LITTLE CELL, EXISTING DAY AFTER DAY, BUT NOT REALLY LIVING.

Before Christ redeemed us, our old master was leading us down the path to eternal damnation. It was as if we were on death row, encaged in a little cell, existing day after day, but not really living. As each day passed, we were moving one day closer to judgment day, the day of our execution.

Perhaps you think that describing our pre-salvation situation this way is being melodramatic. Perhaps that's not the way you see it; but that's the way God says it was. The choice for us is whether we will view our condition in the way that an all-knowing, all-wise, inerrant, infinite God views it, or the way we finite, limited, erring human beings perceive it to be.

To return to our death row illustration: What would you think if you saw a man locked up on death row in his little cage and he was just walking around whistling, laughing, joking, and acting like everything was just great? You would probably think, "Man, don't you know you are going to die? Don't you know you are going to face judgment? This is not a time to whistle and joke around. Everything isn't great. Get serious. Recognize the desperateness of your situation and do what you can do to prepare for that event."

Before God saved us, we may have lived like our condition was not something to be alarmed about. Like many others, we may have walked around, whistling, acting like things were great, acting like everything was wonderful. Yet all the while, judgment day was coming closer and closer. We were children of wrath. The wrath of God was coming upon us. Our fate was certain. We might have pretended like judgment day wasn't really coming. We might have become extremely busy in the things of this world. We might have kept ourselves occupied, doing the things we enjoyed. But all of our pretending couldn't change the reality of our captivity. It couldn't release us from our enslavement. It couldn't stop death, nor could it deliver us from the certain judgment of God (Hebrews 9:27).

God, Who created the heavens, Who causes the earth to shake, Who holds this entire universe in the palm of His hand, to Whom the nations of the earth are like a drop in the bucket, Who can do whatever He pleases, Whose eyes are too pure to look on evil, Who is a jealous and avenging God, was against us (Isaiah 40:21-26; Psalm 115:3; Habakkuk 1:13; Exodus 20:5). The truth is that according to the Bible, prior to being redeemed we were in bondage to sin (John 8:34), and we lived a meaningless, pointless life.

What did we need? We desperately needed to be redeemed. And that, Paul said, is just what Christ did. He redeemed us. Peter told us, in 1 Peter 1:18, that God redeemed us from a futile way of life inherited from our forefathers. We lived a pointless, futile way of life before God rescued us. Nothing we did had any meaning as far as God was concerned; nothing we did had eternal value or worth – everything we did was part of futile way of life. Before salvation we were like a man whose job consists of going to the beach, picking up grains of

ALL OF OUR PRETENDING COULDN'T CHANGE THE REALITY OF OUR CAPTIVITY.

BEFORE SALVATION WE WERE LIKE A MAN WHOSE JOB CONSISTS OF GOING TO THE BEACH, PICKING UP GRAINS OF SAND, AND THROWING THOSE GRAINS INTO THE OCEAN.

sand, and throwing those grains into the ocean. Day after day, year after year, that's what he did. What words would you use to describe this man's manner of life? The same words that Peter used to describe us before redemption. That man was involved in "a futile manner of life," and so were we. Oh, our lives may have been a little more interesting than throwing sand into the ocean, but they were just as empty. We may have tried to satisfy ourselves with pleasure, but trying to satisfy ourselves with pleasure is like a thirsty man thinking he is going to be able to quench his thirst by drinking water out of a glass with no bottom. He pours water in, and where does it go? Right out the bottom. So it was with us. But our sin had so fooled us that we just kept trying. We kept bringing that empty glass up to our mouths thinking that just one more sip would quench our thirst.

Some of us tried to find meaning by pursuing education and wisdom. We thought that if we could just attain more knowledge then we would be satisfied. But what is the use of wisdom and education? According to the Bible, the fate of the fool and the wise man is the same (Ecclesiastes 2:14). Solomon, who had become one of the wisest men in all the world, came to this realization that worldly wisdom was futile. His conclusion: *"Why then have I been extremely wise?...This too is vanity. For now there is no lasting remembrance of the wise man as with the fool, inasmuch as in the coming days all will be forgotten. And how the wise man and the fool alike die"* (Ecclesiastes 2:15-16).

Some of us gave ourselves to our work, and to the pursuit of money. If we could just pay off our house, if we could just wear nice clothes, if we could just get a good car, then our life would be full. We worked hard day; after day; we wanted to get as much money in our bank accounts as we could possibly could. But this too is vanity (Ecclesiastes 2:21-22; 3:10-17). This too is the height of folly, a futile manner of life.

You came into the world with nothing, and when you die, that's all you are going to be able to take with you. When you stand before God on judgment day, He's not going to ask how much money you made. How hard you work and how much you possess isn't going to impress God. These things won't matter to God.

Do you see what we were like? We were like men in a desert chasing a mirage, running hard and leaping and falling face down into the hot desert sand, then getting back up and running after another mirage. Your old masters held you in bondage to wicked deeds.

SOME OF US TRIED TO FIND MEANING BY PURSUING EDUCATION AND WISDOM.

SOME OF US GAVE OURSELVES TO OUR WORK, AND TO THE PURSUIT OF MONEY.

That's the point Paul was making in Titus 2:14. Paul said we have been redeemed from every lawless deed. Sin was our master. We were not free. We were in bondage to lawless deeds. Our old masters ruled over our understanding. Romans 3:11 tells us: *"There is no one who understands."* Sin blinded and corrupted our thinking. Before we were saved we couldn't think straight when it came to spiritual things. In fact, the Bible says our minds were naturally biased towards evil. We were naturally opposed to spiritual truth and to God's Word (Romans 8:5-8; Colossians 1:21).

Sin poked out our spiritual eyes. It even blinded us to the desperateness of our situation. Thomas Watson puts it like this:

> Sin first tempts and then damns. Sin does to a man as Jael did to Sisera. She gave him milk but then she brought him low. Judges 5:26-27, "He asked for water and she gave him milk; in a magnificent bowl she brought him curds. She reached out her hand for the tent peg, and her right hand for the workmen's hammer. Then she struck Sisera and smashed his head, and she shattered and pierced his temple." Sin first brings us pleasures which delight and charm the senses, and then comes with its nail and hammer....[49]

Think about this: If a man dies "in sin he is damned irrecoverably. But still the sinner sports with his own damnation – he continues to sin. Sin has made him not only sick but senseless. Though sin has death and hell following it, yet the sinner is so blind that he sins still."[50]

Our will was enslaved to sin. We desired sin, and even our desires for good were tainted by sin (Ephesians 2:3; Titus 3:3; John 8:44). We were even blind as to how evil and disgusting sin really is. The things that were of the most benefit to us were distasteful, and the things that were of the most harm to us were the most pleasing. When we did things that were sinful, time seemed to fly by. But to have someone talk to us about spiritual things, that was boring.

When friends talked to us about their wicked activities, we couldn't get enough. But if a friend came and talked to us about our soul, we were ready for them to stop talking even before they started. It was painful for us to break off with our worldly activities or to spend any time at all thinking about eternity and about God. Thomas Boston explains that the unsaved man "is sick, yet utterly opposed to the remedy; he loves his disease so much that he loathes the

WE WERE LIKE MEN IN A DESERT CHASING A MIRAGE.

physician. He is a captive, a prisoner, and a slave; but he loves his conqueror, his jailer, and his master; he is fond of his fetters, prison, and drudgery, and has no liking to his liberty."[51]

Our old master would tell us that we would find enjoyment and pleasure in things that actually would lead to our destruction. Sin would give us a cup of poison and tell us to take it up and drink. It had no mercy on us. It would tell us that we would find lasting happiness in things that would only end in sadness. It told us that sin is less evil and dangerous than it really is.

SIN IS LIKE A MASTER
WHO KEEPS TELLING
HIS SLAVES THAT IF
THEY JUST DO THIS OR
THAT, THEY WILL BE
FREE.

Sin is like a master who keeps telling his slaves that if they just do this or that, they will be free, they will find true pleasure and joy, but who knows all along that if they just do this or that, they are going to face terrible consequences and die. Sin is like a slave-master who leads you to the door of the Roman Coliseum and tells you that when that door opens there are going to be thousands of people cheering for you; but he doesn't tell you that they'll be cheering because once you are in the Coliseum you will face all kinds of soldiers and ravenous animals who are going to try to kill you.

What Paul was saying here in Titus 2:14 is that we were slaves and our master was lawless deeds. Christ gave Himself up, He gave His own life as the price of our freedom. Jesus Christ redeemed us from the guilt of our lawless deeds. The penalty of our sins was laid upon Christ. By His death He paid the price to God so that we can be free from the guilt of sin. We've been reconciled to God through Christ. He's discharged our guilt, pacified God's wrath, and made God and us friends. This means that you as a believer are not guilty before God anymore. Jesus paid the price that was on your head.

As mentioned earlier in this chapter, the redemption Christ provides goes beyond freeing us from the guilt of our sins. It also includes redeeming us from the power of sin. That's what Paul was writing about in the context of Titus 2. He wrote about why Christians should, and can, live holy lives – why they don't have to be overcome by problems and live like everyone else in the world. *"Christ Jesus,"* Paul wrote, *"gave Himself for us, that He might redeem us (set us free) from every lawless deed...."* Because of our union with Christ, we have been set free from slavery to the power of sin. Our redemption in Christ is extensive.

Christ completely, not partially, redeemed us from the controlling power of sin in our lives. John Murray explains, "Christ in his death and resurrection broke the power of sin in our lives, triumphed over the god of this world, and by that victory delivered all those who were united to him from the power of darkness and translated them into his own kingdom…"[52]

Write how each of the following scritpures illustrate this truth.

Christ delivered us out of the kingdom of sin and has placed us in the kingdom of righteousness.

Colossians 1:14

_____

_____

Romans 8:1-4

_____

_____

As believers, we can and still do sin.

1 John 1:8-10

_____

_____

1 John 2:2

_____

_____

1 Timothy 1:15-16

_____

_____

Romans 7:14-24

_____

_____

However, the glorious fact is that because of Christ's redemption we don't have to ruled by sin, by lawless deeds.

Romans 6:14

_____

_____

Romans 8:12-14

_____

_____

Romans 8:31-39

_____

_____

Galatians 5:16

_____

_____

Galatians 24-25

_____

_____

Colossians 3:1-5

_____

_____

1 John 2:1

_____

_____

Hallelujah! Christ has redeemed us from our guilt and slavery to lawless deeds. Understanding this is an incredible motivation to godliness. Picture in your mind a man who is a slave to a horrible, cruel master who lies to him, spits on him, doesn't feed him, and tortures him. Then someone comes and frees him from that master. What would you think if you later saw that same man go back to his old, cruel master's house to voluntarily be his slave again? You would probably say to him, "Man, what are you doing? You've been set free. You don't need to be his slave anymore." And how would you respond if this man told you that he enjoyed being treated like an animal; that he liked being controlled by this despot of a master; that he was contented with living a meaningless kind of life? If that were to happen, you'd probably be confused, perplexed because that man's behavior and attitude wouldn't make any sense.

To know Christ has redeemed us from every lawless deed and then to continue to live as though we were still enslaved doesn't make any sense. All too often, we as Christians are like the Israelites in the books of Exodus and Numbers. As Exodus begins, the Israelites were enslaved by the Egyptians who treated them in inhumane ways. The Egyptians were incredibly cruel to the Israelites. They made them kill their babies; they beat them; they forced them to build pyramids; and they made their lives miserable. In fact, Exodus 1 tells us the Israelites were in such pain that they groaned under the burden of their bondage. Well, God responded to their cry by delivering them in a miraculous way. He came and did what only He can do: He saved them from their terrible bondage. Yet a little later when things got tough, just a short time after they left Egypt, what did the Israelites start to say? "Oh, I wish we were back in Egypt!" (Numbers 10-11). That kind of thinking is insane! Go back to that bondage? Something was terribly wrong with the way they were thinking and behaving. Had they forgotten that they had been enslaved?

Yet, let's not be too hard on the Israelites, because that's what Christians who have been redeemed often do. They look on the world with envy and think "Oh, I wish that I could do this, or live like that." That's insane! Go back to that bondage? No, let's not go back. Let's not think that way, because Christ has redeemed us so that we can be free from the control of lawless deeds. And that fact should be a powerful motivation for pressing on in obedience to His will; that should stimulate us to face, and in a godly way solve, whatever problems come into our lives.

MOTIVATED BY THE PURIFICATION THE GOSPEL PROVIDES

But that's not all Paul had to say about the motivating power of the Gospel. He went on to say that *"Christ Jesus gave Himself for us...to purify for Himself a people for His own possession...."* Redemption refers to the power of sin; the term for "purify" is speaking of the guilt and defilement of sin. Christ did not come only to set us free from the power of sin, He also came to make us clean from its stain.

To "purify" literally means "to cleanse, to make clean and to purge, to thoroughly cleanse for sacred use." Imagine your children coming up to you after playing in the mud all day long. They are covered, literally, from head to toe with dirt and grime and all kinds of disgusting stuff. They need to be "purified," or "cleansed," from the dirt that is all over their bodies.

TO "PURIFY" LITERALLY MEANS "TO CLEANSE, TO MAKE CLEAN AND TO PURGE, TO THOROUGHLY CLEANSE FOR SACRED USE."

IF THE WORD
"REDEEM"
PRESUPPOSES
BONDAGE, THE WORD
"PURIFY" PRESUPPOSES
FILTH AND
UNCLEANNESS.

Jesus used this term, "purify," when talking to lepers. Imagine the leper coming up to Him. The leper was an outcast from society. Most folks wouldn't talk to him or even want to look at him. They didn't just shy away when he came near, they ran away. His hands were being eaten away by the disease, he was hunched over, and so he fearfully approached Jesus and said, "Lord, if You are willing, You can make me clean." And the Bible tells us that Jesus stretched out His hand and said, *"I am willing, be cleansed"* (Matthew 8:2-3). The Greek word translated here as "cleansed" literally means "purified." The leper wanted Jesus to purify him of his leprosy, meaning he wanted Him to remove all the ravaging effects of leprosy from his body.

Both of those illustrations help us understand the meaning of word "purify" in Titus 2:14. If the word "redeem" presupposes bondage, the word "purify" presupposes filth and uncleanness. Jesus did not come to cleanse us from physical dirt, or simply take away the ravages of a disease that has affected our bodies. He came to do something much more important. He came to free us from the defilement and awful stains of sin.

Every person born into this world is born with a corrupt and filthy nature. The psalmist says, *"Behold I was shapen in iniquity, and in sin did my mother conceive me"* (Psalm 51:5). When the psalmist, under the inspiration of the Holy Spirit, made that statement, he was saying, "I was born with a corrupt nature."

Scripture teaches that God created man perfect and good (Genesis 1 and 2), but man chose to disobey. It also teaches that because of disobedience and rebellion his very nature became depraved and defiled (unclean, unpurified), (Romans 5:12-19; 3:9-23; Jeremiah 9:23-24). As a result of disobedience (sin), every person is now born a spiritually dead man instead of a spiritually living being. He is born spiritually corrupt and filthy in the sight of God.

This corruption or filthiness sticks to man. It is not merely outside of him; it is inside of him. That's why Paul wrote in Romans 7:18 of *"sin that dwelleth within me."* This corruption goes far beyond our actions to our very hearts. Jesus explained that evil behavior including thoughts, words, desires, and reactions, comes from within, out of the heart. We are defiled by what is already in us, not by what happens to us or around us. Evil propensities come from within because we come into this world with corrupt and defiled hearts (Mark 7:21-23). We do evil things, Jesus said, because we are evil, unclean, and unpurified. Our hearts, as Jeremiah declares, *"are deceitful above all things and desperately* wicked…" (Jeremiah 9:23-24). *"There is none righteous, not even one;…there is none who does good, there is not even one"* (Romans 3:10, 12) because there are none who are good in the sight of God. We do what we do because we are what we are – corrupt and defiled within (Ephesians 2:3). Our evil actions are the overflow of our pre-purified hearts.

Before Christ purifies us we are like a sponge from which ink flows when squeezed. The ink comes out because there is ink within, not simply because the sponge is squeezed. So it is with us. The ungodly actions, reactions, thoughts, words, affections and desires come out of us because of the unpurified condition of our hearts.

What do we need so that our actions, reactions, thoughts, words, affections, and desires in the midst of life and in response to the problems of life will be God-honoring and God-pleasing? We need to be purged and cleaned from our internal filthiness. How? The Gospel of Jesus Christ. We need a Savior who will clean us up on the inside, and we have that in Jesus Christ.

This is why He came, why He lived, why He died, why He rose again, why He ascended, and why He even now lives in heaven interceding for us.

Write out the following scriptures.

Hebrews 7:25

_____

_____

Romans 8:32-34

_____

_____

1 John 2:2

_____

_____

Christ came to purge, or cleanse, us from this internal filthiness. The Bible makes it clear that He does this in two ways.

CHRIST CAME TO PURGE, OR CLEANSE, US FROM THIS INTERNAL FILTHINESS. THIS IS NOT ALL DONE AT ONCE. IT IS A DAILY PROCESS.

1. He has purified or washed us. By obtaining our forgiveness of sins, He has obtained our justification before God. He has sanctified us and set us apart for Himself.

2. He frees us from the dirt and stink of sin.

This is not all done at once. It is a daily process. Christ has purified us, and He is continually purifying us. He continues to work in us so that we desire and have the power to do the will of the Father (Philippians 2:12-13; 1:6).

The word-picture Paul painted in Titus 2:14 of what Christ, as our Savior, does for believers is incredible. We were slaves to the bondage of sin. There we were on the slave auction block with all kinds of marks on our backs; there we were hunched over, worn down by the awfulness of years of life devoted to sin. But then, Christ came and bought us back, purchased our redemption with His blood.

THOSE WHOM JESUS REDEEMS, HE ALSO PURIFIES!

But He did more than that. He took an interest in us and cleansed us on the inside. He purified us so that we are free not just from the power and bondage of sin, but also from all of its terrible stains. Paul indicated that those whom Jesus redeems, He also purifies! He begins this process when we initially repent and believe on Him, and then He progressively and continuously cleans us up internally as we continue to repent and trust in Him. Christ Jesus, our Savior, continues this wonderful process of inner cleansing as we daily develop our relationship with Him through our study and meditation on His Word, through prayer, through worship, through listening to the preaching of His Word, and through the fellowship and ministry of gifted godly people.

Write out the following scriptures.

Psalm 119:9, 11

_____

_____

Acts 20:28, 31

_____

_____

Ephesians 5:26-27

_____

_____

John 15:3

_____

_____

2 Timothy 4:2

_____

_____

Ephesians 3:14-21

_____

_____

Ephesians 6:18-19

_____

_____

Hebrews 3:12-13

_____

_____

Hebrews 10:24-25

_____

_____

Galatians 6:1-3

_____

_____

He does it continuously as our inner man is renewed by the means He has appointed.

Romans 12:1-2

_____

_____

2 Corinthians 4:16

_____

_____

John 15:3

_____

_____

John 17:17

_____

_____

WHY IN THE WORLD WOULD WE WANT TO GO BACK AND LIVE THE SAME WAY WE DID BEFORE WE BECAME CHRISTIANS?

Christ Jesus gave Himself for us to purify us for Himself. Since that's true, why in the world would we want to go back and live the same way we did before we became Christians? To do this would be as senseless as a leper who has been totally healed from leprosy choosing to go back and live as a leper once again. Nor does it make sense for us who have been purified by Christ Jesus to go back and live in the same way that unbelievers live. The grace of God has appeared in Jesus Christ with all the power and motivation we need to live in newness of life. Why would we not therefore avail ourselves of all the help that Christ promises to provide and move forward into a life of obedience and triumph?

THE MOTIVATING POWER OF BELONGING TO JESUS CHRIST

Even with all of that being duly noted, understood, and applied, we still haven't exhausted the motivating impact of the Gospel found in Titus 2:14. Paul continued his motivational message by reminding us, *"Christ Jesus gave Himself for us … to purify us unto Himself, a people for His own possession, zealous of good deeds."*

Think carefully about the fact that Christ Jesus gave Himself for us so that we can be a people for His own possession. The phrase, *"a people for His own possession,"* literally means a prized possession. If you are a Christian, you belong to Christ, and you are His prized possession. He bought you for Himself. Jesus Christ chose you out of this entire world to be His treasure.

JESUS CHRIST CHOSE YOU OUT OF THIS ENTIRE WORLD TO BE HIS TREASURE.

This thought of us belonging to God and of the benefits of this truth for us is developed by Paul in many other places. Interestingly, this great truth is usually mentioned for motivational purposes. In other words, the Bible clearly teaches that belonging to Him ought to be a powerfully motivating influence for godly living. Over and over, the Bible tells us that who we are should make a difference on how we live!

Who we are: *I will dwell in them and walk among them; and I will be their God and they shall be My people....And I will be a Father to you, and you shall be sons and daughters to Me says the Lord Almighty* (2 Corinthians 6:16, 18).

How we should live: *Therefore, come out from their midst and be separate, says the Lord. And do not touch what is unclean* (2 Corinthians 6:17).

Who we are: *Do you not know that your body is the temple of the Holy Spirit who is in you ... and you are not your own? For you have been bought with a price....* (1 Corinthians 6:19-20).

How we should live: *Therefore, glorify God in your body. Flee immorality* (1 Corinthians 6:20, 18).

Who we are: *You belong to Christ...* (1 Corinthians 3:23).

How we should live: *So then let no one boast in men* (1 Corinthians 3:21).

Who we are: *Just as He chose us in Christ from before the foundation of the world...* (Ephesians 1:4).

How we should live: *We should be holy and blameless before Him...to the praise of the glory of His grace* (Ephesians 1:4, 6).

Who we are: *We are the Lord's* (Romans 14:8).

How we should live: *Not one of us lives for himself, and not one dies for himself; for if we live, we live for the Lord, or if we die, we die for the Lord....Who are you to judge the servant of another?...So then each one of us shall give account of himself to God. Therefore, let us not judge one another anymore...* (Romans 14:7-8, 4, 12-13).

There's great comfort in the thought that we belong to Christ, that He gave Himself for us that we might be His prized possession. Think of it – Jesus Christ prizes us. Beautiful, powerful, mighty, wise, loving Jesus takes delight in us.

> OVER AND OVER, THE BIBLE TELLS US THAT WHO WE ARE SHOULD MAKE A DIFFERENCE IN HOW WE LIVE!

You and everything you have belong to Christ.

That's Who we belong to. We are His treasured possession. If it is awful to be the object of Almighty God's wrath (Hebrews 10:27, 31; 12:29; Revelation 6:16-17), how incredible, how wonderful to be the object of the Almighty God's mercy. We belong to Him. He rejoices over us. He calls us His children.

This means your Savior will not forget you. He will not forsake you. He will always watch over you. Do you see the confidence, the rock-solid strength that we as believers can and should have? God is for us! Nothing can separate us from His love for us!

Are you in a difficult situation? Remember this – you belong to Christ. Are you in a dangerous situation? Remember this – you belong to Christ. You are His special possession. Does the world think you are foolish? Does the world reject you? Are you poor in the world's sight? Are you confronted by what appear to be gigantic difficulties and problems? Well, if so, think on this fact – you are Christ's special possession, and the one whom God honors can never be contemptible. So find comfort in this. Delight in it. Let this truth encourage you to run with endurance the race that is set before you. You belong to Him and that means that ultimate victory is assured for you. It can't be otherwise. Because you're His, you can count on the fact that regardless of the difficulties you face, He will provide a way of escape. There is hope for you. (1 Corinthians 10:13)

But understand that this thought is not only comforting, it is also challenging. Remember, you are Christ's possession. This means that you are not your own. You and everything you have belong to Christ. Think about how this fact should radically impact the way you live. You have been set apart by God to belong to Christ and you are to live for Him. You are to be in the world, but not of the world.

Christian, since you belong to Christ, your single aim, your single goal in life should be to live all out for His pleasure. This truth should motivate you to frame your life and your actions to the praise and glory of Jesus Christ, your Master. Your body is not your own; therefore, glorify God with your body. Because you are His prized possession you should follow the example of Paul who said, *"We have as our ambition, that whether at home or absent, to be pleasing to Him"* (2 Corinthians 5:9), and *"my earnest expectation and hope (is) that …Christ shall even now, as always, be exalted in my body, whether by life or death"* (Philippians 1:20).

In the light of the great truths Paul highlighted in Titus 2:11-14, evaluate your purpose for living and the way you respond to and handle the inevitable problems of life. Reflect on the fact that you only live once, then you die and face God. How can you stand to live just to survive?

If Christ gave Himself for us to redeem us from every lawless deed and to purify a people for His own possession, what difference does it really make if we don't have a lot of money? Or if we don't have the most prominent position at work or in the church? Or if other people don't treat us with dignity and respect?

Paul said Christ's special people should be characterized by a zeal "for good deeds." To be zealous means to be eager. It means to be hungry to do good. Note that Paul didn't merely say, "Be somewhat interested in doing good deeds." No, he said we should be zealous for good deeds. His idea is that God's people are to be a focused people. They are to be intense about this. They are not to be content to go through life just trying to make it. No, they are to be so dedicated that doing good works is such a lifestyle for them that they can't stop doing good.

We ought to be zealous to *"let (our) light so shine before men in such a way that they may see (our) good work and glorify (our) Father who is in heaven"* (Matthew 5:16). If Christ Jesus gave Himself for us, how can we be lazy or selfish or indifferent or disobedient? How can we be so ungrateful in light of all that God has done for us?

What about you? Does your life reflect the fact that Christ has set you free from the control and power of sin in your life – that you have been set free from every lawless deed? Does your life reflect the fact that Christ has purified you and continues to purify you in your inner man so that your thoughts, desires, affections, and attitudes are God-honoring? Does the fact that you as a Christian are His prized possession comfort and challenge you to face life and its problems with determination, expectation, and joy? Do you know that you have all you need in Christ in order to escape the corruption that is found in the world and in your heart, and to live soberly, righteously, obediently, and victoriously in this present world?

This chapter has emphasized the crucial role that being properly motivated will play in persevering in the Christian life, and in facing and resolving the inevitable problems we face. I have emphasized that the only motivating factor

YOU ONLY LIVE ONCE, THEN YOU DIE AND FACE GOD. HOW CAN YOU STAND TO LIVE JUST TO SURVIVE?

GOD'S PEOPLE ARE TO BE A FOCUSED PEOPLE. THEY ARE NOT TO BE CONTENT TO GO THROUGH LIFE JUST TRYING TO MAKE IT.

that is powerful enough to keep us going is the Gospel. Fear alone won't do it; guilt alone won't do it; shame alone won't do it; the warnings and exhortations of people aren't enough; a partial Gospel won't do it. Nothing except the power of the full Gospel is sufficient for this job. Nothing except an understanding of and continuous reflection on the many-faceted aspects of Christ as Savior will give you the dynamic power to face and solve your problems and live your life for God's glory. So if you want to solve your problems God's way, I encourage you to preach the full Gospel to yourself regularly. Continuously remind yourself of the truths of Titus 2:11-14. When believed and applied, these truths will serve as a primary means of keeping you motivated to persevere in your Christian life.

QUESTIONS FOR DISCUSSION

1. Why is motivation an important factor in solving life's problems?

_____

_____

2. What reason does Paul give in Titus 2:11-14 that Christians ought to live godly lives? Explain verse by verse.

_____

_____

3. Why did Christ die on the cross? Think this question through. Try to be thorough. Support your answer with Scripture.

_____

_____

4. How do some "cheapen" the work of Christ?

_____

_____

5. Explain why thinking you are a Christian and living in blatant disobedience to God demonstrates a misunderstanding of what it means to confess Jesus as Savior.

_____

_____

6. What does the word "redeem" mean?

_____

_____

7. From what were we redeemed? Support your answer with Scripture.

_____

_____

8. Why do some take their redemption for granted?

_____

_____

9. Describe in detail our pre-salvation condition.

_____

_____

_____

10. In what ways is sin like a slavemaster?

_____

_____

11. Why should the fact that Christ redeemed us motivate us to be holy?

_____

_____

12. What does the term "purify" mean?

_____

_____

13. Why do we need to be purified?

_____

_____

14. How does Christ purify us?

_____

_____

15. Why should the fact that Christ purifies us, motivate us to holiness?

_____

_____

16. Give some examples of how who we are should affect how we live. Support your answer with Scripture.

_____

_____

17. What difference should it make in your life that you belong to Christ?

_____

_____

18. What role should good deeds play in the believer's life?

_____

_____

19. Why is the gospel the only motivating factor powerful enough to keep us motivated?

_____

_____

PERSONAL RESPONSE

1. On a scale of 1 to 10, how motivated have you been recently to live for Christ?

_____

_____

2. What motivates you to live the Christian life? Be honest. Is it the question "What will people think of me?" Is it the thought "I don't want to disappoint others?" Or is it something else?

_____

_____

3. Explain how God has made you personally aware of your sinfulness and hopelessness apart from Christ.

_____

_____

4. Describe your life before and after God saved you. What are some of the major differences?

_____

_____

5. What are some reasons people act as if their pre-salvation condition wasn't all that bad?

_____

_____

6. What are some specific ways you can grow in thankfulness for your redemption?

_____

_____

7. To what sins do you keep returning? Why is continuing to return to sin so sad and dangerous? Support your answer with Scripture.

_____

_____

8. What difference has it made in your life this week that you belong to God? Give a specific example.

_____

_____

9. Why should we be zealous for good deeds? What good deeds have you done recently? What good deeds do you plan on doing this week? Be specific.

_____

_____

10. How are you going to implement the truths of this chapter into your life this week?

_____

_____

CHAPTER 13

MAKING CHANGES THAT STICK

When God confronted Adam with his sin in the Garden of Eden, Adam quickly responded by passing the blame – "It's that woman you gave me!" Much has changed since that day in the garden, but unfortunately, when it comes to responding to confrontation and dealing with sin, we haven't changed all that much.

Thousands of years later men and women still respond just like Adam when they are confronted with their sin. Though they may say it in many different ways – "That's just the way I am." "I was born that way." "I'm just like my parents." "That's my personality." "It's my wife's fault." "You can't teach an old dog new tricks." – they are all trying to get across the same point: It's not my fault. I just can't change! I am a victim, and my sin is a sickness.

GOOD NEWS: YOU CAN CHANGE

I would love to be able to personally sit down with each one of you and say this over and over again: "If you are a believer, you can change and become a more godly person!" Parents, you can become more godly parents! Men you can become more godly husbands, and women you can become more godly wives! You can become more sensitive, more considerate, more loving, more disciplined, and more organized. You can control your anger. You can control your appetite. You can control your lusts. You can become less critical. You can be more cheerful. You can be more truthful. That old statement about old dogs not being able to learn new tricks may be true (though probably it isn't) of dogs. But it isn't true of human beings who have been made in the image of God and redeemed through Christ. These kinds of people not only can, but they must change.

When I make a statement like this, I realize that those who have struggled to overcome sin may be a bit skeptical. They may be thinking, "How can you say so confidently that I can change? You don't know my parents, you don't know my situation, and you don't know me!"

I'M CERTAIN THAT YOU
CAN CHANGE BECAUSE
OF WHAT I KNOW
ABOUT GOD!

Rest assured, I'm not here to boost your self-esteem by intimating that you have the power in yourself to change. You see, I'm not confident that you can change because of what I know about you. Instead, I'm certain that you can change because of what I know about God! Every reader of this book is different and faces many different difficult circumstances; yet God is the same, and we place our confidence in Him!

YOU CAN CHANGE BECAUSE OF THE PLAN AND POWER OF GOD

IF YOU ARE A
BELIEVER, YOU CAN
CHANGE BECAUSE OF
THE PLAN OF GOD.

If you are a believer, you can change because of the plan of God. Paul explained in Titus 2:14 that Jesus gave *"Himself for us, that He might redeem us from every lawless deed and purify for Himself a people for His own possession, zealous for good deeds."* Jesus died to save you from your sin and to make you into a person who is pure and zealous for good deeds. John Owen explains, "It is the eternal and immutable purpose of God that all who are His in a peculiar manner, all whom He designs to bring unto blessedness in everlasting enjoyment of Himself, shall, antecedently thereunto, be made holy."[53] God did not save us because we were holy; but He did save us to be holy. To say that you can't change is to say that the great plan of God will be thwarted by you!

YOU CAN CHANGE BECAUSE OF THE GRACE OF GOD

IF YOU ARE A
BELIEVER, YOU CAN
CHANGE BECAUSE OF
THE GRACE OF GOD.

If you are a believer, you can change because of the grace of God. Paul wrote in Titus 2:11-12 that *"the grace of God has appeared bringing salvation to all men, instructing us to deny ungodliness and worldly desires and to live sensibly, righteously and godly in the present age…."* It is ludicrous to say that a Christian can't change. The grace of God has come not only to save us from the penalty of sin, but also to save us from the power of sin. Paul was saying, "The grace of God brings salvation; it teaches us to say no to sin and yes to godliness. That's what grace does." Therefore, if you are not learning to say no to sin and yes to godliness, you haven't experienced the grace of God. J. Gresham Machen explains: "A Christian life that permits a man just to knock along in very much the same way, making a poor, ineffectual battle against evil habit, is not a true Christian life at all."[54] To say that you can't change is to say that the grace of God is woefully inadequate.

YOU CAN CHANGE BECAUSE OF THE PROMISES OF GOD

If you are a believer, you can change because of the promises of God. We read in 1 Corinthians 10:13, *"No temptation has overtaken you but such as is common to man, and God is faithful, who will not allow you to be tempted beyond what you are able, but with the temptation will provide the way of escape also that you may be able to endure it."* God promises that you will not be given more than you, by His grace, can handle. So you don't have to sin when you are in the midst of temptation. You can overcome! To say that you can't change is to say that the promises of God are lies.

YOU CAN CHANGE BECAUSE OF THE COMMANDS OF GOD

If you are a believer, you can change because of the commands of God. Paul commanded us in Ephesians 4, *"Don't walk anymore as the Gentiles walk."* In other words, you were walking like the Gentiles (i.e., like unbelievers, non-Christians) walked, but now that you've become Christians, you've learned of Jesus Christ, you're being renewed by the Spirit, and therefore you must no longer live as the Gentiles live! You need to put off your ungodly habits, patterns, and lifestyles, and you've got to put on godly ones. What would be the point of that command if it were impossible to obey? Paul expects Christians to change. Change is not an option. It's a command. To say that you can't change is to say that the commands of God are futile.

THE PROCESS AND METHOD OF CHANGE

The Bible makes it abundantly clear that if you are a Christian you can change. The question is how? It's very nice to say that change is possible, but perhaps you've tried, and nothing has seemed to work. Sure, you make changes for a short period of time, but you can't seem to make those changes stick.

How do you change an ungodly lifestyle and become godly? How do you change from being insensitive to being sensitive? How do you change from being critical to being appreciative? How do you change from being a person who is a deceiver to being one who is truthful? How do you change from being a lazy person to being a person who works? How do you change from being a selfish person to being a person who is giving and generous? How do you change from pride to humility, from holding grudges to having a forgiving spirit,

IF YOU ARE A BELIEVER, YOU CAN CHANGE BECAUSE OF THE PROMISES OF GOD.

IF YOU ARE BELIEVER, YOU CAN CHANGE BECAUSE OF THE COMMANDS OF GOD.

TO SAY THAT YOU CAN'T CHANGE IS TO SAY THAT THE COMMANDS OF GOD ARE FUTILE.

GAS
TANK

from lustful thoughts to thoughts that are pleasing to God? How do you become a godly person?

If you are going to make changes that stick, you must be converted. Don't rush by this important truth. It is absolutely impossible to change in a God-honoring way unless you are born again. Imagine a man driving a car down the highway when suddenly it sputters and comes to a stop. The fuel tank is empty. He gets out and takes a good look at his car, wondering what could possibly be wrong. He notices that there are bugs on the windshield, so he wipes it clean. He sees that the tires are dirty so he gets down on his hands and knees and scrubs the tires until they are "spic-and-span." By the time he's done cleaning the outside of the car, it looks brand new. But has he fixed the problem? Of course not! He can clean the outside of the car all he wants, but if that car doesn't have gas, he's not going to be able to drive it anyplace.

The same is true in our lives. Unbelievers may be able to clean up the outside of their lives, but they will not be able to deal with their fundamental problems unless they are converted. They will continually be frustrated in their attempts to make changes that stick because their problems go much deeper than the surface; they go straight to the heart.

Ephesians 2 describes our pre-conversion condition, *"You were dead in your trespasses and sins, in which you formerly walked according to the course of this world, according to the prince of the power of the air, of the spirit that is now working in the sons of disobedience. Among them we too all formerly lived in the lusts of our flesh, indulging the desires of the flesh and of the mind, and were by nature children of wrath, even as the rest."*

WE WEREN'T JUST SICK. WE WERE DEAD.

Don't be fooled. It wasn't just our actions that were bad; it was also our slavery to our lusts. We had a nature that was opposed to God; we were His enemies, and we were ungodly. We were completely alienated from God, totally inactive when it came to the things that please God, and constantly pursuing the things that God hates. We weren't just sick. We were dead.

Write out the following scriptures.

Ephesians 2:1-3

_____

_____

_____

Romans 8:5-8

_____

_____

Jeremiah 17:9

_____

_____

Mark 7:21-23

_____

_____

Colossians 1:21

_____

_____

Trying to change apart from a real and vibrant relationship with Jesus Christ is like telling a dead man to walk and expecting him to be able to obey. You can yell, "Get up and walk!" at him all you want, but he's not going to go anywhere. You can dress him up in a designer suit, but no matter how nice you make him look, he's not walking anywhere, because he's dead. The only way for a dead man to walk is for him to be raised from the dead, to be given new life!

The only way for you to begin to walk in a way that honors God is to be born again! God's grace is magnified in our salvation because He's not just healing the sick, He's raising the dead. When you truly repent of your sins and put your faith in Christ, something remarkable happens. A definite change occurs in your life. Your old self dies (Romans 6:2). You are given a new nature, one that loves God and desires to obey Him. This means that when you are saved, God frees you from slavery to sin and He gives you a love for righteousness (Romans 6:18). You became dead to sin and alive to God. You have changed, so you can change!

What is more, when we come to Christ in repentance and faith, God gives us His Holy Spirit. The Holy Spirit indwells us, and acts as a divine Helper who guides us to truth. By the power of the Holy Spirit we can develop godly lifestyles. Apart from a new nature and the Holy Spirit, it is absolutely impossible to change in ways that honor God. But perhaps you are thinking, "Look, I am a Christian and yet I find it very difficult to put off some ungodly

WHEN YOU ARE SAVED, YOU BECAME DEAD TO SIN AND ALIVE TO GOD. YOU HAVE CHANGED, SO YOU CAN CHANGE!

BECOMING A CHRISTIAN IS NOT THE END OF THE PROCESS; RATHER, IT'S THE BEGINNING!

YOU MUST BE COMMITTED TO DOING WHAT GOD SAYS IS NECESSARY.

YOU ARE GOING TO HAVE TO DISCIPLINE YOURSELF...THE WAY AN ATHLETE TRAINS FOR COMPETITION.

habits and patterns. Plus, I know other people who are Christians and they have ungodliness in their lives."

That's because becoming a Christian is not the end of the process, rather it's the beginning! If you are going to make changes that stick, you must be committed to doing what God says is necessary for real changes to occur. And that requires a commitment to discipline. Paul exhorted Timothy in 1 Timothy 4:7-8, *"On the other hand, discipline yourself for the purpose of godliness; for bodily discipline is only of little profit, but godliness is profitable for all things, since it holds promise for the present life and the life to come."*

Timothy was a Christian. Paul wasn't questioning his Christianity. Yet Paul said, "Timothy, if you are ever going to become godly, you are going to have to discipline yourself." Godliness is not something that comes automatically. It's not something that comes miraculously. It's not something that comes magically. It's not something that comes easily.

When I was born I began to breathe automatically. I didn't have to say to myself, "Come on breathe. Come on now, breathe, breathe, breathe." No, I automatically, began to breathe. When I was born I didn't have to say to my heart, "Heart, beat, beat, beat!" No, my heart just beat automatically.

A lot of things happen to us automatically. Godliness isn't one of those things. Paul says that if you are going to become godly, you are going to have to discipline yourself.

When Paul said this, he was drawing an illustration from the world of athletics. The term he used for "discipline" was a term used to describe the way an athlete trains for competition. It implies vigorous exercise and strenuous effort. Paul was saying, "Timothy, you've got to be your own personal trainer in an exercise program designed for godliness, because biblical change does not take place without a serious commitment to discipline."

In commenting on this passage, William Hendriksen, wrote:

> What Paul had in mind, accordingly, must have included one or more of the following comparisons:
> (a) Just as a youth in the gymnasium exerts himself to the utmost, so you, too, by God's grace and power, must spare no effort to attain the goal.

(b) Just as that youth discards every burden or handicap in order that he may train the more freely, so you, too, should divest yourself of everything that could encumber your spiritual progress.

(c) Just as that youth has his eyes on a goal – perhaps that of showing superior skill on the discus range, that of winning the wrestling match or boxing-bout in the palestra, that of being the first to reach the post which marked the winning point on the running track, at least that of improving his physique – so you should be constantly aiming at your spiritual objective, namely, that of complete self dedication to God in Christ.[55]

Imagine a person who says that he wants to run in the Boston Marathon, but never trains. He just sits on his couch all day, watches sports on television, plays video games, and talks about running in the marathon. When the day of the Boston Marathon actually comes, he won't get very far, because he failed to train, to discipline himself. If you want to be a great athlete, you have to make sacrifices; you have to do things that are difficult; you have to get up off that couch; you have to be committed.

THE PROBLEM IS THAT MOST OF US DON'T LIKE THIS WORD, DISCIPLINE!

The problem is that most of us don't like this word, discipline! One of the primary reasons believers do not grow in godliness is because they are not willing to work hard at becoming godly. There are many lazy Christians, and the results are devastating. They profess to be Christians, but because of a lack of spiritual discipline they are living pathetic lives. To make matters even more tragic, they are willing to discipline themselves for the purpose of excelling in their jobs, but they refuse to discipline themselves for the purpose of godliness. They are earnest and serious about the things of this world, but they are absolutely unwilling to strive for the good of their souls. Sadly, this is true not only of people outside of the church, but also of many who are professing Christians and members of the body of Christ.

Donald Whitney comments:

I've seen Christians who are faithful to the church of God, who frequently demonstrate genuine enthusiasm for the things of God, and who dearly love the Word of God, trivialize their effectiveness in the kingdom for lack of discipline. Spiritually they are a mile wide and an inch deep. There are no timeworn channels of communing discipline between them and God. They have dabbled in everything but disciplined themselves in nothing.[56]

Godliness does not come instantaneously. The word "discipline" is in the present tense, which means that this matter of becoming godly is something you have to continually work at. Years ago when I was in high school and college I played football. I had to exercise and discipline myself like never before to be a good football player. Hour after hour, year after year, I had to train to get in shape for football. As a result, I was in the best shape of my life. My stomach was hard, my muscles were hard, and I could run for miles. But then I graduated from college and went to seminary. Suddenly, I wasn't able to exercise nearly as much. Do you know what happened? Even though I had been in great shape, even though it had taken me a long time to get in that shape, when I stopped exercising I quickly started getting flabby again! That's because it requires continuous effort and discipline in order to remain in top physical condition.

IF YOU ARE GOING TO BECOME GODLY YOU'VE GOT TO DISCIPLINE YOURSELF DAILY.

So it is with godliness. If you are going to become godly you've got to discipline yourself daily. "There are no 'gains without pains' in spiritual things any more than in temporal. That roaring lion the devil will never let a soul escape from him without struggle....The world with all its opposition and temptations will never be overcome without a conflict."[57]

Every day you've got to study the Word. Every day you've got to deny yourself. Every day you've got to evaluate yourself. Every day you've got to seek the Lord's help. Hour by hour, moment by moment. Not just for a year or two, but every day until Christ takes you home. You can't be a spiritual couch potato and expect to effectively run the marathon of the Christian life for God's glory.

YOU CAN'T BE A SPIRITUAL COUCH POTATO AND EXPECT TO EFFECTIVELY RUN THE MARATHON OF THE CHRISTIAN LIFE FOR GOD'S GLORY.

Any good physical trainer will tell you that in order to become physically fit, you must stop doing certain things and start doing others. The same is true when it comes to godliness. In order to become godly, you must discipline yourself to avoid ungodly teaching (1 Timothy 4:7; Psalm 1:1), tempting activities, practices, and places (Romans13:14; Matthew 5:28,29; Proverbs 4:14-15, 27; 7:6-21), bad company (1 Corinthians 15:33; Proverb 1:10-19; 13:20), sinful thinking (James 1:13-14; 2 Corinthians 10:3-5), and unbiblical actions (1 Peter 2:9; Colossians 3:5-9).

One writer explains, "Christianity is not the gentle, easygoing thing that it is sometimes mistaken for....It involves heroic self-denial; it means the uncompromising relinquishment of sin."[58]

To make changes that stick, you need to evaluate your life and think specifically, "What needs to be put off?" Are you filling your mind with the world's perspective on sin? Do you place yourself in tempting situations? Are your friends distracting you from your pursuit of Christ? What are you doing that is disobedient to God's commands?

But it's not enough just to put off these things. If you are to become godly, you must discipline yourself to develop a desire for sound teaching (1 Peter 2:2; James 1:21-22; Psalm 1:2), a commitment to prayer (Colossians 4:2, 12), a pattern of biblical thinking (Romans 12:2; Philippians 4:8; 2 Corinthians 10:5; Psalm 1:2), a practice of obedient living (Galatians 6:9; Luke 11:28; James 1:21-25), a support team of biblical friends (Hebrews 3:12-13; Proverb 13:20; Hebrews 10:24-25), and a habit of God-honoring speech (Ephesians 4:29; Colossians 4:6). You must dedicate yourself to implementing biblical principles into the fabric of your life. You've got to stop just listening to Scripture; you've got to start applying it!

THE INESTIMABLE VALUE OF CHANGE

As you can see from everything that has been written thus far in this chapter, growing in godliness (making changes that stick) takes great effort and great discipline. It requires blood, sweat, and tears. All this talk about effort, commitment, and discipline might leave some of you wondering why you should do this. The answer is very plain: Your most important priority in life is to become a godly person, because godliness has value for absolutely everything.

Paul told us in 1 Timothy 4:8 that *"bodily discipline is only of little profit, but godliness is profitable for all things, since it holds promise for the present life and also for the life to come."* Catch what Paul was saying. He was saying that there is nothing, no activity, no relationship, no aspect of life on which godliness does not exercise an influence for good! To say it another way, godliness is valuable in this life, and it is also valuable in the life to come. If you are godly, you have the best of both worlds!

CHANGE FOR FUTURE

THE VALUE OF GODLINESS IN THE FUTURE

ALL MEN DIE BUT THE ONLY ONES WHO ARE GOING TO BE HAPPY WHEN THEY DIE, ARE THE GODLY.

Death helps put the value of godliness in perspective. All men die, but the only ones who are going to be happy when they die are the godly. Ungodliness has no value for the life to come.

Jesus tells the story of an ungodly man in Luke 12. This man wasn't as bad as he could possibly be. Jesus doesn't say that he was an adulterer. Jesus doesn't tell us that this man was a murderer or a terrible blasphemer. Many people think that doing things such as that is the essence of ungodliness. Not so! Doing such things is certainly a manifestation of ungodliness, but it is not the sum total or essence of ungodliness. Ungodliness may involve those things, but ungodliness is much more than that.

Ungodliness is simply not living your life according to the will of God and for the glory of God. Ungodliness involves not having a right attitude and response toward the true and living God. It consists of not having God at the center of your thought life. It involves a lack of reverence and respect for God. It involves focusing on your own desires, your own values, and your own priorities rather than God's. It includes seeking to please yourself rather than God, being driven by self-interest rather than God's interests. In essence, it is worshiping self rather than worshiping God.

The man described in Luke 12 was ungodly because he was living for himself. He had his own values, his own standards. He was seeking the things that he wanted to seek. He was a rich man. In fact, he had crops that produced so much that he had to build bigger barns. He had a very simple plan for his life: "Eat, drink, and be merry." Probably sounds like many people you know.

FOR THE RIGHTEOUS, DEATH IS A DOORWAY TO EVERLASTING JOY.

The world will tell you that this man was doing just fine; he was living the high life! But the Bible says that he was a fool. God came to him and said, *"You fool, this very night your soul shall be required."* God called this man a fool because he had the absolutely wrong idea about what was truly valuable. He was living for the temporary rather than the eternal, worshiping himself rather than the true and living God, focusing on what pleased him rather than what pleased God, seeking first his own kingdom rather than the kingdom of God (Matthew 6:18-33).

If somehow you were able to go to hell today and interview that man, and you were able to ask him, "Were the things you lived for and the lifestyle you chose, valuable for the life to come?" he would cry out, "No!" Ungodliness has no value, none at all, in the life to come.

But, how different it is for those who have made godliness their goal in life! For the righteous, death is a doorway to everlasting joy. Death is not something to be dreaded but anticipated, because *precious in the sight of the Lord is the death of His godly ones*" (Psalm 116:15). Though certainly God does not take delight in the painful experiences that may accompany the death of the godly, He is happy when they die, because one of the reasons God saved us was to pour out His love on us for all eternity!

Paul wrote in Ephesians 2:4-7 that God saved us because of His great mercy and love, and He made us alive together with Christ. He raised us up with Him, "*in order that in the ages to come He might show the surpassing riches of His grace in kindness towards us in Christ Jesus....*" It's as if the believer is standing in front of a great dam. Behind that dam is the great ocean of God's love, and when we go to heaven, God's grace and kindness is going to break through the dam and we will swim in the great ocean of God's love for all eternity. We have experienced the great love of God here on earth, but it's nothing like what we will experience in heaven!

In Revelation 7, John described a group of believers who arrive in heaven. These people were godly men and women; the context makes that clear. Their lives on earth may have been very difficult, they may have had to endure great persecution, but now they are at peace. They serve God in His temple day and night. They have immediate access to God. They hunger no more; they thirst no more; they never are burned by the sun; they are led by the Lamb of God Who is in the midst of the throne. God Himself wipes away every tear from their eyes! And if you were somehow able to visit heaven and interview the people that are there, you'd discover that all of them would tell you that godliness is valuable in the life to come. For the godly, "*to live is Christ, and to die is gain!*" Discipline yourself for godliness because for the godly, the best is yet to come!

THE VALUE OF GODLINESS IN THE PRESENT TIME

Paul tells us that godliness is not only valuable for the life to come, it's also valuable in the present life! Christianity gives us a quality of life right now that

JESUS CHRIST DID NOT COME TO MAKE US MISERABLE NOW AND HAPPY LATER.

is unparalleled in the world. True believers would not exchange the joy they experience as a result of godliness for all the treasures in the world. Jesus Christ did not come to make us miserable now and happy later. He came to give us a portion of eternity right now. *"I have come that they might have life, and that right now, they may have it more abundantly"* (John 10:10).

Godliness is valuable physically. Proverb 14:30 says that *"a tranquil heart is life to the body, but passion is rottenness to the bones."* If you are content, it is good for you physically, but if you are envious, it will destroy you physically. Solomon tells us in Proverb 17:22, *"A joyful heart is good medicine, but a broken spirit dries up the bones."* Sin is not only bad for you spiritually, it is bad also for you physically!

Godliness is valuable for your marriage and family. The godly man will love his wife as Christ loves the church. He will nourish and cherish her; he will be devoted to her welfare; he'll seek her good before his own; he'll listen to her – and that's good for a marriage. The godly wife will devote herself to being her husband's helper. She will seek to cooperate with her husband; she'll support her husband; she'll do everything she can to encourage her husband – and that's good for a marriage.

Godliness means that parents will want to be the kind of parents that God says they should be. They won't provoke their children to wrath. They'll seek to bring their kids up in the discipline and the counsel of the Lord. And that's good for families.

Godliness is valuable in your business life. The godly man will be a better employee. Paul tells us that the godly man works in order to make the gospel look beautiful in every way (Titus 2:10). By watching the way the godly man works at his job, people are attracted to his Savior! The way he works is so striking because he works not just to please his boss on earth, not just to look good to men, but to please God, Whom he fears (Colossians 3:22-24).

Joseph is one of the first biblical examples of a godly employee, and we read in Genesis 39:5 that the Lord blessed *"the Egyptian's house on account of Joseph, the Lord's blessing was upon all that he owned, in the house and in the field."* Joseph, because he was a godly person, was conscientious, diligent, a hard worker, trustworthy, and honest. Joseph's diligence as an employee brought blessing not just on him, but also on the house of Potiphar.

But godliness does not only make a man a better employee, it also makes a man a better employer. Paul challenged employers in Colossians 4 saying, *"Masters grant to your servants justice and fairness, knowing that you too have a Master in heaven."* The godly employer realizes that he is a servant of Christ, and that the way he treats his employees should reflect the character of God. He will have a high regard for his employees; he won't abuse them or use them; he'll be concerned about them, he won't threaten them; but rather he will treat them in a manner consistent with the grace that God has shown him. Godly people make the best employees, and the best employers!

Godliness is valuable to you in your witness for Christ. Jesus told the disciples in Acts 1:8, *"You shall receive power when the Holy Spirit has come upon you; and you shall be my witnesses...."* Notice carefully what Jesus did not say. Jesus did not say, "You shall witness." To witness is something you do primarily with your mouth. We should witness, but that's not Jesus' point here. Jesus said, "You shall be my witnesses," and what He meant was that their lives were to be witnesses for Him and the gospel. You as a person are going to be a witness. Your life can draw men to Christ, or your life can bring shame to your Savior.

That was Paul's point in Titus 2. He urged Titus to teach the believers in Crete to live in a way that matched sound doctrine. One of the primary reasons it's so important is because the way that believers act can either make the Gospel look beautiful or ugly to unbelievers. We can either dishonor the Word of God by our behavior (Titus 2:5), or we can adorn the doctrine of God in every way (Titus 2:10).

Several years ago, my son Wayne took a job to support himself while going through college and law school. Not long after he started the job, his employer came to him, knowing that he was a Christian, and said, "If you have a brother at home who is anything like you, I want to hire him." Well, he did have a younger brother at home, who got a job because of the way his older brother worked.

A little while later, his boss came back to him and said, "Do you have any friends who are Christians and are looking for a job? I like the way Christians work."

You see, my sons were a testimony for Jesus Christ by the way they worked. So if you want to influence people for Christ, it's not simply a matter of what you say with your lips; it's also a matter of how you live your life.

Paul's words are absolutely true. *"Godliness is profitable in every way."* Please note the words "every way." Underline those words at least in your mind. Mark them down as solid gold. We've actually considered only a few of the ways in which godliness is beneficial. There are many more, such as:

1. It is beneficial for you personally because you will be contented, full of peace, joy, patience, self-control, and stability (1 Timothy 6:8; Philippians 4:10-13; Galatians 5:22-23; Matthew 6:33).

2. It is beneficial for your country in that it will make you a good citizen, a good neighbor, and a good friend (Romans 13:1-14; Genesis 39:1-14).

3. It is beneficial in terms of your fulfilling the purpose for which God made you and saved you, because godly people bring honor and glory to God and make an impact on others for God (1 Timothy 4:9-16; 1 Peter 3:15; Acts 4:13).

4. It is beneficial for your relationship with God because God shares His secrets with, draws near to, and manifests Himself to the godly person (Psalm 4:3; 25:1-15; John 14:21-23; Proverbs 1:7, 10:9, 14:26-27).

Just how is godliness beneficial? The answer is: *"In every way."* Believe it, or rather, believe God who inspired Paul to write those words. There are many other ways in which godliness is beneficial. We've only scratched the surface of the meaning of these three words.

Take God at His Word and commit yourself to doing whatever is necessary for you to become a more godly person. "In every way" means that it is absolutely impossible for you to spend too much effort in your pursuit of godliness. It means that you should let nothing distract you from studying the Word of God, from spending time in prayer, from fellowshiping with other believers, from listening to sound doctrine, and from meditating on the truth. Fight against the lusts that wage war against your soul (1 Peter 2:11-12).

> REMEMBER, IF YOU ARE A BELIEVER YOU CAN BECOME GODLY.

Remember, if you are a believer you can become godly. By God's grace and your obedience to the command of 1 Timothy 4:7, you can solve your problems and make changes that stick. Godliness is valuable for both the present life and the life to come. So I urge you to go for it! Orient your life toward and discipline yourself for the purpose of godliness. If you do, what happens in eternity and in this world will reveal that you made a wise choice.

QUESTIONS FOR DISCUSSION

1. What are some common excuses people give for sinful behavior?

_____

_____

2. Why do you think people seek to excuse their sin?

_____

_____

3. Give four reasons that confirm the fact that a believer can overcome sin. Support your answer with Scripture.

_____

_____

4. Explain in your own words John Owen's statement, "It is the eternal and immutable purpose of God that all who are His in a peculiar manner, all whom He designs to bring unto blessedness in everlasting enjoyment of Himself, shall, antecedently, thereunto, be made holy."

_____

_____

5. Why is saying that you can't change actually saying that the grace of God is woefully inadequate?

_____

_____

6. Defend with Scripture J. Gresham Machen's statement: "A Christian life that permits a man just to knock along in very much the same way, making a poor ineffectual battle against evil habits, is not a true Christian life at all."

_____

_____

7. What two things must be true of you if you are going to become a more godly person?

_____

_____

8. What does regeneration have to do with change?

_____

_____

9. Describe what takes place when you are converted.

_____

_____

10. Can an unbeliever change in ways that honor God? Why or why not?

_____

_____

11. Explain what the Bible has to say about the nature of the unbeliever.

_____

_____

12. What difference does it make that not only our actions, but also our very natures were bad?

_____

_____

13. What does the word "discipline" teach us about what it takes to become godly? From what sphere of life does Paul borrow this term? What does that indicate to us about what it takes to become godly?

_____

_____

14. What difference does it make that the word "discipline" is written in the present tense?

_____

_____

15. Specifically, what must you discipline yourself to do if you are going to become godly?

_____

_____

16. What motivation does Paul give us for godliness?

_____

_____

17. How does death put godliness in perspective?

_____

_____

18. What is ungodliness?

_____

_____

19. Prove from Scripture that godliness is valuable for the life to come.

_____

_____

20. What are several ways that godliness is valuable in this present age?

_____

_____

PERSONAL RESPONSE

1. If someone came to you and said, "I just can't change!" how would you respond?

_____

_____

2. What are some excuses you have made for not changing?

_____

_____

3. Are there any other reasons than the ones mentioned in this chapter that make it certain that a believer can change?

_____

_____

4. Why is it that believers still struggle with sin?

_____

_____

5. Give several reasons why people who claim to be believers may sometimes be defeated by sin?

_____

_____

6. With what areas in your life have you consistently struggled? Do any of the reasons you just listed above explain why you have continually struggled with this particular sin?

_____

_____

7. What do the grace of God and conversion have to do with change?

_____

_____

8. Why is "the only way for you to begin to walk in a way that honors God" to be born again?

_____

_____

9. In what areas in your life have you not been committed to change?

_____

_____

10. What does J.C. Ryle mean when he says that "there are no 'gains without pains' in spiritual things any more than temporal?"

_____

_____

11. In what specific ways are you exercising yourself for godliness?

_____

_____

12. What must you put off and put on in order to become a more godly person? Refer to the list of things that need to be put off and examine yourself. What do you need to put off? Bad teaching? Tempting activities? Bad company? Sinful thinking? Unbiblical actions?

_____

_____

13. Refer to the list of things that need to be put on and examine yourself. What do you need to put on? A desire for sound teaching? A commitment to prayer? A pattern of biblical thinking? A practice of obedient living? A support team of biblical friends? A habit of God-honoring speech?

_____

_____

14. What areas in your life are ungodly?

_____

_____

15. What steps are you going to take to implement the truths you learned in this chapter into your life?

_____

_____

CHAPTER 14

HOW TO SAY NO TO TEMPTATION

Late one night, Michael* picked up the telephone and made a frantic call. He began the conversation by saying, "Pastor, please just talk to me for the next hour. The liquor stores close at 11 and I just don't know if I can make it until then. I don't want to give in, but I'm weak and I can't resist the temptation." He then went on to pour out his heart, relating how his abuse of alcohol had been devastating to his life. He acknowledged that alcohol abuse had been one of the causes of his divorce from his first wife and was now causing major problems in his new marriage. His present wife was threatening to divorce him. His excessive drinking had resulted in his losing several different jobs, and had even played a major role in sending him to prison for several years. Yet he still wanted to go to the liquor store! His desire to turn to the bottle seemed overwhelming. He felt trapped.

Later, when Michael came for person-to-person counseling, he wept uncontrollably as he described his constant failure in battling the same temptation. He was living a vicious cycle. He would be convicted of his sin in church, determine he wouldn't yield in those areas any longer, and yet, just a short while later, when the determination wore off, he would find himself succumbing to the same old temptations. After his failure he'd start over, make a fresh determination, and fall yet again. Determining to change and then falling to temptation became the norm in his life. Time after time he repeated the same pattern. In the past there had been times when he thought he could see a little light, but then the door would be slammed shut on him once again. The result? His hopes were crushed and he began to think that victory over the bottle was impossible. So for the most part, he ended up thinking he could not overcome, and he was resigned to the idea that he would always lose in his battle with temptation. He was convinced that the temptation to drink was one of life's problems that he simply couldn't overcome.

Have you ever felt trapped? Anyone who has been trapped physically will tell you that it is a horrible experience. But it's even worse to feel trapped morally and spiritually. Oh, perhaps your temptation doesn't come in the form of a bottle. Perhaps yours comes in the form of a temptation to lose your temper

HAVE YOU EVER FELT TRAPPED?

Name has been changed.

259

when things don't go the way you want them to go; or in the form of a pattern of gossip, slander, or speaking evil of people; or in the form of a critical, judgmental spirit; or in the form of sexual lust; or a temptation to be greedy or discontented; or in the form of a hundred other things. The list of potential sources of temptation is almost endless.

Can you identify with this man about some temptation(s) that you face? Like Michael, you might have an area or areas of temptation that are especially problematic for you. And like Michael, you may have tried to overcome your temptation but failed and consequently have almost come to the point where you think you can't ever overcome. In fact, like Michael you may have resigned yourself to the idea that succumbing to your particular temptation(s) is a given, a norm for your life.

While serving Christ as pastor and counselor, I've found that although Michael's particular story may be unique, his feelings of desperation and hopelessness are not. I've often had people tell me they feel trapped by certain difficulties and temptations they face. I've heard them say, "I really don't want to give in to this temptation, and I've often said after I've given in, 'I'll never do that again.' But when I'm confronted by the temptation again, I find myself giving in and doing what I said I would never do. It's hopeless. I can't overcome. I'm trapped." Years of counseling experience have convinced me that this is the attitude that many professing Christians have about their encounters with certain temptations. They really don't think they can overcome.

WHY IS IT THAT SO MANY PROFESSING BELIEVERS THINK THEY ARE TRAPPED, DOOMED TO GIVE IN, LACKING POWER TO RESIST AND OVERCOME TEMPTATION?

Why is it that so many professing believers think they are trapped, doomed to give in, lacking the power to resist and overcome temptation? Scripture indicates that several different answers could be given to this question. Many times people fail in their attempts to resist temptation because they aren't truly regenerate. They have never really been born again (1 Peter 1:22-2:3) and given a new nature (2 Corinthians 5:17). Consequently, they are not indwelt by the Holy Spirit Who gives power to resist and overcome temptation (Romans 8:10-14; Ephesians 3:15-17). In other cases, they seem powerless to resist temptation because they are ignorant of the Word, and thus don't know how to change (Ephesians 5:15-17; Colossians 1:9-10). Sometimes they don't change just because they are lazy and unwilling to work (Proverbs 14:23; Philippians 2:12-13; Hebrews 12:1-3). Then, too, Scripture teaches that one of the primary reasons believers fail in their attempts to change is that they don't understand the nature of temptation. Here they are, going into battle, but they have no idea who or what they are fighting! Many believers don't really know why they do the bad things they do, and thus don't even know where to begin in their fight against temptation.

In James 1:13-18, the apostle James wrote the following to a group of believers who were confused about sin and temptation:

> *Let no one say when he is tempted, I am being tempted by God for God cannot be tempted by evil, neither does he tempt anyone with evil. But each one is tempted when he is carried away and enticed by his own lust. Then when lust has conceived it gives birth to sin, and when sin is accomplished it brings forth death. Do not be deceived my beloved brethren, every good thing bestowed and every perfect gift is from above, coming down from the Father of lights, with whom there is no variation or shifting shadow. In the exercise of His will He brought us forth by the Word of truth so that we might be as it were the first fruits of His creatures.*

This gives us several key insights into the nature of temptation that if properly understood and applied by God's grace will help you gain your freedom!

EVERYONE IS TEMPTED

Notice how James began in verse 13, *"Let no one say when he is tempted…."* He did not say, "if he is tempted," but "when he is tempted." He stressed this once again in verse 14, where he continued: *"each one is tempted…."* He didn't write, "There is a possibility that you are going to be tempted," or, " Many of you are going to be tempted," or even, "Most of you are going to be tempted." Instead, he said, "Each one is tempted."

We're not all tempted in the same way, but the truth is, we all will be tempted. You can count on it! That may sound simple, but it has some profound and important implications. Since everyone is tempted, you shouldn't be surprised when temptation comes! Many times we give in to temptation because it catches us off guard. Temptation sometimes surprises us because we are proud. Pride puts blinders on our hearts so that we don't see temptation coming, and it deadens our spiritual senses so that we aren't aware when temptation sneaks up on us. We've deceived ourselves into thinking that we are stronger than we really are, so when temptation proves so enticing, we are shocked by it – and often end up giving in to it. *Pride comes before a fall* (Proverb 16:18).

ONE OF THE PRIMARY REASONS BELIEVERS FAIL IN THEIR ATTEMPTS TO CHANGE IS THAT THEY DON'T UNDERSTAND THE NATURE OF TEMPTATION.

WE'RE NOT ALL TEMPTED IN THE SAME WAY, BUT THE TRUTH IS, WE ALL WILL BE TEMPTED.

Other times, temptation surprises us simply because we are spiritually lazy. Temptation presents itself to us, but because we aren't prepared for it, we fall into it. Jesus warned his disciples, *"Keep watching and praying that you may not enter into temptation; the spirit is willing, but the flesh is weak"* (Matthew 26:41). Peter challenged: *"Be of sober spirit, be on the alert. Your adversary, the devil, prowls about as a roaring lion, seeking someone to devour"* (1 Peter 5:8). If you don't stand guard, if you aren't ready, if you aren't watching, you're going to fall to temptation. It's that simple. You can't escape being tempted but you can escape from falling into temptation. The way that you do that is by watching and praying so that you don't enter into it, so that you are not surprised by it when it comes!

John Owens explains:

> Be always awake, that you may have an early discovery of thy temptation, that you may know it to be so. Most men do not perceive their enemy until they are wounded by him. Yes, other people may sometimes see them deeply engaged, while they themselves are utterly insensible; they sleep without any sense of danger, until others come and awaken them by telling them their house is on fire…Few take notice of it until it is too late, and they find themselves overcome and entangled, if not wounded."[59]

YOU SHOULDN'T BECOME DISCOURAGED WHEN TEMPTATION COMES

One of the enemy's tricks when we are struggling with severe temptation is to get us thinking that we are in this fight alone. As a result, we become extremely discouraged and are more likely to give in and lose the battle.

In a powerful scene in John Bunyan's *Pilgrim's Progress*, Christian was walking through the valley of the Shadow of Death. Bunyan described the valley as a Land of Drought and Desolation. Christian faced incredibly severe trials as he walked through this lonely valley. The path was so dark that "often when he picked up his foot to go forward, he had no idea where he should step next." He experienced terrors of sight and sound. He became confused, desperate, and often felt like giving up. But just at the breaking point, Christian experienced something that gave him strength to carry on:

> IF YOU DON'T STAND GUARD, IF YOU AREN'T READY, IF YOU AREN'T WATCHING, YOU'RE GOING TO FALL TO TEMPTATION.

After Christian had traveled this disconsolate condition for quite some time, he thought he could hear a man's voice somewhere ahead of him. The voice was saying, "Even though I walk through the Valley of the Shadow of Death, I will fear no evil, for You are with me." Then Christian was glad for a number of reasons: First, he gathered from this that he was not alone but that others who feared God were in the Valley as well.

Second, he realized that God was with them even though they were in a dark and dismal place…And third, he hoped that if he could soon catch up with someone, he would then have company. So he ventured on, calling out to whoever was up ahead. There was no answer, however; it was evident that the person thought he also was alone."

Bunyan's point was that it's good to know that you are not alone when facing temptations. Perhaps you are thinking that's easy to say, but you want proof.

You can be confident that you are not alone because Jesus understands the temptations you face. The writer of Hebrews told us *we do not have a high priest who cannot sympathize with our weaknesses, but one who has been tempted in all things as we are, yet without sin* (Hebrews 4:15). There isn't any temptation that you or I could ever face that Jesus Christ, at least in principle form, has not faced.

Well, you think, that's Jesus. Yes. But Paul added something to that in 1 Corinthians 10:13. *"No temptation has overtaken you but such as is common to man…."* In other words, there is no temptation that you have ever faced that somebody else hasn't faced or that somebody else isn't facing right now. You are not some special case. You are facing the same kind of conflicts, the same kind of struggles that others have faced. Don't be discouraged by temptation because it is the common lot of all Christians.

In a very helpful exposition of 1 Corinthians 10:13, Jay Adams used the illustration of something that happened to him while visiting the "Garden of the Gods" outside Colorado Springs. He wrote:

In this beautiful natural wonder you can see rocks balanced on a pinpoint and vividly colored scenery on every side. As you drive slowly, viewing the marvels about you, suddenly you are confronted with a problem: directly ahead of you looms a wall of sheer rock, and the road

YOU ARE FACING THE SAME KIND OF CONFLICTS, THE SAME KIND OF STRUGGLES THAT OTHERS HAVE FACED.

on which you are traveling disappears into what seems to be a crack so narrow that it looks as though you'd have a hard time driving a VW through it. Looking around for a place to turn and go back your eye falls upon a small white sign. It reads: NARROWS. YES YOU CAN. A MILLION OTHERS HAVE. And what do you know – a minute-and-a-half later, a million and one have done it.[60]

On one occasion, I was counseling a young lady who was going through some difficult trials in her life. She was brokenhearted, and said to me, "Dr. Mack, I just want to run. I just want to give in and give up. I don't think I can handle it. It's more than any human being can bear." I understood that she was hurting, and I wanted to find a way to strengthen her in the Lord. I happened to know that there were other people involved in this same difficult trial who, in some ways, had actually had more of a struggle than she was having. Without inferring that her situation was a "piece of cake" and without specifically identifying who these people were, I mentioned the situations these people were facing and the struggles they were having. I also related how many of these people were finding God's help for handling their challenges in a God-honoring, constructive way.

I then asked her what she thought these people were experiencing as they went through their times of difficulty. What might they have been thinking or feeling? She responded by saying that they were probably hurting badly, feeling overwhelmed, and thinking about giving up. I affirmed that was she said was accurate. Then I put a question to her, "What do you personally learn from what I have described to you about these people, their situations, and their reactions?" She smiled and said, "I've learned that I'm not alone. I've also learned that others have made it through and if they can do it, maybe I can too." Being reminded that others had faced similar situations and with God's help, had made it through was a tremendous encouragement to her. It was a "YES YOU CAN. MANY OTHERS HAVE" experience for her.

YOU SHOULD LEARN FROM OTHERS WHO HAVE FACED TEMPTATION

We ought to pay attention to the experiences of others in temptation and learn from their victories and their failures. Don't be a lone-wolf Christian. If others have faced temptation, we'd be foolish not to learn from them.

We can learn from the failures of others. Immediately before I went to pastor my first church, several godly older pastors pulled me aside and shared various stories about the mistakes they had made. That was extremely helpful, because it pointed out pitfalls I wasn't even aware of, and helped me avoid them. We should do this when it comes to temptation. Paul wrote in 1 Corinthians 10:6, *"Now these things happened as examples for us, that we should not crave evil things as they also craved."* Then in verse 11, he once again wrote, *"Now these things happened to them as an example, and they were written for our instruction, upon whom the end of the ages have come."* In other words, God uses the examples of the Israelites as a spiritual lesson for us to learn from. We should learn from their mistakes. If we don't, we are doomed to repeat them.

We can also learn from the successes of others. You can begin by studying the example of our perfect Savior. The writer of Hebrews explained. *"We do not have a high priest who cannot sympathize with our weaknesses, but one who has been tempted in all things as we are, yet without sin."* What a great privilege! Our God understands the temptations we face. And even better – He defeated them all. He never failed. He never caved in. We should read the gospels and learn from Christ's example, how He as a man conquered the incredible temptations that he experienced.

God will often use the affliction, trials and temptations of one believer to encourage and strengthen another. Paul pointed this out in 2 Corinthians 1:3-4, 6 when he wrote, *"Blessed be the God and Father of our Lord Jesus Christ…who comforts us in all our affliction so that we may be able to comfort those who are in any affliction with the comfort with which we ourselves are comforted by God…But if we are afflicted, it is for your comfort and salvation; or if we are comforted, it is for your comfort…."*

You are not in this fight alone. Take every opportunity to learn from others who have faced temptation and won. You ought to ask yourself what you can learn from the experience of Paul. What can you learn from the failures and victories of others as they face temptation? What can you learn from your own experience, past and present, that will help you as you face temptation in the future, or that you could share with others in order to be helpful to them?

James wanted you to know that every one of us is going to be tempted. So be on the alert; know that you are not in this fight alone; learn from those who have gone before you. Others have faced temptation; others are facing it; others have overcome!

> WE CAN LEARN FROM THE FAILURES OF OTHERS. WE CAN ALSO LEARN FROM THE SUCCESSES OF OTHERS.

THERE IS A DIFFERENCE BETWEEN SIN AND TEMPTATION

James continued, *"Each one is tempted when he is carried away and enticed by his own desire, and then when desire and lust conceive it gives birth to sin."* Sin and temptation are connected, but they are not synonymous. Temptation may give birth to sin, but temptation is not sin.

This means that you don't have to sin when you are tempted. Joseph didn't. In Genesis 39 we learn that he was tempted time and time again by Potiphar's wife; and time and time again he said no. Shadrach, Meshach, and Abednego didn't sin. Daniel 3 tells us their lives were on the line, and they were tempted to bow down and worship the image but they said no. Jesus didn't sin. The book of Hebrews tells us that Jesus was tempted in all points, just as we are, yet He was without sin. It's possible to be tempted, and yet not give in!

Temptation becomes sin when we stop struggling against it; when we cooperate with it, yielding to the thought and the desire for it; and when we allow ourselves to be carried away and enticed by it. Isn't that how James put it? *"Each one is tempted when he is carried away and enticed by his own lust, and when lust is conceived it gives birth to sin, and when sin is accomplished it brings forth death."* Temptation becomes sin when we give in and yield, when we stop fighting the thought, and instead just allow the desire to take over.

Jesus explained in Matthew 5:28 that *whoever looks upon a woman to lust after her in his heart has committed adultery already with her in his heart.* He is not talking about a person who happens to see a woman who is scantily clad and is tempted to think evil thoughts or have evil desires, but who immediately begins to struggle with it and pushes it out of his mind. Jesus is talking about a person who goes around looking to lust. He's not struggling with temptation; he's not fighting; there's no battle going on; there's no struggle. His lusts and desire have won. He continues to feed it internally, even if he never follows it through externally. He's encouraging and promoting his sinful desire. He is looking to stir up his lust. He is sinning!

Picture the process by which temptation leads to sin. An evil thought enters your mind. You allow that evil thought to remain. That evil thought then inflames your desire. Your evil thoughts and evil desires impel you toward yielding to that temptation. Finally, you yield to those evil thoughts and actions.

TEMPTATION MAY GIVE BIRTH TO SIN, BUT TEMPTATION IS NOT SIN.

James 1:13-16

TEMPTATION BECOMES SIN WHEN WE STOP STRUGGLING AGAINST IT, COOPERATE WITH IT, YIELD TO THE THOUGHT AND THE DESIRE FOR IT, AND ALLOW OURSELVES TO BE CARRIED AWAY AND ENTICED BY IT.

When the yielding comes, the struggles cease and you've allowed your lust to have control. At that point, it has become sin.

Knowing this helps in the fight against temptation. You need to learn to recognize temptation when it comes so that you can immediately and decisively resist it. You must not allow it to linger in your heart. If you are going to overcome temptation, the best time to overcome it is at the beginning, before it gets a hold, not after it's been around for a while.

Think back to your old Sunday school days. Do you remember the stories about Joseph and Potiphar's wife, and David and Bathsheba? Both David and Joseph faced serious temptations to lust, didn't they?

Both were known as godly men. Both were "heroes of the faith." Both had at one point a deep, intimate, real relationship with God. Yet one fell and the other didn't. Why did Joseph remain pure, and David fall to impurity? One of the primary differences was that Joseph fled temptation; David stayed and toyed with it. Joseph overcame temptation at the beginning point; David allowed it to get a hold of his heart! Don't play with temptation. Renounce it and resist it! God is not to blame for your temptation. *"Let no one say when he is tempted I am tempted by God. For God cannot be tempted by evil and He Himself does not tempt anyone with evil or to evil"* (James 1:13). James began this chapter by telling us to count it all joy when we encounter various kinds of trials because God brings those trials into our lives to produce spiritual fruit.

James was a wise old pastor and counselor. He knew the tendencies of the human heart. Our first instinct when we fall to temptation is to pass the blame. "Aha! God must be at fault because He allowed this situation to come into my life." We sometimes lay the blame right at God's feet. "Lord, if You hadn't made me endure this circumstance, I never would have sinned. God, it's Your fault, because You created me this way. If You hadn't allowed evil into the world, there's no way I would have sinned, so how can You hold me responsible for my actions?"

James said, "No! You must not blame God for your sin, because God never entices you to do evil."

Most of us know enough not to directly blame God for our sin. So instead, we blame other people. We blame our parents. "If only they hadn't raised me the

> WHY DID JOSEPH REMAIN PURE, AND DAVID FALL TO IMPURITY? JOSEPH FLED TEMPTATION; DAVID STAYED AND TOYED WITH IT.

> YOU MUST NOT BLAME GOD FOR YOUR SIN, BECAUSE GOD NEVER ENTICES YOU TO DO EVIL.
>
> JAMES 1:13

WE HAVE BECOME VERY SOPHISTICATED IN THE WAY WE PASS THE BLAME FOR OUR SIN ON TO OTHERS.

WHEN YOU PLAY THE VICTIM, YOU ARE CASTING THE BLAME FOR YOUR SIN AT GOD'S FEET.

way they did, I wouldn't be the way I am." Or we blame our circumstances. "If only I had more money, there is no way that I would have done what I did." Sometimes we blame our personalities. "I can't help it; that's just the way I am."

We have become very sophisticated in the way we pass the blame for our sin on to others. Perhaps that's because we've had so much practice. How did Adam respond when God confronted him with his sin in the garden? By passing the blame onto Eve! But ultimately, who was Adam really blaming for his sinful behavior? God Himself. "It's that woman You gave me!" The same is true for us.

When you play the victim, you are casting the blame for your sin at God's feet. Commenting on this thought from James, Jerry Bridges wrote the following:

> King Saul felt this way (i.e., that God had put him in a situation where he had no choice but to disobey) in his first major campaign against the Philistines (1 Samuel 13). Before going into battle Saul was to wait seven days for the Prophet Samuel to come and offer a burn offering and ask the favor of the Lord. Saul waited the seven days for Samuel.
>
> When he didn't come, Saul became anxious and took it on himself to offer the burnt offering. Saul felt he had no other alternative. The people were fearful and had begun to scatter; the Philistines were assembling for battle; Samuel was overdue. Something had to be done! God had put him in a place where he had no choice, it seemed, but to disobey God's explicit instructions.
>
> But because Saul disobeyed God's express will, he lost his kingdom (1 Samuel 13:13-14). What about us? Do we sometimes feel we have no choice but to shade the truth a little, or commit just a slightly dishonest act? When we feel this way, we are in effect saying that God is tempting us to sin, that He has put us in a position where we have no alternative.[61]

We are so much like the little boy who said to his teacher after he had taken home a bad report card, "Teacher, I want to warn you so you won't get in trouble with my Dad. You see, after he looked at my report card, he said, 'If you don't get better grades on your next report card, someone is going to be sorry.'" Like this little boy, and like Saul in 1 Samuel 13, we want to put the blame for our yielding to temptation on something or someone outside ourselves. We want to say it's not really our fault. It's the fault of our circumstances, or it's the fault of other people. And though we would probably not acknowledge that this is what we're doing, we really put the blame on God for our downfall because He is the One Who is in control of all things. After all, He could have prevented the circumstances from occurring. He could have prevented other people from doing what they did; He could have made them do what they didn't.

IDENTIFYING THE REAL PROBLEM

James understood this propensity to blame everything and everyone but ourselves. So he made it crystal clear that the problem is not up there, it's not out there, it's inside us. It's in our heart! *"Each one of you,"* wrote James, *"is tempted when you are carried away and tempted by your own desires!"* You are the reason you fall to temptation. The problem is your desires. What this means is that if you are going to overcome temptations, you need to stop blaming everyone else for your sin, and deal with your own heart. You do what you do, you say what you say, you react as you react because you want what you want. And often what you really want is the wrong thing. So if you're going to resist temptation, you need to get your desires purified. You need to clean up the inside, because if you get the inside cleaned up, the temptation won't overcome you.

Write out the following scriptures.

Proverb 4:23

_____

_____

Proverb 23:7

_____

_____

Proverb 27:19

_____

_____

Matthew 5:8

_____

_____

YOU DO WHAT YOU DO, YOU SAY WHAT YOU SAY, YOU REACT AS YOU REACT BECAUSE YOU WANT WHAT YOU WANT.

Acts 8:18-22

_____

_____

WHAT MAKES
TEMPTATION
TEMPTING IS WHAT'S
GOING ON IN OUR
HEARTS.

Galatians 5:16

_____

_____

Hebrews 4:12

_____

_____

James 4:8

_____

_____

Some people, for example, really enjoy cheesecake. Others hate it. Put a cheesecake in front of some people, and they will be eager to eat all of it. Yet do the same with other people and they won't even take a bite. Why? It's the same piece of cheesecake. The difference is in their desires. The point is this: What makes temptation tempting is not so much the thing itself; instead, it's what is going on inside our hearts. We wouldn't respond sinfully to temptation if there weren't sinful desires already in our hearts.

Why does one man overcome temptation and another man fall? It's not necessarily because their temptations were so different, but because their hearts were. Jesus explained, *"A good man out of the good treasure of his heart brings forth good things, and an evil man out of the evil treasure brings forth evil things"* (Matthew 12:35). Jesus was specifically talking about our speech, but the principle holds true for all temptations. Why does a man say or do evil things? Because of the evil that lies in his heart! The heart is like a treasury or a bank. In our hearts we store either good or bad desires. Then when temptation comes, we draw from that bank and either respond properly or sinfully, depending on what is stored up in our heart.

THE GREATEST PRESERVATIVE AGAINST THE POWER OF TEMPTATION

Mark this well and accept it as absolutely true: If you are going to overcome temptation, you must make sure that you war against the evil desires that reside in your heart and replace them with godly thoughts and longings. Picture your heart as a fortress. Often, when an enemy comes near a fortress to overtake it, if he sees that the fortress is well-manned, furnished with provisions for battle, and well-equipped to hold out, he will withdraw and won't even assault it.

You need to lay up provisions in your heart so that you are prepared when the temptation comes. John Owen explains it thus:

> If Satan, the prince of this world, comes and finds our hearts fortified against his batteries, and provided to hold out, he not only departs but as James says, he flees: "He will flee from us." (James 4:7) For the provision to be laid up, it is that which is provided in the gospel for us. Gospel provisions will do this work; that is, keep the heart full of a sense of the love of God in Christ. This is the greatest preservative against the power of temptation in the world. Joseph had this; and therefore, on the first appearance of temptation, he cries out, "How can I do this great evil, and sin against God?" and there is an end of the temptation as to him; it lays no hold on him, but departs. He was furnished with such a ready sense of the love of God as temptation could not stand before....[62]

To prosper in your battles with temptation, you must reject the counsel of the ungodly even if that counsel comes from your own heart. You must delight in the law of the Lord, and meditate in His law (think about, fill your mind with, and reflect on His Word) day and night (Psalm 1:2-3). To put it in the words of Paul, if you are going to have victory over wicked desires that lead you into the influence and power of temptation – desires that entice, seduce, and carry you away – you must "walk by the Spirit."

This important statement of Paul in Galatians 5:16 about overcoming temptation contains both a command and a promise. The command of this verse, which is in the present tense, means that we must constantly do what this verse tells us to do. The command includes the word "walk" which means that we must make what the command tells us to do our lifestyle, the habit of our lives. It can't be an on-again/off-again matter. We must train ourselves to walk in the way this verse prescribes.

But how is it that we are to walk? Paul wrote, *"Walk by the Spirit."* What does it mean to walk by the Spirit? It means that we must walk in dependence on the

KEEP THE HEART FULL OF A SENSE OF THE LOVE OF GOD IN CHRIST.

YOU MUST "WALK BY THE SPIRIT."

IT CAN'T BE AN ON-AGAIN/OFF-AGAIN MATTER.

Spirit. We must recognize that we must not go through life depending on our own strength, but we must make it a lifestyle to rely on and trust in the power of the Holy Spirit to live the life He wants us to live. Walking by the Spirit means that we will make prayer a lifestyle, that we will be constantly calling out to Him for His help and strength, that we will be constantly communing with and thinking about God.

Write the following scriptures:

Psalm 50:15

_____

_____

Psalm 55:22

_____

_____

Isaiah 41:10

_____

_____

Romans 8:10-13

_____

_____

Galatians 5:16

_____

_____

Ephesians 3:16

_____

_____

1 Thessalonians 5:17

_____

_____

Walking by the Spirit also means walking in obedience to the Spirit. It means that we must fill our minds with the desires of the Holy Spirit and then actually do what He wants us to do. It means that we must focus on emptying our hearts of our desires and filling them with thoughts about what the Holy Spirit desires. It means that we will choose to trust Him for the strength to do what He wants us to do and then move out to do it. It means that we will marinade our minds with God's Word because that is where we learn the thoughts and desires of the Holy Spirit.

Earlier, we learned that Galatians 5:16 contains a command and a promise. We've examined the command, but what about the promise? The promise is that if we will fulfill the command, we will not be overcome by temptation. Note Paul didn't say, "Walk by the Spirit and you will sometimes not be carried away by the desires of the flesh." Nor did he say, "Walk by the Spirit and you will probably not be carried away by the desires of the flesh." No, he said, "Walk by the Spirit and you will not be carried away by the desires of the flesh." This is a rock-solid, take-it-to-the-bank promise, a guarantee from the God Who can't lie. In effect, He is guaranteeing that if we walk by the Spirit we will be able to say no to temptation; we will not be enticed and carried away by our own evil desires. We will be able to do what God desires rather than what our sinful hearts desire.

Do you feel trapped, hopeless, overwhelmed, or helpless when confronted by temptation? You don't have to be, if you are a believer. You can overcome! Victory begins with understanding the nature of temptation. Remember, you are going to be tempted, so get ready for it. Recognize the difference between temptation and sin. Don't think that just because you are tempted, it means you have to give in. Stop blaming your circumstances, other people, and even God. Take full responsibility for your responses. Recognize the fact that when you yield to temptation, you are being enticed and carried away by your own desires. Focus your attention on your heart. Devote yourself to constantly cleaning up your heart, your thoughts, and your desires, and filling them with God's Word.

To resist and overcome temptation you must, *let the Word of Christ richly dwell within you* (Colossians 3:16); you must learn to make walking by the Spirit a lifestyle. The good news is, God guarantees that as you do, you will be able to say no to temptation. Failure in this endeavor most certainly means that you are neglecting God's appointed means of victory.

THE PROMISE IS THAT IF WE WILL FULFILL THE COMMAND, WE WILL NOT BE OVERCOME BY TEMPTATION.

THIS IS A ROCK-SOLID, TAKE-IT-TO-THE-BANK PROMISE.

QUESTIONS FOR DISCUSSION

1. Why are people sometimes overcome by temptation?

_____

_____

2. Why is understanding the fact that everyone will be tempted important for overcoming temptation?

_____

_____

3. Describe the scene from *Pilgrim's Progress* and identify what this has to do with overcoming temptation.

_____

_____

4. What does Matthew 26:41 have to do with overcoming temptation?

_____

_____

5. What does Hebrews 4:15 have to do with overcoming temptation?

_____

_____

6. Explain the difference between temptation and sin.

_____

_____

7. What point does the illustration of Joseph and Potiphar's wife suggest in reference to overcoming temptation?

_____

_____

8. Explain the relevance of Matthew 5:28 to the temptation/sin process?

_____

_____

9. Why did Joseph succeed and David fail in resisting temptation?

_____

_____

10. Describe the biblical illustration Jerry Bridges used to describe a propensity to which many people are prone when they yield to temptation.

_____

_____

11. Why is blaming other people and our circumstances for our yielding to temptation a subtle way of blaming God?

_____

_____

12. Why is accepting responsibility for our response to temptation such an important part of overcoming temptation?

_____

_____

13. What truth does the cheesecake example illustrate?

_____

_____

14. What answer is given to the question, "Why does one man overcome temptation and another man fail?"

_____

_____

15. What is meant by the phrase, "the heart is like a treasury bank?"

_____

_____

16. What do Luke 6:42-43 and Matthew 12:35 indicate about success or failure in overcoming temptation?

_____

_____

17. According to John Owen, what must people do if they want to overcome temptation? What does a person have to do to resist the temptations of Satan?

_____

_____

18. Explain the relevance of Galatians 5:16 to overcoming temptation. What command is found in this verse? What does this command mean? What is the promise found in this verse? How does this promise relate to overcoming temptation?

_____

_____

PERSONAL RESPONSE

1. To what temptations are you most susceptible? Which ones do you struggle with the most?

_____

_____

2. When you are tempted to do something that God doesn't want you to do, how do you respond?

_____

_____

3. What have you learned from the victories and failures (biblical, historical, or contemporary) that others have experienced as they faced temptation? How has that been of help to you in your confrontations with temptation?

_____

_____

4. How have you failed or succeeded in the temptation/sin process mentioned in connection with Matthew 5:28?

_____

_____

5. When you are tempted, are you prone to respond as David did or as Joseph did?

_____

_____

6. When you yield to temptation, do you accept full responsibility for your response, or do you blame someone or something else?

_____

_____

7. Who or what are you most likely to blame? What excuses do you sometimes use for your failure?

_____

_____

8. When you yield to temptation, do you accept the biblical fact that the reason is inside you rather than outside of you?

_____

_____

9. Can you honestly say that you are warring against the evil desires that lurk in your heart?

_____

_____

10. What are you storing in your heart?

_____

_____

11. In keeping with what you've learned about the meaning of walking in the Spirit, how well are you doing in this area?

_____

_____

12. What are you doing to empty your heart of evil desires and fill your heart with the desires of the Holy Spirit?

_____

_____

13. What insights have you gained or been reminded of in regards to overcoming temptation?

_____

_____

14. What changes should you make in your life so that you will be more successful in saying no to temptation?

_____

_____

15. What changes will you make? When will you begin to make these changes? How will you make these changes?

_____

_____

ENDNOTES

[1] C.H. Spurgeon, "Sovereignty and Salvation," *New Park Street Pulpit, Volume 2,* (Passmore and Sons, London, 1857).

[2] C. H. Spurgeon, "The Priest Dispensed With," *Metropolitan Tabernacle Pulpit, Volume 21,* (Pilgrim Publications, Pasadena, Texas, 1991).

[3] Sinclair B. Ferguson, *The Christian Life* (Banner of Truth, Carlisle PA, 1989) 57-60.

[4] John Blanchard, *Right With God* (Banner of Truth, Carlisle PA, 1975) 82, 90.

[5] B.B. Warfield, *The Inspiration and Authority of the Bible* (P&R Publishing, Phillipsburg, NJ, 1948) 133.

[6] John MacArthur, *Our Sufficiency in Christ* (Word Publishing, Dallas, TX, 1991) 38-39.

[7] John MacArthur, *I Corinthians* (Moody Press, Chicago IL, 1984) 61.

[8] Jay Adams, *How to Help People Change* (Zondervan Publishing, Grand Rapids, MI, 1986) 30.

[9] Adams, ibid, 31.

[10] Adams, ibid, 139-140.

[11] Iain Murray, *Pentecost Today?* (Banner of Truth, Carlisle PA, 1998) 78.

[12] Jerry Bridges, "Does Divine Sovereighty Make a Difference in Every Day Life?," *Still Sovereign*, Thomas Schreiner and Bruce Ware, ed., (Baker Books, Grand Rapids, MI, 2000) 298.

[13] Jerry Bridges, *Transforming Grace* (NavPress, Colorado Springs, CO, 1991) 143.

[14]Oswald Chambers, *If Ye Shall Ask* (Christian Literature Crusade, London, 1963) 12.

[15]A.T. Pierson, *George Mueller of Bristol,* Appendix N, "Wise Sayings of George Mueller" (Revell, Westwood, NJ, n.d.)

[16]S.D. Gordon. *Quiet Talks on Prayer* (Baker Books, Grand Rapids, MI, 1984) 19.

[17]John Piper, *A Godward Life* (Multnomah Press, Sisters, OR, 1997) 164-165.

[18]Cited by E.M. Bounds, *Power through Prayer* (Baker Book House, Grand Rapids, MI, 1972) 483.

[19]Jay Adams, *A Consumer's Guide to Preaching* (Victor Books, Wheaton, IL, 1991) 14.

[20]John MacArthur, *Our Sufficiency in Christ* (Word Publishing, Dallas, TX, 1991) 131.

[21]J.I. Packer, "Introduction," *Knowing Scripture,* by R.C. Sproul (IVP, Downers Grove, IL, 1977) 9.

[22]Jay Adams, ibid, 12-13.

[23]John Calvin, *Commentaries on the Epistles to Timothy, Titus and Philemon* (Baker Book House, Grand Rapids, MI) 250.

[24]Jay Adams, ibid, 40.

[25]John MacArthur, *Our Sufficiency in Christ* (Word Publishing, Dallas, TX, 1991) 103-104.

[26]Sinclair Ferguson, *The Holy Spirit* (IVP, Downers Grove, IL, 1996) 154.

[27]John Owen, *The Works of John Owen, Volume 3* (Banner of Truth, London, Eng, 1966) 488, 435.

[28]Sinclair Ferguson, ibid, 156.

[29]John Owen, ibid, 471, 477.

[30]John Owen, ibid, 496.

[31]Jay Adams, *The War Within* (Harvest House, Eugene, OR, 1989) 59, 71.

[32]Jay Adams Ibid, 71.

[33]John MacArthur, *MacArthur New Testament Commentary on Galatians* (Moody Press, Chicago, IL, 1987) 152-154.

[34]Charles Sykes, *A Nation of Victims* (St. Martins Press, New York, NY, 1992) 11.

[35]Charles Colson, *Loving God* (Zondervan Books, Grand Rapids, MI, 1987) 96-97.

[36]Charles Sykes, Ibid, 13, 15.

[37]John MacArthur, "Rediscovering Biblical Counseling," *Introduction to Biblical Counseling,* ed. Wayne Mack, 1994, p.7.

[38]Alan Ehrenhalt, "Assessments," *Governing,* April 2001.

[39]Martyn Lloyd Jones, *Old Testament Evangelistic Sermons* (Banner of Truth, Carlisle, PA, 1995) 198.

[40]Ed Welch, *Blame it on the Brain* (P&R Publishing, Phillipsburg, NJ, 1998) 13.

[41]Stanton Peele, "My Genes Made Me Do It," *Psychology Today,* July/August 1995: 50.

[42]Barshinger, LaRowe, and Tapia, "The Gospel According to Prozac," *Christianity Today,* August 14, 1995: 35.

[43]Ibid, 35.

[44]Stanton Peele, ibid, 51.

[45]Gary Almy, *How Christian is Christian Counseling* (Crossway Books, Wheaton, IL, 2000) 293-294.

[46]Cited by Dr. Bob Smith, *Christian Counselor's Medical Desk Reference* (Timeless Texts, Stanley, NC, 2000) 65.

[47]Cited by Gary Almy, ibid, 119.

[48]Dr. Bob Smith, ibid, 68-69.

[49]Thomas Watson, *The Mischief of Sin* (Soli Deo Gloria Publishing, Pittsburgh, PA, 1994) 210.

[50]Thomas Watson, ibid, 55.

[51]Thomas Boston, *Human Nature in Its Fourfold State* (Banner of Truth, London, 1964) 54.

[52]John Murray, *Collected Writings of John Murray, Vol.2* (Banner of Truth, Carlisle, PA, 1977) 289.

[53]Cited by Octavius Winslow, *The Work of the Holy Spirit* (Banner of Truth, Carlisle, PA, 1984) 109.

[54]J. Gresham Machen, *The New Testament: An Introduction to Its Literature and History* (Banner of Truth, Carlisle, PA, 1981) 362.

[55]William Hendriksen, *Exposition of the Pastoral Epistles* (Baker Book House, Grand Rapids, MI, 1957) 151.

[56]Donald Whitney, *Spiritual Disciplines of the Christian Life* (NavPress, Colorado Springs, CO, 1991) 19.

[57]J.C.Ryle, *Practical Religion* (Thomas Crowell Corp., New York, 1959) 22.

[58]J. Gresham Machen, ibid, 362.

[59]John Owen, *Temptation and Sin* (Zondervan Publishing, Grand Rapids, MI, 1958) 134-135.

[60]Jay Adams, *Christ and Your Problems* (P&R Publishing, Phillipsburg, NJ, 1983) 6.

[61]Jerry Bridges, *The Pursuit of Holiness* (NavPress, Colorado Springs, CO, 1978) 27.

[62]John Owen, ibid, 133-134.

ENDORSEMENTS

FROM PASTOR GEOFFREY THOMAS

God's Solution to Life's Problems is an extremely helpful book. Lucidly written, it examines the enormous dilemmas of modern man and earths its analyses and answers in historic Christian teaching. This is no stilted, predictable, simplistic response. The book is a page-turner full of illustration, contemporary example, memory, and apposite quotation. All this is grounded in the exegesis of the Bible and solid theology. One's admired teachers and authors are referred to in these chapters, Dr Lloyd-Jones, J.I.Packer, John MacArthur, Thomas Watson, Thomas Boston, John Owen, Gresham Machen, John Murray, and William Hendricksen. As guided by the Macks, one is taught how to become a more courageous, wiser pastor and counselor. In many places, truths are so freshly written and illustrated that they simply jump off the page. Preachers will find the book invaluable in preparing sermons, and they will wish that it had been written ten years ago. But the way it encourages all of us to solve life's problems is by a manner that is accessible to every single Christian. The book was a means of grace to me.

—GEOFF THOMAS
    Pastor, Alfred Place Baptist Church (Independent), Aberystwyth, Wales
    Conference speaker

FROM JERRY MARCELLINO

Once again, we are indebted to Dr. Wayne Mack for providing solid biblical counsel for living in our morally depraved and biblically illiterate age. In the author's familiar writing style, he takes the reader continuously through a plethora of Scriptures as he directs us in the way to solve our problems God's way. The result? We are constantly assured throughout that our problems can be tackled God's way by the approach Mack uses both to address and then answer each of our familiar struggles and even some of the shockers. This means that this book is a needed guide for our crooked age. Every believer, and especially every pastor, needs to read it a few times and consult it often. The Christian life is lived out in a real world, and this tool shows believers how to live realistically and therefore repentantly to the glory of God. I believe the fruit of this book will not only be the help it offers to our individual Christian lives, but also in how it will help us to become what we need to be for our brethren!

—JERRY MARCELLINO
    Pastor, Audubon Drive Bible Church, Laurel, Mississippi
    Director of Audubon Press and Christian Book Service
    Moderator of Fellowship of Independent Reformed Evangelicals (FIRE)

FROM DR. RICHARD L. MAYHUE

One of my personal heroes in the faith is Dr. Wayne Mack because of his unwavering commitment to the gospel of our Lord Jesus Christ and to the time-honored Christian doctrine that the Holy Scriptures are sufficient for all that pertains to life and godliness. I heartily commend Dr. Mack's multi-volume work **God's Solutions to Life's Problems** *as a spiritual resource which will serve as both preventative and corrective spiritual medicine for the soul. To read the refined wisdom from Dr. Mack's lifetime study and ministry of the Scriptures is to be blessed abundantly.*

—DR. RICHARD MAYHUE
   Executive Vice President, The Master's College and Seminary
   Author
   Pastor

FROM DR. FRANK CATANZARO

For years I have been reading and using in my classes many resources written by Dr. Wayne Mack. In this current edition, joined by his son, Joshua, the Macks have given us another wonderful tool to be used in fulfilling God's calling on our lives. On every page we are reminded of the usefulness and sufficiency of God's Word, His faithfulness, and His sovereignty. Thank you, Wayne and Joshua Mack, for a wonderful, useful tool that will assist me and my students in becoming better equipped for a lifetime of ministry.

—DR. FRANK J. CATANZARO, III
   Associate Professor of Pastoral Care and Counseling
   Southeastern Baptist Theological Seminary, Wake Forest, North Carolina

FROM DR. JAY ADAMS

Wayne Mack has written an eminently valuable book entitled **God's Solutions to Life's Problems**. *In the book, Mack shows what a Christians is/is not, that his nature has been changed so as to enable him to make changes that truly solve problems God's way, and what he must do to make such changes. It is a helpful volume that every counselor/pastor/believer should own.*

—DR. JAY ADAMS
   Author of many books on a variety of subjects
   Former pastor
   Seminary professor
   Seminar speaker

FROM DR. STEVEN VIARS

*Reading the book, **God's Solutions to Life's Problems**, is like opening a toolbox. The Macks provide a biblical framework to address the problems you and I face. You will find solid help from two men who demonstrate a knowledge of God's Word and an understanding of the challenges of real life. I heartily recommend it.*

—DR. STEVE VIARS
  Pastor of Faith Baptist Church, Lafayette, Indiana
  President of the National Association of Nouthetic Counselors
  Seminar speaker

FROM DR. TED TRIPP

***God's Solutions to Life's Problems** by Wayne Mack and Joshua Mack is a primer on the Christian life. The chapters of this book brim with encouragements to Bible study, personal discipline for Christian growth, motivation for obedient living, and careful guarding of the heart. You will find two things you need here: biblical direction and hope for victory rooted in Christ. Any book that does that is worth reading.*

—DR. TEDD TRIPP
  Pastor
  Seminar speaker
  Author of *Shepherding a Child's Heart*

FROM DR. DAVID POWLISON

What do "your problems" have to do with such Bible words as "sin and temptation, grace and truth, Christ and the Spirit, repentance and faith, obedience and discipline?" Everything! But we often need help drawing out the immediate connections. Wayne and Joshua Mack trace out the "how do you change?" implications of the theological worldview that has been so well articulated by writers such as Sinclair Ferguson, John Owen, Jerry Bridges, Jay Adams, and John Calvin. He calls believers to the long race. He teaches us about an intentional and carefully lived life, about lifelong immersion in Scripture, about utter reliance on the grace and power of the Holy Spirit, about vigilant self-examination and willing self-denial, about devotion to Jesus Christ whole and simple.

—DR. DAVID POWLISON
  Editor in Chief of the Journal of Biblical Counseling
  Teacher of pastoral counseling at Westminster Theological Seminary

FROM DR. JOHN D. STREET

*Christians today are taught how to cope with problems, not solve them. Many believe that the tough issues of modern life are beyond the Bible's range of answers or that it provides authoritative answers to get to heaven but not how to live here on earth. **God's Solutions to Life's Problems** is a persuasive argument to the contrary. It demonstrates that insightful theology is not only practical, it is functional for resolving deep-seated problems in life. It is obvious that this series is the product of good pastoral theology and a rich life-experience of counseling people-problems. The Macks are to be commended for providing yet another helpful tool for Christians serious about changing and growing.*

—DR. JOHN D. STREET
  Chairman, MABC Graduate Program
  The Master's College & Seminary
  Vice President of the National Association of Nouthetic Counselors

FROM DR. LANCE QUINN

Dr. Wayne and Pastor Joshua Mack have given the Church a most wonderful volume of Biblically-based teaching on a variety of sanctification subjects. You could call it a "handbook on spiritual surgery for the soul!" Mack and Mack are skilled, spiritual physicians, taking the delicate, dynamic instrument of the Word of God and powerfully, yet appropriately using it to slice into the spirit of a man, dissecting their way to not only discovering the initial causes of the malady, but also offering the only viable, life-sustaining healing — God's solutions to life's problems. It is a most commendable effort. Oh, how the Body of Christ needs these kinds of books! The various and insidious diseases which inflict the Body are crippling its effectiveness. Please pray along with me that the church would diligently seek the remedy given herein, for the sole glory of the Great Physician."

—DR. LANCE QUINN
  Pastor and teacher
  The Bible Church of Little Rock
  Little Rock, Arkansas

Real Problems... Real People... Real Life... Real Answers...

THE INDISPUTABLE POWER OF BIBLE STUDIES

Through the Bible in One Year
Alan B. Stringfellow • ISBN 1-56322-014-8

God's Great & Precious Promises
Connie Witter • ISBN 1-56322-063-6

Preparing for Marriage God's Way
Wayne Mack • ISBN 1-56322-019-9

Becoming the Noble Woman
Anita Young • ISBN 1-56322-020-2

Women in the Bible — Examples To Live By
Sylvia Charles • ISBN 1-56322-021-0

Pathways to Spiritual Understanding
Richard Powers • ISBN 1-56322-023-7

Christian Discipleship
Steven Collins • ISBN 1-56322-022-9

Couples in the Bible — Examples To Live By
Sylvia Charles • ISBN 1-56322-062-8

Men in the Bible — Examples To Live By
Don Charles • ISBN 1-56322-067-9

7 Steps to Bible Skills
Dorothy Hellstern • ISBN 1-56322-029-6

Great Characters of the Bible
Alan B. Stringfellow • ISBN 1-56322-046-6

Great Truths of the Bible
Alan B. Stringfellow • ISBN 1-56322-047-4

The Trust
Steve Roll • ISBN 1-56322-075-X

Because of Jesus
Connie Witter • ISBN 1-56322-077-6

The Quest
Dorothy Hellstern • ISBN 1-56322-078-4

God's Solutions to Life's Problems
Dr. Wayne Mack & Joshua Mack • ISBN 1-56322-079-2

A Hard Choice
Dr. Jesús Cruz Correa & Dr. Doris Colón Santiago
ISBN 1-56322-080-6

11 Reasons Families Succeed
Dr. Richard & Rita Tate • ISBN 1-56322-081-4

Problemas reales... Gente real... Vida real... Respuestas reales...

EL INDISCUTIBLE IMPACTO DE LOS ESTUDIOS BÍBLICOS

A través de la biblia en un año
Alan B. Stringfellow • ISBN 1-56322-061-X

Preparando el matrimonio en el camino de Dios
Wayne Mack • ISBN 1-56322-066-0

Mujeres en la Biblia
Sylvia Charles • ISBN 1-56322-072-5

Parejas en la Biblia
Sylvia Charles • ISBN 1-56322-073-3

Decisión Difícil
Dr. Jesús Cruz Correa y Dra. Doris Colón Santiago
ISBN 1-56322-074-1